D1378272

The State Under Contract

Edited by Jonathan Boston

Marshall, Missouri
Missouri Valley College 65340
Murrell Library

First published in New Zealand in 1995 by
Bridget Williams Books Ltd, PO Box 11-294, Wellington

© The contributors, 1995

This book is copyright under the Berne Convention. All rights reserved.
No reproduction without permission.
Inquiries should be made to the publishers.

ISBN 0 908912 71 4

Cover design by Mission Hall Design Group, Wellington
Internal design by Afineline, Wellington
Typeset by Archetype, Wellington
Printed by GP Print, Wellington

Contents

Acknowledgements

Most of the chapters in this volume were first presented at a conference of the New Zealand Politics Research Group at Victoria University of Wellington in early July 1994 on 'The Reconfiguration of the State in New Zealand'. Numerous people assisted with the organization of this conference, or have subsequently commented on chapters and helped in various ways with the publication of this book. The editor would particularly like to thank Elizabeth McLeay for her support and encouragement with the project, and the secretarial staff of the Department of Politics at Victoria University. He would also like to thank Colleen Flood for deputizing, at very short notice, for Michael Trebilcock at the conference, and those who acted as commentators: Philippa Howden-Chapman, John Morrow, Sir Kenneth Keith and June Pallot. Finally, he acknowledges with gratitude the financial assistance for this project provided by Victoria University (in the form of a research grant from the Faculty of Commerce and Administration).

With respect to individual chapters, the following acknowledgements are due:

Chapter 1: this is derived from a larger study, *The Prospects for Reinventing Government*, published by the C. D. Howe Institute (Toronto, 1994) and is published here with the permission of the C. D. Howe Institute.

Chapter 4: the author would like to thank Gary Hawke, Sir Kenneth Keith, John Martin, Martin Matthews and Nicola White for their helpful comments on an earlier version of this chapter.

Chapter 5: this is a revised version of an article published in the *New Zealand Law Journal* (1994) and is published here with the permission of the editor.

Chapter 6: this is a revised version of the author's Inaugural Lecture presented to Macquarie University, October 25, 1994. The author wishes to thank Alex Matheson, Andrew Ladley, Barbara Sullivan and Margaret Wilson for their assistance.

Chapter 7: this is a revised version of an article published in the *Economics and Labour Relations Review* (1993) and is published here with the permission of the editor.

Chapter 9: the author would like to thank Joe Atkinson, Gillian Brock and John Morrow for their comments on an earlier version of this chapter.

Preface

Governmental renewal, reinvention and restructuring has been much in vogue during the past decade. In Britain, there has been a vigorous programme of state asset sales, the 'Next Steps' initiative has transformed most government departments, and numerous public services at both the central and local government level have been contracted out to private-sector suppliers. In Australia, there have been major reforms at the federal and state levels in financial management, human resource management and the machinery of government. Likewise, the Canadian federal government, under the 'Public Service 2000' programme, has embarked on a comprehensive series of changes designed to enhance the performance of the public sector. Meanwhile, in the United States the Clinton Administration has made governmental reform a top priority. In 1993 the Vice-President, Al Gore, chaired a taskforce known as the National Performance Review, the principal aim of which was to ensure that government 'works better and costs less'. Subsequently, Congress passed the Government Performance and Results Act which requires the introduction of a new system of performance assessment throughout the federal government.

Within the OECD, probably the most radical and comprehensive programme of state-sector reform has been pursued in New Zealand. Spurred on by a perception of bureaucratic rigidity, inefficiency and waste, and galvanized by the combined afflictions of high inflation, rising unemployment, large fiscal deficits, mounting public debt and low rates of economic growth, recent governments — first Labour and then National — have undertaken thorough-going changes to the structure, role and management of the public sector. Broadly speaking, these changes have conformed to the principles and practices of managerialism. For instance, there has been a strong emphasis on the devolution of management responsibilities (or 'letting the managers manage'), the privatization of commercial state assets, the commercialization of many departmental functions, the institutional separation of public funding and provision, and the separation of the functions of policy advice, regulation and policy implementation. These changes have not only brought about a radical reshaping of the bureaucratic landscape, but also contributed to a dramatic 'downsizing' of the core public sector and the development of a new managerial ethos.

Three features of the new model of public management that has emerged in New Zealand since the late 1980s are particularly worth highlighting. The first is the increasing resort to competitive tendering and the contracting-out of publicly funded services. This has occurred at both central and local government levels. As a result, private-sector organizations are now delivering a wide range of public services, some of which were previously the exclusive domain of government departments. Of course, this growing reliance on 'third-party government' or 'government by proxy', as it is sometimes termed, is not unique to New Zealand. Nevertheless, it is an important development here and poses various issues in relation to risk management, institutional learning, the contract management skills of public agencies, political accountability and responsible government. Equally important, it raises serious questions about the nature of the distinction between 'public' and 'private', the proper boundaries between the state and the market, and whether this trend towards 'virtual' government is in the public interest.

A second feature of the New Zealand model is the prominence policy-makers have given to the new institutional economics, and more specifically the application of agency theory to a wide range of relationships within, and between, public-sector organizations. According to agency theory, those who seek a particular good or service are called 'principals' and those with whom they contract are called 'agents'. Hence, voters can be seen as principals who purchase various services from their agents, namely MPs and Parliament. Likewise, ministers can be seen as principals who purchase various services from their departments and other agencies. The costs of undertaking these transactions and of preventing opportunistic behaviour by the parties involved are referred to as agency costs. In designing institutional arrangements and governance structures, agency theorists argue that one of the aims should be to minimize these costs. For instance, it is claimed that agency costs are lower when an agent serves only one principal rather than multiple principals. Hence, dual accountability systems are generally not favoured by agency theorists.

A third, and related, feature of the New Zealand model is its strong emphasis on contractual relationships and the language of contract. One of the key manifestations of this 'contractualism' or 'new contractualism', as it is variously called, has been the introduction of a wide range of contractualist instruments (e.g. purchase agreements, performance agreements, ownership agreements, and so on). For instance, in addition to their contracts of employment, departmental heads now have performance agreements with their portfolio ministers. Indeed, performance agreements have become an increasingly common instrument of control and accountability at all levels in public organizations. Similarly, formal contracts of various kinds are now used to govern the relationships between public organizations (e.g. between funders and purchasers, purchasers and providers, funders and regulators, and so on). While some of these contracts are legally binding, others are more in the nature of mutual undertakings. Regardless of their legal status, however, the aim of these contracts is to specify as precisely as possible the requirements of the principal and to ensure that agents can be held to account for their performance.

The new model of public management in New Zealand, and especially the increasing reliance on third-party government, agency theory and contractualist modes of governance, raises numerous questions. What kinds of contract are now in use, and how do they differ? What are the strengths and weaknesses of using contractualist instruments to manage inter-personal and inter-institutional relationships? Are the often high transaction costs associated with the new arrangements undermining the quest for greater efficiency? Why have contractualist doctrines acquired such prominence at this juncture in history, and what relationship, if any, is there between contemporary contractualism and the ideas of the social contract theorists in the seventeenth and eighteenth centuries? What are the strengths and weaknesses of agency theory? Can it be applied to complex constitutional relationships and, if so, with what consequences? What are the implications of the growing use of competitive tendering and external contractors by public agencies? In particular, what impact is this development having on the accountability of the executive, the ethos of the public service and the core capabilities of public agencies? Are there certain government functions which should never be contracted out?

What implications do the various changes in public-sector management have for the role of the courts and the scope for judicial review? And does the increasing reliance on market mechanisms and consumer preferences rest on secure philosophical foundations?

To explore these and related matters, the New Zealand Politics Research Group sponsored a conference in early July 1994 on 'The Reconfiguration of the State'. Seven papers were presented at this conference, two from overseas contributors. These papers — some significantly revised — furnish the bulk of the essays in this volume (chapters 1–5, 8 and 9). In addition, two essays, both by Australian academics, have been included (chapters 6 and 7), in each case because they touch on one or other of the central themes of the conference.

The essays in this collection vary a good deal in their subject matter, theoretical orientation and methodological approach. Some deal primarily with public management developments in New Zealand; others have a broader international orientation. Some have a strong empirical focus; others are much more philosophical in nature. Some indicate broad support for the changes in public management during the past decade; others are much more sceptical. As conference organizer and editor, I have been concerned not to strive for theoretical consistency among the contributors, let alone to impose a narrow, doctrinal uniformity. On the contrary, my aim has been to bring together contributors from various disciplinary backgrounds (e.g. law, political philosophy, public administration and sociology) and from different theoretical traditions in the interests of providing a range of perspectives on issues concerning the future shape and role of the state both in New Zealand and beyond. Although this volume is primarily concerned with the reconfiguration of the state and the rise of contractualist approaches to governance, its coverage is by no means complete. The analyses offered here are intended to stimulate further discussion, not to provide a definitive treatment. It is to be hoped, therefore, that other scholars will take up the challenge to extend and refine some of the work begun here.

Let me briefly outline the key themes and issues addressed in each chapter.

Michael Trebilcock, in chapter 1, begins by exploring some of the pressures which have led governments within the OECD to embark on the 'reinvention' of the state. Against this background, he examines the various policy levers or governing instruments available to policy-makers:

bureaucratic provision, contracting out, management contracts, franchising, licensing and individual contracting. Three sets of criteria, he argues, ought to bear on the choice of instrument: efficiency, distributive justice, and political considerations. Under the heading of efficiency, Trebilcock gives particular attention to the burgeoning literature on agency theory and provides a very useful summary of the nature of agency costs and the application of agency cost concepts to the public sector. In considering the politics of instrument choice, Trebilcock makes some telling observations about the relationship between means and ends. Rejecting the assumption of the technical efficiency thesis that means and ends can be readily distinguished, he contends that many of the so-called objectives identified and pursued by policy-makers – price stability, lower unemployment, improved educational standards and so forth – are in fact not ends in themselves but rather the means for achieving more ultimate ends. He also rejects the common assumption that once a specific policy objective has been selected it is possible to choose the best policy instrument in an ethically neutral manner.

Contracting and accountability is the theme of chapter 2. Here John Martin reflects on what is meant by the term 'contract' and explores the various kinds of contract that have emerged in the public sector, especially in New Zealand, since the late 1980s. Three kinds of contract are distinguished – spot, classical and relational (or implicit) – and the applicability and relevance of each to public agencies is discussed. Two case studies illustrate the new kinds of contractual arrangement which have emerged. The first explores the government's evolving relationship with the Plunket Society, a voluntary agency which has been providing post-natal services since 1908. Whereas Plunket once received a grant from the central government to cover input costs, it now contracts with regional health authorities to provide outputs. The second case study deals with the Civil Aviation Authority, an advisory and regulatory body established by the Civil Aviation Amendment Act 1990. Under this Act, the authority is required to have a service charter and to enter into an annual performance agreement with the Minister of Transport; its performance is monitored by the Ministry of Transport. Martin argues that the new network of contracts has brought various benefits, particularly in technical efficiency and the tighter specification of objectives. Against this, the move away from traditional hierarchical control mechanisms in the public sector may be reducing political accountability and the responsibility of elected representatives.

Similar concerns are raised by Robert Gregory in chapter 3. Gregory takes as his starting-point the conceptual framework developed by James Q. Wilson, a leading American political scientist and writer on public bureaucracy. Wilson differentiates among public organizations according to, on the one hand, the observability of their outputs and, on the other hand, the observability of their outcomes. He identifies four kinds of task — production, procedural, craft and coping — each of which is characterized by a different type of management culture and a different mix of employee incentives and sanctions. According to Gregory, New Zealand's state-sector reforms have been based on the assumption that public agencies should operate as if all their functions fall within the 'production' category (i.e. that the outputs and outcomes of every function can be readily observed and measured). But such an approach is open to serious objections. For one thing, many of the tasks undertaken by public organizations do not produce easily observable outputs and/or outcomes. For another, to treat all tasks as if they are amenable to a 'production' culture runs the risk of generating goal-displacing behaviour by employees. Worse, according to Gregory, it may result in less responsible, even corrupt behaviour. Gregory acknowledges that his analysis is tentative and, in part, speculative. However, given the number of cases involving official corruption which have come to light in New Zealand recently, Gregory's analysis of the possible ethical implications of managerialism is timely.

While the focus of chapters 2 and 3 is on the merits of the contractualist and managerialist emphasis of the state-sector reforms in New Zealand, chapter 4 addresses the question of whether there are any 'inherently governmental functions' which should not be contracted out to the private sector. In short, can the state be reduced to a mere contractor for services or are there certain public functions which only government employees should carry out? Although such issues have attracted little attention in New Zealand, they have generated increasing concern in the United States. As a result of investigations in the early 1990s, the General Accounting Office reported that many federal agencies were contracting out functions of an inherently governmental nature and that this posed serious questions about the capacity of departmental officials to exercise adequate control over the use of public power. In this chapter I review the arguments advanced by the General Accounting Office and consider their relevance to New Zealand. I then use agency theory and transaction-cost analysis to explore the merits of recent proposals for contracting out most, if not all, of the policy advice services of government departments. My argument is that such proposals encounter four major difficulties: limited contestability between suppliers, the difficulties of specifying and monitoring contracts, the problems generated by political uncertainty, and the increased risk of opportunistic behaviour. Such problems do not imply that the provision of policy advice to ministers should never be contracted out. Nonetheless, they suggest that there are sound reasons for maintaining a permanent, professional, non-partisan policy advice capability within the public sector.

In chapter 5, Mai Chen turns her attention to the implications for the courts of the recent changes to governance structures within the public sector, especially the increasing reliance on profit-oriented Crown-owned companies. A central issue here is whether the commercial decisions of such bodies should be subject to judicial review. Senior jurists are deeply divided on such matters. Proponents of expansive judicial review argue that the decisions of public bodies with public effects should be subject to review by the courts. Indeed, some maintain that all decisions with public effects should, in principle, be open for the courts to review, even if the body making these decisions is private. By contrast, those opposed to expansive judicial review question the competency of the courts to second-guess the merits of companies' commercial decisions. Further, intervention by the courts is likely to thwart Parliament's intention that commercial decisions be left to the boards of Crown-owned companies. In general, Chen supports the latter position. At the same time, she acknowledges the need for public bodies to be accountable to Parliament. In this context she is hopeful that the new system of proportional representation will enhance Parliament's capacity to exercise its scrutiny functions.

Chapters 6 and 7 provide perspectives on contemporary contractualism from Australian academics. In chapter 6, Anna Yeatman analyses the origins, nature and ethos of contractualist doctrines and considers the various critiques to which they have been subjected. The distinguishing feature of contractualism, she argues, is its emphasis on the mediation of social obligation via some form of individualized enquiry, judgement and consent. More narrowly, it is about the freely undertaken and legally sanctioned contractual choices of individuals. Contemporary contractualism, she observes, draws heavily on a number of theoretical discourses, especially rational choice theory and the new institutional economics. According to Yeatman, rational choice theory is more sophisticated than many of its critics recognize. For instance, contrary to the arguments of some, it does not preclude individualized desires of a non-egocentric nature. Nevertheless, she questions one of its central foundations, methodological individualism (i.e. the notion that the whole is never more than the sum of its parts and that collective desires and beliefs do not exist). The chapter then explores two broad lines of attack on the new contractualism: first, internal critiques which focus on the adequacy of the notion of individualized agency; and second, external critiques which focus on the theoretical gaps in contractualist discourses. In sum, Yeatman calls for a critical engagement with the new contractualism and contends that in some contexts (e.g. employment relations and wage bargaining) the best approach is not to oppose contractual arrangements but rather to make them more adequately contractual, or fairer.

While chapter 6 addresses some of the broader philosophical issues of the new contractualism, chapter 7 by Glyn Davis and Margaret Gardner focuses directly and pointedly on the dilemma of applying agency theory to members of Parliament. The context for this discussion is the 1992 proposal of the opposition Liberal and National parties in Australia to model Australian industrial relations policies on those introduced in New Zealand under the Employment Contracts Act 1991. Shortly after the Liberal/National Coalition announced its new policy, John Howard, the Shadow Minister for Industrial Relations, was asked by a journalist whether MPs would be subject to the same wage-fixing procedures as everyone else. Howard responded that, although there might be a case for politicians to negotiate their employment conditions with representatives of the electorate, in practice it would be very difficult for such a system to work. He therefore preferred the existing arrangements by which the salaries of MPs are related to the salary movements of members of the senior executive service in the Australian public service. But, as Davis and Gardner contend, if there is a case for MPs being treated as special — perhaps on the ground that direct negotiations with representatives of the electorate would produce unjust or unfavourable outcomes — presumably other groups of workers could also claim dispensation on similar grounds. After all, when the parties to a contract are in an asymmetric power relationship, as often occurs in industrial relations, the application of simple principal–agent models is likely to produce outcomes which are systematically biased against the weaker party. The arguments presented in chapter 7 are particularly pertinent to New Zealand, not merely because of their relevance to the continuing debates over the Employment Contracts Act but also because of the recent advocacy of performance-based pay for MPs: if Davis and Gardner are correct, remunerating MPs in accordance with their presumed performance is likely to produce highly adverse consequences.

The author of chapter 8, Donald Kettl, is one of America's leading authorities on contracting out and third-party government. In this chapter he explores the recent initiatives of the Clinton Administration to 'reinvent government', and in particular its attempts to introduce more effective performance management systems within the federal government. Accordingly, the chapter focuses on the Government Performance and Results Act (GPRA) 1993. This legislation, passed by an overwhelming majority in Congress, commits the federal government to a ten-year reform programme which includes the development of five-year strategic plans for every federal agency, the introduction of comprehensive performance measures, and the regular monitoring of progress against these measures. Despite the high level of congressional support for the GPRA, Kettl raises serious doubts about whether the Act will achieve its promised goals. The problems of measuring the outputs of government agencies are daunting — a fact which has not been lost on New Zealand reformers in recent times. Another problem, of special significance in a federal system like that of the United States, is that many federal programmes are implemented at the sub-national level and it is often very difficult for federal agencies to hold state and local government administrators accountable. A further problem is the complex nature of the relationships between the various branches of the federal government in America. Above all, however, Kettl argues that if performance-based management is to succeed it must be understood as having more to do with the the art and craft of political communication than with the technical issues of measuring outputs and outcomes.

Underpinning many of the recent market-oriented and contractualist reforms is the assumption that markets provide the most efficient way of allocating scarce resources. But, as is well recognized, markets are efficient in an allocative sense only if certain conditions apply — among them that people behave rationally and that individuals are the best judges of their own interests. In the final chapter, Martin Wilkinson explores some of the philosophical foundations of welfare economics. He begins by examining the nature of rationality and the requirements which must, at least according to economists, be satisfied for agents to act rationally. In this context, he critically assesses the merits of the completeness and transitivity axioms. He then discusses the various ways in which individuals' actions may fail to satisfy their rational interests (e.g. because of mistaken beliefs or preferences). Following this, he explores one of the central assumptions underpinning the principle of consumer sovereignty: the claim that individuals are the best judges of their own interests. His argument is that the 'best judge' view applies to most relatively mundane market transactions undertaken to satisfy a person's short-term self-interested preferences (e.g. buying food and clothing). However, it is less readily applicable to many other transactions, especially those involving altruistic preferences, judgements about a person's long-term self-interest, and complex matters requiring specialized knowledge. Wilkinson does not explore in depth the policy implications of his analysis, but his conclusions highlight the fact that maximizing individuals' choices will not always enhance human well-being.

In an age now so dominated by the ideology and rhetoric of market liberalism, such simple verities risk being all too quickly forgotten.

Jonathan Boston
December 1994

CHAPTER ONE

Can Government Be Reinvented?

Michael J. Trebilcock

We can no longer afford to pay more for — and get less from — our government. The answer for every problem cannot always be another program or more money. It is time to radically change the way the government operates — to shift from top-down bureaucracy to entrepreneurial government that empowers citizens and communities to change our country from the bottom up. We must reward the people and ideas that work and get rid of those that don't.

Bill Clinton and Al Gore

Our goal is to make the entire federal government both less expensive and more efficient, and to change the culture of our national bureaucracy away from complacency and entitlement toward initiative and empowerment. We intend to redesign, to reinvent, to reinvigorate the entire national government.

Bill Clinton[1]

Introduction

In their recent national best-seller, *Reinventing Government,*[2] David Osborne and Ted Gaebler argue that the entrepreneurial spirit is transforming the public sector of the United States and can transform it even more dramatically in the future. According to the front cover, President Clinton claims that the book 'should be read by every elected official in America. This book gives us the blueprint.' A recent commentary[3] notes that this must be 'the first public administration book in history to become a best-seller', probably reflecting the degree of current citizen dissatisfaction and disaffection with the quality of public governance and concerns over run-away government budgetary deficits or debt burdens.

Osborne and Gaebler argue that, in an era of high budget deficits or debt levels and fiscal austerity, the options of more government borrowing to finance public spending, or higher taxes, or dramatic reductions in many public services, are all viewed as strongly unacceptable by a large percentage of American voters. This leaves as the only option the provision of the same, or more, or better-quality public services at less cost (i.e. a dramatic enhancement in the efficiency and productivity of the public sector). In order to achieve this, the authors argue that private-sector organizational analogues should be applied much more comprehensively and rigorously to the public sector. In particular, they conceive of government playing a catalytic role in establishing policy priorities but distinguishing this role sharply from itself delivering goods or services according to these priorities. They call this approach 'steering rather than rowing'. They also argue for substantial devolution or decentralization of government functions to community organizations ('empowering rather than serving'); for more competitive government through injecting competition into service delivery; for mission-driven and result-oriented government, entailing the transformation of rule-driven organizations by funding outcomes and not inputs; for customer-driven government designed to meet the needs of the customer and not the bureaucracy; and for enterprising government that maximizes its possibilities for raising non-tax revenue rather than simply spending tax revenues. The book is replete with numerous examples of all these precepts drawn from recent public-sector experience in the US at federal, state and local government levels.

The recently released National Performance Review,[4] chaired by Vice-President Gore, echoes many of these precepts, again accompanied by numerous examples of proposed changes in programme design or delivery. The Gore Task Force argues for (i) cutting red tape, by streamlining the budget process, decentralizing personnel policy, streamlining procurement, eliminating regulatory overkill, and empowering state and local governments; (ii) putting customers first, by reducing the number of internal monopolies, encouraging contracting out, and harnessing market incentives to improve bureaucratic performance; (iii) empowering employees to get results, by decentralizing decision-making authority, flattening managerial hierarchies, enhancing skills-training opportunities and incentives, and improving the quality and accessibility of information technologies in the workplace; and (iv) cutting back to basics by eliminating special-interest subsidies or perks, utilizing more user charges for government services and collecting more efficiently outstanding charges or debts, making more long-term capital and other investments in enhanced bureaucratic productivity. The Gore Task Force estimates that over a five-year period (1995–99) its proposals, if fully implemented, will generate net savings of US$108 billion, reduce the federal civilian payroll by 252,000 positions (12 per cent), and provide better government for less.

I do not mean to deprecate the highly suggestive proposals in Osborne and Gaebler's book, but its reliance on a combination of messianic fervour and casual empirical vignettes leaves to others the task of developing the rigorous theoretical frameworks and detailed empirical investigations that would enable hard policy choices to be made among alternative governing instruments in particular sectors of government activity. While the *Gore Report* is commendably more specific in its proposals, it too relies heavily on rhetoric and passion in its commitment to more 'entrepreneurial' government, and the feasibility of its proposals along several dimensions requires careful evaluation. In this chapter, I make a start at outlining some of the difficult theoretical and empirical issues that must be resolved if a radical transformation of government is to be attempted.

Before I embark on this task, a cautionary note is in order. The demand for the elimination of 'waste and inefficiency' in government has been a recurrent theme in most industrialized countries, including New Zealand, over the past few decades, voiced most intensely in difficult economic times. In such times, rival political parties aspiring to office routinely promise to cut public spending by attacking public sector 'waste, in- efficiency, duplication and overlap'. Typically, they do not specify in advance what they have in mind or what fiscal magnitudes might realistically be entailed and, having attained office, they largely ignore the issue or confine themselves for the most part to moving bureaucratic organizational charts around.

Despite the revelatory tone of Osborne and Gaebler's book, for close students of government these issues carry strong elements of *déjà vu*. In most industrialized economies, the organization of government has been the subject of detailed and repeated study over the years. For example, in Canada, the federal government's white paper *Public Service 2000: The Renewal of the Public Service of Canada*[5] in 1990 identified many of the same concerns and responses relating to the performance of the public sector.

In 1986, the Neilsen Task Force,[6] in a department-by-department review, identified countless areas of potential savings. In 1979 and 1981, the Economic Council of Canada issued two detailed reports recommending extensive reforms of the regulatory process.[7] In 1979, the Lambert Royal Commission on Financial Management and Accountability[8] proposed detailed recommendations for improving the management of the public sector. In 1963, the Royal Commission on Government Organization (the Glassco Commission) also advanced detailed proposals for enhancing the efficiency of the federal civil service. The *Gore Report* chronicles a similar history of efforts to enhance the efficiency of the public sector in the US — a summary of the table of contents alone of these reports apparently filled 83 notebooks.[9] Dalliances with 'scientific' public-sector management techniques like Planning, Programming and Budgeting Systems (PPBS), Management by Objectives (MBO), zero-based budgeting, sunset laws, cost-benefit and cost-effectiveness analysis, and value-for-money public audits, date back in Canada[10] and the US at least to the early 1960s. A cynic might conclude that these exercises were largely diversions or distractions initiated by politicians unable or unwilling to make hard political choices. The rejoinder might be, however, that the severity of the fiscal crisis now confronting governments renders past experience little guide to the future: now politicians have no choice but to act. As Dr Johnson noted, the prospect of a hanging wonderfully concentrates the mind. In short, good economics and good politics may have sharply converged. The extent of this potential convergence is a major focus of this chapter.

Criteria for Instrument Choice

I will argue that three sets of considerations should or will bear on the question of instrument choice: (i) technical or efficiency considerations, designed to identify the policy instrument that is likely to lead to the realization of a given policy objective at least cost, in terms of economic resources deployed; (ii) principled distributive justice considerations, reflecting concerns over ability to pay and avoiding excessive burdens on the least advantaged members of society in terms of how consumption or use of the goods or services in question should be financed — in short, who should pay for these goods and services; (iii) whatever the normative implications for instrument choice suggested by efficiency and distributional considerations, the incentive structure of our political system may,

may, as a matter of positive analysis, imply a different set of instrument choices. In this sense, political considerations can be viewed as a constraint on the application of efficiency and distributional considerations to instrument choice.

Efficiency Considerations

Agency Cost Theory

One of the most rapidly burgeoning bodies of literature in law and economics pertains to agency cost theory and the theory of the firm (or more generally theories of corporate governance).[11] These two related bodies of theory attempt to explain diverse organizational and governance structures observable in the private sector.

Agency costs arise whenever one person or organization (the principal) contracts with another person or organization (the agent) to perform a service for the principal, and the performance of this service necessitates the delegation of some decision-making authority from the principal to the agent. The agency problem is the difficulty of ensuring that the principal is faithfully served and that the agent is fairly compensated in situations where the agent's interests do not coincide with those of the principal and where the principal has incomplete control over the agent and the agent has incomplete information about the principal's interests.[12] Michael Jensen and Clifford Smith identify three types of agency costs.[13] First, there is the cost of structuring the contract so as to require the agent to perform the desired service as a proxy for the principal. Second, there is the cost of enforcing the contract.[14] Third, there are residual losses.[15]

Different organizational arrangements have different inherent incentive structures that yield different agency costs. For example, owner-managed firms, and firms that are managed by professional managers and in which the owners (shareholders) have little involvement in day-to-day control of organizational activities, are major representative types of private-sector organizational structure. In owner-managed firms (e.g. small businesses or professional partnerships), agency costs are minimized by the fact that ultimately the owners are in charge. While owners may be required to delegate a certain amount of decision-making authority to their subordinates, ultimate authority remains in their hands. In exercising this ultimate authority and control, they will be motivated by the fact that the more efficiently the firm operates, the greater the profits that accrue to them as the owners (residual claimants). Consequently, they have strong incentives to ensure that the behaviour of their subordinates is as efficient as possible. In contrast, in the case of firms where ownership and management are separated — typically firms whose stock is publicly traded on the stock market — these firms have widely diffused owners (shareholders) who collectively delegate responsibilities to professional managers. The agency problem arises because the managers will often be tempted to act in their own self-interest, not in the best interests of the company as represented by the shareholders as residual claimants, who face a collective action problem in co-ordinating monitoring efforts.[16]

The recent literature identifies three main factors that help align the interests of principals and agents in publicly traded corporations: the market for managers, the output market, and the market for corporate control. First, competition in the market among and for managers encourages greater efficiency, greater innovation and lower agency costs.[17] Second, competition among firms in their output markets requires firms to act efficiently if they are to survive and managers are to retain their jobs.[18] Third, private capital markets where firms must raise equity or debt capital will discipline weak management. More specifically, open-market trading of stock contributes to the minimization of agency costs, in part because senior management is frequently compensated at least in part based on stock performance, and firms considering hiring new managers often evaluate candidates on their previous performance with other companies as reflected in the stock performance of those companies.[19] In addition, where a firm's shares are traded on the stock market, corporate takeovers are possible whenever a company is being poorly managed and hence its assets depreciated (the market for corporate control). Since takeovers often result in management being replaced by a new team, existing managers will be motivated to perform their functions efficiently so as to ensure that a takeover does not occur.[20]

Of course, these factors cannot perfectly align managerial and shareholder interests. While they do significantly reduce agency costs, there will always remain some room for managerial and employee inefficiency. Moreover, there is likely to be more room for inefficient behaviour in a professionally managed firm than in an owner-managed firm where the owner's residual interest in profits is simply a stronger constraint on agency costs than the constraints on the professionally managed firm.[21]

If one relates these agency cost concepts to the public sector, it is easy to see why the problem of agency costs is likely to be much more severe there. First, the owners of public-sector activities (i.e. the electorate or taxpayers) exert little control over the managers of public-sector agencies and are therefore likely to be ineffective at minimizing agency costs. Their control over management is even weaker than that of shareholders in large publicly traded corporations. This is due primarily to the extremely diffuse nature of ownership of public agencies. Electors could increase the control they exert over management by banding together in large powerful groups. However, individual electors have little incentive to do this because their share of the cost of an agency's inefficiency is infinitesimally small and collective action (free-rider) problems are likely severely to undermine attempts at concerted action.[22] While the market for government debt has some disciplinary effect on government fiscal management, this typically operates at a highly aggregated level, and will not finely differentiate the performance of different government agencies.

Second, the other factors that minimize agency costs in large publicly traded corporations are not as prevalent in the public sector. Competition among managers is muted by highly formalized rules for promotions. Moreover, public-sector agencies rarely face competition in their output markets and therefore cannot be driven out of business by competition; nor can taxpayers easily compare the cost or quality of their public services with those of alternative providers.

Third, shares in public-sector agencies are not traded on the open market and consequently there is no risk of corporate takeover. Furthermore, evaluating the performance of senior management without the aid of the stock market is more difficult. While it might be argued that politicians can act as monitors of the efficiency of public agencies and attempt to minimize agency costs, unless taxpayers as the ultimate shareholders are able to hold the politicians accountable for their monitoring role, politicians are likely to have weak incentives to do so and raise an agency cost problem in their own right (the dual agency problem). Moreover, there are likely to be some beneficiaries from public-sector inefficiency, such as sub-sets of public servants and private-sector constituencies, who may represent powerful interest groups and may resist attempts by politicians to take effective measures to contain agency costs in public institutions.[23] One person's notion of waste will be another person's notion of rents.

The Theory of the Firm

Economic literature on the theory of the firm has attempted to explain why some private-sector economic activity is organized within firms and others through the market (the 'make or buy' decision). For example, if General Motors requires tyres for its cars, it may purchase them from a tyre-manufacturing company or it may create its own tyre-manufacturing division. Why do firms sometimes produce their own inputs and at other times contract out the provision of inputs? Ronald Coase's pioneering analysis of this question focuses on the transaction costs inherent in organizing an activity through either the market or the firm.[24] Where a transaction is organized through the market, information on available prices and quality must be obtained. As well, contracts must be negotiated, monitored and enforced for each purchase. Each of these steps is costly. However, internalizing production is also costly because information on the value and scarcity of inputs, which would otherwise be provided by the market, is replaced by less accurate internal proxies.[25] Subsequent theorists have stressed the relative costs of different forms of opportunism under contracting-out and internal production regimes.[26] In the case of contracting out, there are incentives for the outside contractor to engage in pecuniary forms of opportunism by chiselling on features of the contract that are difficulty to specify, monitor or enforce. Where production is moved in-house on an employment basis, there are incentives to engage in non-pecuniary forms of opportunism, such as consumption or slacking on the job, given that remuneration is typically not closely tied to output. Alternative arrangements for the supply of inputs all entail contractual arrangements of one form or another, although with different incentive structures. Indeed, it is now common to view a firm as simply a 'nexus of contracts' of various kinds with different stakeholders.[27]

The implications of this literature are, on the one hand, that market provision of needed inputs may well be more efficient when needs can be easily specified and are relatively constant, when compliance with contractual terms is easily monitored, when negotiation of contracts is relatively inexpensive, and when highly differentiated inputs with few economies of scale and scope but large returns to specialization are entailed. On the other hand, 'in firm' production becomes preferred when needs become more difficult to specify or are in a state of continuous evolution and change, when compliance with contractual terms becomes more difficult to monitor and hence there is an increased risk of chiselling by contractors, and when contract negotiations become more complicated and expensive.[28]

The relevance of the theory of the firm for the choice of public-sector organizational arrangements is obvious. When a government decides to embark on a new activity it faces the following choices:[29] (i) performing the activity itself 'in house', either by using public servants on a conventional employment basis within a government department or 'corporatizing' the activities by creating a state-owned enterprise with institutional structures analogous to those of a private-sector enterprise and with greater autonomy in decision-making about both inputs and outputs than the public service at large; (ii) contracting out; (iii) management contracts; (iv) franchising; (v) licensing; (vi) individual contracting (subject, where appropriate, to regulation). I will briefly review the incentive properties associated with each of these organizational options.

Alternative Arrangements for the Provision of Public Goods
(i) Bureaucratic Provision
Recent proposals for reorganizing the public sector explicitly invoke private-sector analogies. For example, the Canadian federal government's white paper *Public Service 2000*[30] recommends: increased reliance on output measures and mission statements for government departments and agencies; reduced reliance on input regulation through more flexible job-classification systems and enhanced ability of senior managers to hire, fire and set appropriate rates of remuneration for employees; greater use of pecuniary and non-pecuniary reward systems for outstanding individual performance or innovative or productivity-enhancing ideas; more flexible budgetary arrangements which permit deviations from line-item budget constraints, which permit all or some percentage of cost savings realized during a fiscal year to be retained by a department rather than surrendered to central agencies, and which avoid budget reductions in ensuing years that penalize cost savings in prior years; encouraging flatter, less hierarchical and more participatory internal department structures; and greater reliance on consumer-satisfaction surveys in order to ensure responsiveness to citizen expectations. Progress reports issued by the Public Service 2000 Taskforce provide encouraging examples of action in a number of departments on many of these fronts.[31] Reforms of the public sector in New Zealand and elsewhere in the 1980s have adopted a similar orientation.[32] As noted earlier, the recent *Gore Report* in the US strongly espouses similar reforms.[33]

However, the argument for 'management by objectives' rather than detailed system-wide prescription of inputs has a long genesis in various government studies and the public administration literature, and in general has not led to radical transformations in the organization of bureaucracies. There are several reasons for this. While for some government services it may be possible to specify outputs with some precision, for many services departments often have multiple missions, sometimes conflicting mandates, and overlapping functions with other departments. Profitability, or rate of return on invested capital, in the private sector has no close analogue in the public sector. To take an extreme case, specifying the desired output from the Canadian Department of Foreign Affairs or the Department of Defense is likely to entail largely meaningless bromides. With activities in the large spending categories of health, education and welfare, stipulating outputs in a sufficiently precise way so that the performance of a department can be meaningfully evaluated against its progress towards these objectives may be next to impossible. Even with relatively routine functions, like processing tax returns, specifying (as the Canadian Department of National Revenue has done in response to *Public Service 2000*) waiting time by taxpayers with inquiries at local offices or in making telephone inquiries may incompletely capture the relevant objectives. For example, while many taxpayers' inquiries might be processed in a given period of time, if the advice is incorrect, or if tax returns are being inaccurately processed by achieving the stipulated rate, efficiency has gone down rather than up. Or, to take other examples, expenditures per client served in Ontario from 1977–78 to 1991–92 in constant dollars show dramatic increases for hospitals, schools and the public service, and relatively constant or declining per capita expenditures for universities and colleges, with a more erratic trend line for correctional services. In order to be confident of what these numbers mean, however, one would need to know whether universities and community colleges, in spending less money per student processed, are offering an enhanced, constant or declining quality of education, which presumably can be determined only by much more sophisticated measures of subsequent student performance in job markets, graduate schools, and so on, than indicated by a simple through-put count. In the case of elementary and secondary schools where total school costs per pupil in constant dollars have dramatically escalated over the period, this might be efficient if the increases in expenditure were accompanied by equal or larger increases in the quality of students graduating from the system. Many citizens of Ontario believe this not to be true, relying on international comparative testing of numeracy and literacy,[34] but again one would want to look at trend lines over time. Similarly, if increased hospital expenditures per patient day were accompanied by an even more dramatic improvement in the health status of the population, these expenditures may be efficient. Without admittedly elusive measures of this kind, however, we really have no accurate measure of the efficiency of these expenditures. In short, *outputs* are not to be confused with *outcomes*.

The problems of specifying desired outcomes with sufficient precision so as to constitute meaningful performance measures against which government agencies can be evaluated without reliance on input measures (i.e. specifying an output objective but not prescribing a production function) are graphically illustrated by James Q. Wilson in a recent article in the *Wall Street Journal*:

> In 1956 Congress passed the Federal Aid Highway Act. In 28 pages, it authorized the interstate highway system, levied the taxes to pay for it and set the (few) rules to be followed in building it. Thirty-five years later, Congress reauthorized it by passing the Intermodal Surface Transportation Efficiency Act of 1991. The new law was over 10 times as long as the original one and not only told the Secretary of Transportation to 'finish the interstate highway system' but gave him, by my count, over 20 new goals and constraints. Among these were: preserve historic sites, reduce erosion, encourage the use of seat belts, control outdoor advertising, hire Indians, reduce drunken driving, use recycled rubber in making asphalt, give 10% of the construction to businesses owned by women or other 'disadvantaged' individuals, buy iron and steel from American suppliers, require metropolitan area planning, and limit the use of calcium acetate in performing seismic retrofits on bridges. I doubt that this law, whatever its merits as public policy, will help make the Department of Transportation the kind of lean, flexible, mission-driven, customer-oriented agency of which the *Gore Report* speaks.[35]

There are other problems with a more outcome-oriented, more decentralized bureaucracy with greater decision-making autonomy in relation to inputs (the production function) at the departmental or sub-departmental level. Relaxing centralized constraints ('red tape') on personnel decisions, budgetary expenditures, government procurement and contracting out, and decentralizing decision-making in these areas to a much greater extent to individual agencies or departments of government in order to promote flexibility, adaptability, innovation and dynamism, as *Public Service 2000* and the *Gore Report* recommend, risks discounting excessively the historical reasons for the evolution of these constraints: preventing the abuse of political and bureaucratic discretion through self-dealing, conflicts of interest, improper inducements, personal or political favouritism, and so forth. Relaxing these constraints is likely to increase the incidence of these alleged abuses or simply the good-faith errors of judgement that a more entrepreneurial, risk-taking public-sector environment will generate. Such abuses or errors of judgement, even if relatively isolated and outweighed by improvements in systemic performance, will attract high-profile media attention, while the improvements, because less focused, will not. Risk-averse politicians and bureaucrats will then face incentives to reduce these risks, leading to the resurrection, at least in part, of centralized, input-oriented constraints ('red tape') on decentralized bureaucratic decision-making.

A final and important irony with outcome-oriented bureaucratic policy prescriptions must be confronted. If desired outcomes can be politically agreed on and technically measured with reasonable precision, then this is one of the key conditions that in general make contracting out or external delegation of service provision feasible (albeit with the political implications already reviewed above). If all feasible contracting out or external delegation has occurred, then the remaining bureaucratic functions are, by definition, unlikely to be readily evaluated by output-oriented criteria. Hence, not only for political but also for technical reasons, we would be driven back to primary reliance on input regulation of these functions, or at least to making second-best judgements about the relative magnitudes of organizational 'slack' under alternative regimes.

(ii) Contracting Out

This is the most common form of private provision of a public good. The government hires or subsidizes a private company to provide a needed service to all or a segment of the population. Under such an arrangement, the service commonly remains a public good in that it is paid for on behalf of all citizens by the government.

This approach to the provision of public goals has been extended to natural monopolies. In such cases, Harold Demsetz[36] argues that, if competitive bidding is instituted for the contract, the abuse of monopoly power is eliminated because firms, in bidding for the contract to service the market at the lowest cost, will drive the prices to be charged down from the monopoly level to the competitive level. Demsetz argues that, while *competition within the market* is inefficient and should not occur with a natural monopoly, there is an alternative to regulation: the organization of *competition for the market*. Demsetz argues that such a procedure would eliminate the need to regulate prices charged by natural monopolies.

Oliver Williamson[37] raises two problems with Demsetz's argument. First, how does one design a long-term contract that accounts for unforeseeable future changes in service objectives, technology, input costs or other factors? As input costs change or technology evolves, it may be necessary to alter the contractually agreed-upon service arrangement and prices. Service objectives are not always static or explicitly quantifiable and may require periodic modification. Given these factors, contracts with the 'low bid firm' for the provision of monopoly services must be flexible. In fact, there may be so much flexibility built into the contract that the firm can adapt to future changes in such a way as to exercise some monopoly power. This bilateral monopoly problem becomes more severe the longer the contract lasts.

A second difficulty with Demsetz's theory is that incumbent contract-holders often have a considerable advantage at renewal time over their competitors. Government will not want the potential disruption of changing contractors. Also, because the current contract-holder already owns the relevant assets, has a specialized staff and is better informed about operating costs, it is in a significantly better position at renewal time than its competitors, who must start from scratch in bidding for the contract renewal and must purchase all the necessary assets, often from the incumbent where the assets are highly specific. As a result, the degree of competition for the market is reduced and the risk of prices rising above the competitive level re-emerges. This problem is greatest when the good or service in question is supported by durable investments in transaction-specific human or physical assets.[38]

For both of the reasons identified by Williamson, the contracting-out of natural monopolies may in some cases enable the contractor to earn above-normal profits in the absence of regulation. Williamson concludes that:

> where significant investments in durable specific assets are required and contracts are subject to technological and market uncertainties, . . . bidding in practice requires the progressive elaboration of an administration apparatus that

differs mainly in name rather than in kind from that which is associated with
... regulation.[39]

With many government functions, problems in defining and monitoring the desired output are likely to be severe, and may engender serious
risks of pecuniary opportunism by contractors on unconstrained
contractual margins, or alternatively the use of second-best proxies for
desired outputs.[40] In some of these contexts, Henry Hansmann[41] has
persuasively argued that another option is the subsidization of service
provision, either directly by government or through the tax system, by
non-profit organizations in the so-called 'third sector'. This may be a more
efficient option than either private for-profit provision or centralized
provision. Because non-profit organizations typically do not have residual
claimants to their revenue stream, there is less incentive than with private
for-profit providers to engage in pecuniary forms of chiselling on
commitments to public- or private-sector donors. Agency costs, however,
are not eliminated entirely by the non-profit form. The non-profit provider
of a good or service has less incentive to be efficient than a profit-
maximizing provider because cost savings do not accrue to such a provider
as profit. We would therefore expect more 'slack' in a non-profit enterprise
and also more transforming of profits into perquisites (or perks). However,
according to Richard Posner,[42] there are reasons why all revenues do not
get transformed into non-pecuniary perquisites. First, beyond a point soon
reached, the utility conferred by a perk may be only a small fraction of
its cost. Second, both private and public donors will not donate to a non-
profit organization whose employees are known to over-indulge in perks.
Third, an enterprise that constrains profit-making may attract as employees
people less preoccupied with money-making than comparable employees
of profit-making enterprises. They may be more risk averse and hence
more willing to trade money income for job security, or their utility
functions may be dominated by non-pecuniary sources of utility.[43]

While the problems of defining, monitoring and enforcing desired
outcomes with respect to the contracting-out of public services are
pervasive and arise in most major areas of public expenditure, such as
health, education and social welfare, the problems can perhaps best be
illustrated with a contemporary and controversial example: the contracting-
out of correctional services.

An intense public and academic debate is in progress in the US, Britain,
New Zealand and elsewhere on the potential role for private prisons.[44] The

argument made in favour of private prisons is that which is generally made for contracting out government services: costs to the public sector can be reduced by putting up for competitive tender the operation of correctional facilities, on the assumption that a private operator will have the usual economic incentives to minimize costs of operation. These in turn will be reflected in the competitively determined service fee, which one might expect to be lower than the costs entailed in public provision where this competitive discipline is absent.

A number of problems arise with this proposal. First, even in an economic framework, there is the difficulty of being confident that a competitive bidding process can be sustained over time if private operators are expected not only to operate but to build or own the facilities in question. Given the highly specialized nature of these assets and the sunk costs entailed, it seems unlikely that at contract renewal time there will be other private bidders with alternative facilities. This problem might be overcome by the state owning the facilities and leasing them to the successful bidder for the period of the contract at a pre-determined price, with the operating contract being essentially a management contract. But there would still be legitimate concerns, reflecting the implications of agency cost theory and the theory of the firm reviewed above, that the private operator would have incentives, once a contract has been entered into, to chisel on various kinds of costs (e.g. in feeding and clothing prisoners and providing adequate services and amenities).[45] Many of these forms of chiselling may not be readily observable to the public-sector overseer. Even if these problems can be overcome, there is a major question of determining what the private contractor is to be remunerated for. If the contractor is paid on a prisoner *per diem* basis, there would be perverse incentives to promote recidivism or at least not to promote rehabilitation. If the contractor is paid on some combination of a *per diem* rate and a royalty reflecting rehabilitation rates, thus creating an incentive to provide rehabilitative services, then defining and measuring recidivism or rehabilitation rates and determining how to attribute these to particular correctional institutions would have to be resolved.

Setting aside such problems of writing contracts that specify appropriate outcomes and monitoring and enforcing contractual obligations, one might well expect resistance to this proposal at a political level from at least two quarters. First, current public-sector employees in the correctional services system might resist strongly the contracting-out of these functions.

Second, many members of the public might view the 'privatization' of correctional services as violating an important moralism in that, when punishment is imposed on wrongdoers, it is important that this be unambiguously perceived both by them and by other potential wrongdoers as the collective judgement and retribution of the community, acting directly through the agency of the state. That is to say, crimes should be seen as violations of community values, and the community should signify, as clearly and directly as possible, its disapprobation through direct state administration of an appropriate punishment.

All of these concerns may still leave some room for more disaggregated contracting-out by the state (e.g. of catering, janitorial and maintenance services in the correctional services system). Indeed, this may also be a feasible strategy for other public-sector functions where no generalized 'bottom-line' can be precisely defined.

(iii) Management Contracts

Management contracts represent a type of contracting out that has been suggested as a partial solution to some of the problems raised by Williamson and others. Under a management contract, a private firm is hired to provide a public service, but the assets used to provide the service are owned by the government. For example, a hydro-electric plant may be owned by the government but its operation contracted out to a private-sector firm. This enables the government to benefit from the improved efficiency associated with private-sector service provision, while avoiding one of the major problems with contracting out: the contractor's ownership of specialized assets. When a management contract comes up for renewal, the incumbent contractor does not benefit from a competitive advantage associated with specialized asset ownership because the physical assets in question are owned by the government, although the possession of specialized human capital may still confer some advantage on the incumbent.

In drafting management contracts, particular attention must be paid to structuring the relationship so as to align the management contractor's interest with that of the assets' owner (e.g. the government). For example, a management contractor may be tempted to cut costs by neglecting properly to maintain government-owned assets. A properly designed management contract will utilize incentives to maintain the assets properly. However, designing, monitoring and enforcing a management contract that accounts for all such agency costs can be quite problematic.

(iv) Franchising

Franchising is similar to contracting out, but with two important differences. First, under a franchise arrangement, the franchisee is generally paid directly by citizens for services rendered rather than being paid by the government out of general tax revenues. Second, because of the payment arrangement, citizens are able to save money under a franchising arrangement by not purchasing the service from the franchisee. While they cannot purchase the service from another company, they can choose to reduce their consumption or to provide the service themselves. Under contracting out, these choices would be valueless to the citizen since the citizen has already paid for the service through taxes.

Franchising enjoys virtually all the advantages of contracting out, with two exceptions. First, because the franchise-holder is paid directly by citizens, and not by the government, the franchise-holder must incur expenses involved in billing and collecting not incurred by the contractor. Consequently, franchising may entail higher transaction costs than contracting out. Second, the government may feel compelled to consider the need for direct subsidies to low-income members of society who would be unable to pay for the service on their own.

The main advantage of franchising is that it requires most citizens to pay for the service according to the degree they choose to use it, and thus utilizes the price mechanism to ration demand. Furthermore, the franchise-holder can be required to pay the government for permission to hold the franchise. Therefore, this system not only reduces government expenditures but also raises revenue. However, once again, such a form of private-sector service provision is valuable only if it is desirable for most citizens and not the government to pay for the service. In making this decision, the government should consider whether the service is used at different rates by different citizens and whether it is practical and distributionally de-fensible to calculate a price and charge each service-user individually according to consumption.

(v) Licensing

Under this arrangement, the government allows (but does not require) one or more private firms to provide the service to citizens. A licensing arrangement where there is only one licence-holder in an area is almost identical to franchising. The more common form of licensing, however, is to allow several, sometimes many, competitors to enter the market. The licence is usually associated with a variety of restrictions and regulations concerning the private firm's activities. As well, the threat of licence cancellation serves as a bonding mechanism to ensure adherence to the prescribed conditions.

Such a system ensures that relatively competitive prices emerge without relying on Demsetz's theory of competition for the market or on price regulation. This form of competition is therefore not subject to Williamson's criticisms of Demsetz's theory, although obviously it is not a feasible option in industries with natural monopoly characteristics.

However, the requirement for a licence implies that competition may be limited. This makes collusion among licensees easier and makes it more likely that the market price will be somewhat higher than the truly competitive level. This risk is particularly significant when existing licensees are able successfully to resist the granting of new licences.

(vi) Individual Contracting (with Regulation, Where Appropriate)
Individual contracting contemplates a largely open market in which a number of firms compete and customers individually contract for service provision from the firm of their choice. It is different from licensing in that no limits are placed on the number of firms that can compete. Since entry is unrestricted, there is less opportunity for collusion among service suppliers. Even so, government may be interested in regulating the behaviour of the competing companies. While pricing is unlikely to be the subject of regulation, the government may still wish to regulate the industry so as to protect, for instance, worker safety, citizen safety, environmental safety or consumer welfare.

Such regulation is more difficult and costly to implement in an individual contracting arrangement, with many participants and frequent entry and exit, than under a licensing regime, for several reasons. First, under a licensing arrangement, the number of firms requiring regulation and their identities are known to and controlled by the licensing authorities. Second, under a licensing arrangement, firms can be informed of all regulations and have their compliance with these regulations monitored as part of the licensing and licence-renewal process. Finally, under a licensing arrangement, the threat of cancellation of a licence acts as a bonding device which helps to ensure that firms comply with regulations.

All of these factors, which render the process of regulation easier to administer, are absent from an individual contracting arrangement. Consequently, while individual contracting provides for more effective price discipline than licensing arrangements, regulation of non-price factors may prove more difficult.

Licensing or regulation may be either directly undertaken by government, or delegated to a specialized independent agency created by government, or delegated to self-regulating professional or trade associations. In addition, a regulatory regime may focus principally on outputs or outcomes, or principally on inputs. For example, a regulation that prescribes a limit on the quantity of a pollutant that a firm may emit would focus on outputs, while a regulation that prescribes what abatement technology a firm must employ would focus on inputs.

(vii) Summary

Once the decision to use a private-sector service provider is made, one of five principal private-sector organizational options must be chosen: contracting out, management contracts, franchising, licensing or individual contracting (subject to regulation, where appropriate). All of these options can be viewed as entailing explicit or implicit contracts of various kinds between government and private-sector agents. In an economic framework, choices among them or combinations of them would turn on relative transaction and agency costs of various kinds. Contracting out, management contracts and franchising are best suited to situations where economies of scale favour monopolistic service provision. Among these three, contracting out is to be preferred when the government wishes to continue paying for the service. Management contracts may be preferred when specialized assets must be used in providing the service. Franchising is to be preferred when the government wants citizens to pay directly for the services they receive.

If the service is not a natural monopoly, a choice must be made between licensing and individual contracting. Between these two, individual contracting allows for greater competitive discipline in prices. However, if the government wishes to regulate non-price factors or to control externalities, this may be easier to achieve through a licensing arrangement.

Each option has relative strengths and weaknesses that must be matched with programme objectives in order to choose the most effective private-sector organizational arrangement. Much of the thrust of Osborne and

Gaebler's book is that governments at all levels rely excessively on 'in house' production of public goods ('rowing') and unduly discount the efficiency gains likely to be realized from the various private provision options reviewed above ('steering'). Indeed, extensive studies that have compared the relative efficiency of private- and public-sector provision of various services have found substantial productive efficiency gains from private provision, thus corroborating the implications of agency cost theory and suggesting substantial gains from governmental delegation of service provision under these options, as implied by the theory of the firm.[46] In most cases, government-provided services range from being 30 per cent to 90 per cent more costly than equivalent private-contractor service provision.[47] Moreover, notwithstanding common claims to the contrary, these cost differences are principally explained not by wage differences between the public and private sectors, but rather by the greater productivity of the private sector in providing most of these services. However, where public-sector agencies are required to compete with private-sector providers, these productivity differences often largely disappear.[48]

The puzzle that remains to be explained is why governments have not chosen to invoke these policy instruments more frequently. In other words, if, following Stephen Breyer and Charles Schultze,[49] there are such pervasive 'mismatches' of policy instruments and policy objectives, is this a reflection of chronic but curable ignorance or stupidity on the part of public-sector decision-makers, or are there more systemic and enduring forces at play that explain these instrument choices? This requires us to turn from economic theories of choice of governing instrument in the private sector to the second and third classes of consideration bearing on public-sector instrument choice: distributional considerations, and political theories of instrument choice.

Distributional Considerations

The efficiency considerations canvassed above all relate to the question of how to generate a desired policy output or outcome at least cost in terms of the economic resources deployed in producing that output or outcome. However, it will be obvious that in many contexts the incidence of the costs of providing the goods or services in question on different groups in the community will legitimately engage principled distributional concerns. These concerns relate to differential ability to pay for 'essential' goods and services (so-called 'merit goods') and the desirability of not imposing undue burdens on the least-advantaged members of the community.[50] I distinguish sharply these concerns from redistributional or rent-seeking activities pursued by special interests through the political process, which do not legitimately engage distributive justice values.

It is important to stress at the outset that public or private provision of public goods does not correlate closely with public or private payment for the goods or services produced and consumed. Collectively supplied goods can be provided free of charge, at a nominal charge, at full cost or according to a variable means-tested charge to consumers. Just as a collective decision to ensure the provision of a higher quantity or quality of goods or services than unregulated markets would provide does not pre-ordain whether these goods or services should be publicly or privately provided, so also legitimate distributional concerns that might favour either universal access to goods or services or targeted assistance to less-advantaged citizens do not pre-ordain public or private provision. In choosing among alternative policy instruments for the realization of given policy objectives, clarity of analysis requires that these issues not be elided.

Clarifying the relationship between these issues is facilitated by thinking through the sequence of decisions that a government might make, having decided, for example, that some form of government intervention is required in the provision of infrastructure goods or services. Where the activity in question involves physical infrastructure, it is useful to distinguish the various roles that the government might play in *building* new infrastructure and then in its subsequent *operation*. In the case of a highway or the construction of new airport terminals, say, the government might decide that it will *operate* these facilities itself after construction, but in most cases it is unlikely actually to build these facilities itself using public-service employees. In fact, it would be conventional for the government to contract out the construction of various aspects of these facilities to prime contractors and sub-contractors through a competitive bidding process. This presumably reflects the superior efficiencies of private-sector agents in doing this work and the returns to specialization it often entails. But if the government finances the initial construction of the facility and assumes directly the responsibility for its subsequent operation, clearly the government (and its taxpayers) are the residual risk-bearers in the project. These risks might include cost over-runs in the initial construction, design errors, and errors in estimating the subsequent demand for the services associated with the facility. If the facility is a natural or protected monopoly, the costs associated with these risks presumably can, as a matter of policy choice, be passed on to users of the facility through user charges. If the facility is not a monopoly, the government's ability to pass on these costs will be limited by the availability of substitutes. Even where it is a monopoly, the government's ability to pass on these costs through user charges will be constrained, in some cases, by distributional considerations, which may dictate that the government absorb user costs itself in their entirety, or at least absorb these costs with respect to some targeted portion of the user population.

An alternative risk-minimizing strategy would be for the government to contract out both the initial construction and subsequent operation of the facility to a private-sector firm, perhaps through a competitive bidding process. Here, most of the relevant risks (e.g. cost over-runs, design errors, or mis-estimation of subsequent demand) are shifted to the successful private-sector builder and operator. In effect, this exemplifies the franchising option described earlier in this chapter. If the government wishes to avoid entirely paying for the initial construction costs and to shift these costs and related risks to a private-sector firm, this obviously will come at a cost. After all, private-sector firms will wish to be compensated for these costs and risks through an appropriate return on the facility, presumably generated subsequently either through user charges paid directly by consumers (with the option of reimbursement in all or some cases by government), or alternatively by a government contract with the facility owner stipulating levels of operating subsidies to be provided (financed out of general tax revenues) if the government is committed to providing universal free access. Existing physical infrastructure could also be sold off to the private sector on a competitive bidding basis, with similar subsequent operating options.

Each of these options raises different efficiency/equity trade-offs. The comprehensive (build and operate) franchising option, at first sight, has attractive efficiency properties in that it provides some kind of market-based test of whether the proposed facility has a positive net present value, sufficient to attract private bidders into the market. However, this judgement probably depends on whether the initial capital costs and subsequent operating costs can be covered (along with an adequate rate of return on invested capital) out of subsequent user fees. If usage costs are not privately borne, but subsidized directly or indirectly by government, this judgement becomes much more speculative and error-prone. Moreover, in the absence of market-determined and privately borne usage costs, there will be no obvious mechanism for rationing usage rates with the facility and demand may be socially excessive. Conversely, even if usage costs are privately borne but the facility is a natural or protected monopoly, in the absence of contractual or regulatory constraints imposed by government on subsequent usage charges, the private owner of the monopoly facility is likely to charge excessive prices for the services generated, in which case the opposite problem of socially sub-optimal usage will arise.

In determining how the incidence of usage costs should ultimately be borne, governments will also confront different levels and forms of transaction costs associated with different subsidization mechanisms. Obviously, these costs are minimized if the government simply pays the private provider for all services provided and then makes them available to all members of the public free of charge, recouping these costs out of general tax revenues. However, this distributional choice entirely abandons any reliance on market mechanisms to ration demand and creates, in effect, a moral hazard problem in the form of incentives for excessive use. Alternatively, more targeted forms of subsidization, such as voucher systems, on the one hand preserve market incentives in rationing access to the facility or service to a greater extent, but on the other hand entail higher transaction and administrative costs in means-testing recipients of vouchers. In addition, there are likely to be some social costs from overt stigmatization of recipients of these subsidies.

Obviously, these efficiency/equity trade-offs are likely to prove more acute in some contexts than others. For example, private construction and operation of an airport terminal that caters primarily for business and leisure travellers may not strongly engage legitimate distributional concerns. Similarly, private construction and operation of toll roads or bridges, while impacting on a broader cross-section of the community, may be thought to involve relatively modest financial impositions (like driver licence fees or public utility charges) and therefore to warrant no service-specific distributional response beyond general redistributive policies reflected in our tax-and-transfer system. The provision of health-care services and educational services, however, engages these trade-offs in a much more acute form. Here, user charges will raise serious

GARNETT LIBRARY
SMSU-WEST PLAINS

distributional concerns, as well as negating some of the positive externalities that may be associated with universal access, although the absence
of such charges will remove important market-based incentives to ration
demand and allocate supply. If a collective decision has been made
favouring universal access to a particular good or service (like health care
or education), then direct government provision, or contracting out with
the government directly compensating the provider of the good or service,
or a universal voucher system with users contracting directly with service
providers, seem the most attractive options on distributional grounds. If
more restricted targeted assistance, reflecting ability to pay, is preferred,
then targeted voucher or demand-side indemnification for costs incurred
to private providers by qualifying users may best meet distributional
objectives. All these options entail transfers in kind. If transfers in kind
are not collectively thought justifiable in given contexts — perhaps because
it is thought desirable to utilize the price mechanism as a rationing device
or because in-kind transfers in some contexts are regarded as excessively
paternalistic — then the uneven financial impact of private provision on
users of different means can be left to be accommodated, to some extent,
by the general tax-and-transfer system.

Political Considerations

A substantial body of recent economic analysis of the political process —
often referred to as public choice theory or rational choice theory — reflects
an extension of the logic of conventional economic behavioural postulates
to collective decision-making.[51] Instead of conceiving of the role of the
state as a *deus ex machina* which will eliminate one or another unfortunate
allocative consequence of market failure, public choice theory assumes,
first, that rational self-interested behaviour implies that people are unlikely
to have any *ex ante* preference for the market allocation of resources over
collective allocation of resources, and presumably will choose to invest
resources in pursuing their economic self-interest through either market
activity or political activity, depending on where their net gains are likely
to be greater. Second, as with private markets, whose functioning is
presumed to be dominated by self-interest, so in political 'markets' one
should assume that the relevant actors — voters (demanders), politicians
(suppliers), bureaucrats, regulators and the media — tend to be motivated
principally by self-interest. Thus, economists have gradually come to

recognize that the central role of the state in a modern representative democracy is to mediate interest-group conflicts over distributive claims. This has led to some measure of modesty about what economics as a discipline can contribute in determining appropriate policy objectives for the state.

With this retreat from the relevance of economics to shaping the state's policy goals well advanced, economists have more recently begun to make another point. While conceding that any of several possible policy goals may be adopted by governments, including openly and often perhaps perversely redistributive goals, it is argued that, at the very least, everybody's interests would be best served by governments choosing the most efficient instrument available to accomplish any given policy objective.[52] This might be called a concept of technical, as opposed to allocative, efficiency. The argument is that, whatever the policy objective, it ought to be achieved at the lowest social cost: nobody gains by needlessly dissipating resources. On the face of it, this seems an attractive decision principle for guiding the selection of instruments of intervention, and makes relevant many of the considerations canvassed earlier on economic theories of governance. However, I and several colleagues (Professors Hartle, Prichard and Dewees) have previously argued that a careful public-choice framework cannot in fact readily sustain this sharp distinction between means and ends.[53]

First, the technical efficiency thesis assumes a dichotomy between means and ends that in many cases is non-existent. It is true that often in political discourse such things as reducing inflation, unemployment, the trade deficit, poverty or traffic congestion, or increasing economic growth or the level of education or health status of the population, are described as 'policy objectives' (ends) for which 'means' must be selected to accomplish them. These so-called objectives or ends, however, are themselves means to more final objectives.[54] For example, reducing inflation or increasing levels of educational attainment are not ends in themselves, but means to achieving some more ultimate ends. In a public-choice framework, the more ultimate ends of the stated 'ends' are likely to relate to the objectives of salient interests. These interests, in turn, will be pursuing these objectives for more ultimate ends. The process of translating objectives or ends into more ultimate objectives or ends therefore involves almost infinite regress. Thus, the determination of both 'policy objectives' in the conventional sense and the means by which those objectives are to be pursued will be weighed against the ultimate calculus of maximizing political support. The choice of both policy means and ends will be subsumed in this political objective: nothing about this exercise can be viewed as predominantly technocratic.

Second, an even more fundamental difficulty raised by the means–ends relationship implicit in the technical efficiency thesis is the assumption that, once a policy objective has been specified, the choice of instrument is a valuationally neutral exercise. If this were so, one could probably agree that generally, in choosing an instrument to accomplish a given objective, one should choose an instrument that uses fewer rather than more resources. This assumes, however, that the alternative instruments implicate no other policy objectives. If what we understand here by objectives are values or interests espoused by politically salient groups of voters, then any instrument that advances policy objective A, no matter how efficiently, while at the same time impairing policy objective B, will not necessarily be consistent with the end of the policy-making process. In the real world, few policy instruments are so circumscribed in their effects that a choice among them simply reduces to the question of which one involves the least resources in attaining a given policy objective. As Charles Lindblom points out, it is only in the process of choosing among alternative policy instruments that choices can be made about trade-offs among different policy objectives, whether they be values or interests.[55] This point is also conceded by Schultze, in the course of making the argument that greater weight should be attached to technical efficiency considerations in the choice of governing instruments:

> The suggestion that the political debate be confined to ends, while technicians and experts design the means once the ends have been decided, is facile and naive. Ends and means cannot and should not be separated. In the real world they are inextricably joined: we formulate our ends only as we debate the means of satisfying them. No elected politician can afford to turn over the crucial question of how social intervention is to be designed to supposedly apolitical experts.[56]

In our earlier analysis, we developed a number of positive political axioms governing instrument choice:[57]

1. It is in the interest of the governing party to choose policies that confine the benefits to marginal voters and confine the costs to infra-marginal voters. By marginal voters, we mean voters in marginal ridings who are likely to switch political allegiances fairly readily if not offered some desired set of policies.

By infra-marginal voters, we mean voters who are strongly committed to a given party, largely irrespective of the choices made by that party with respect to the set of policies in issue, or are strongly committed to a rival political party, largely irrespective of the policy choices made by the incumbent party.

2. In order to overcome the information costs faced by marginal voters, it is in the interest of the governing party to choose policies that provide benefits in concentrated forms, so that their visibility is enhanced, and to impose the costs in dispersed forms, so that their lack of visibility is enhanced.

3. In order to secure the co-operation of bureaucracies in implementing policy, a governing party is likely to attach special weight to the views of bureaucrats in formulating policies. Bureaucrats, in advocating policies to their political overseers, will have a tendency to favour policies that have a heavy bureaucratic orientation, and entail more jobs, larger fiefdoms, and more power and prestige. The virtues of decentralized forms of resource allocation are likely to be systematically depreciated.

4. Where, in order to confer benefits on a relatively dispersed group of marginal voters, it is necessary to impose costs on a relatively concentrated group of marginal voters, it will be in the interests of a governing party to choose a policy instrument that minimizes real costs over time, while obscuring the erosion of real benefits through the provision of symbolic reassurances to the beneficiaries of continuing commitment to the initial policy, and exploiting the information asymmetries between the two groups.

5. Given the short electoral time-frame in which political parties operate, it will be rational for the governing party to choose policy instruments that confer benefits, or perceived benefits, on marginal voters throughout, or at least late in the current electoral cycle, while attempting to defer the real and perceived costs borne by other marginal voters to some point in time beyond the current electoral cycle, where causal connections are attenuated.

If these political axioms have any plausibility as descriptions of the political process, then the profit maximization problem that private-sector firms must solve may not readily be transposed into the political support maximization problem that political parties face. More explicitly, the problem of systematic 'mismatch' between policy instruments and policy objectives, of which commentators like Breyer and Schultze are critical, is unlikely to be the random product of mistakes, ignorance or stupidity on the part of collective decision-makers, but in many cases is likely to reflect systematic incentive structures that we as a community have built into our political system.

I should acknowledge here the limitations of this framework of analysis.

When I and my colleagues undertook our study of the choice of governing instrument in the early 1980s we were sceptical about the prospects of serious tax reform, privatization and deregulation, even if in many contexts such reforms were likely to be efficient. We were equally sceptical about the prospects of serious regulatory reform (e.g. the substitution of more incentive-based, output-oriented regulatory instruments for command-and-control-based, input-oriented instruments) and for serious reform of the public expenditure process. In a number of respects, as we have subsequently acknowledged,[58] our pessimism has proved unfounded. In many countries — not least New Zealand — during the 1980s and early 1990s, whether governed by right-of-centre or left-of-centre administrations, major policy initiatives have been made particularly in tax reform, privatization and deregulation.[59] Moreover, significant experiments have now been undertaken with incentive-based forms of regulation (e.g. in the environment), as well as significant reforms of the budgetary expenditure process and the contracting-out of the provision of public services. Thus, we assumed that the 'iron triangle' of special-interest groups, politicians and bureaucrats (or regulators) was more impervious to change than subsequent events have proven. While various explanations of these changes in the choice of policy instrument can be offered, many of them particular to the activity or sector in question, I believe that more generally we underestimated the power of ideas in the political system.

While not denying the significance of self-interest in the political process, Steven Kelman, in a recent important book,[60] demonstrates that the public-choice view of the political process dramatically underestimates the role of what he calls 'public spirit', or 'civic virtue', or simply non-self-interested ideas in the political process. As John Maynard Keynes once argued, in the long run ideas (for good or ill) matter more than vested interests in our collective policy-making processes.[61] Thus, politics is partly about what are thought to be good ideas as well as what are thought to be politically salient interests. Exactly what weight each carries is not clear in the theoretical literature. However, it is clear that persuasion has important currency in the political process, in a reciprocal sense: voters and interest groups may persuade politicians, bureaucrats and regulators of the virtues of a position or idea; similarly, political leaders, bureaucrats or regulators may persuade interest groups and voters of the wisdom of an idea. Just as in private markets, where it must be conceded that many preferences are not innate, so preferences are not fixed and immutable in the political process. Thus, I acknowledge the irony that economists, who stress the dynamic qualities of private markets and the forces of innovation and new entry in breaking down entrenched market positions and inducing consumers to try new products or services to meet old or new preferences (the 'perennial gale of creative destruction', in Joseph Schumpeter's famous words),[62] are inclined to view the political process in such static terms and the role of policy innovations and policy entrepreneurs as so limited. It may be especially so that, in the current environment of fiscal restraint, economic and political rationality may converge more sharply than at other times.

However, having acknowledged the potential for greater convergence between economic and political perspectives on choice of policy instruments, I believe that it would be a serious mistake to assume that this convergence is complete or that the technical efficiency thesis advanced by economists for choice of public policy instruments will, in many cases, be easy to achieve. In short, serious tensions continue to exist between these two perspectives, which suggests that future attempts to 'reinvent' government will require a broad political economy perspective.

Conclusions

In reflecting on the implications of the previous discussion of the choice of governing instruments and the potential for 'reinventing' government, I conclude with several modest points.

First, both the technical (or, if one prefers, economic) and political constraints on dramatic improvements in public-sector productivity within existing programmes are easily underestimated. This is not to espouse a deterministic view of the policy-making process — that (according to Gary Becker) 'the methods used to accomplish any given end tend to be the most efficient available, in the public as well as the market sector'.[63] But, in general, I think that the most we can reasonably aspire to is a multitude of changes on small margins. To 'reinvent' bureaucratic government in any fundamental sense entails reinventing the essential features of democratic politics as we have at present designed them. The notion that bureaucracies can be required or induced to engage in collective decision-making on criteria that are sharply at variance with the criteria by which their political overseers make collective decisions is naive.

Second, while I believe that there are many margins in which improved choices of governing instruments may permit the realization of existing policy objectives at lower cost, I am profoundly sceptical that the cost savings are likely to prove so substantial that the painful exercise of deciding whether some policy objectives and related programmes should be abandoned altogether can be avoided. That is to say, choices among policy instruments for the realization of given policy objectives are not a substitute for choices among policy objectives (or political interests or values). Rethinking *how* governments might do their work better is not to be confused with rethinking *what* governments should be working at. For example, the *Gore Report* estimates the savings from its sweeping proposals, even if fully implemented, to be about US$20 billion per year — a significant figure — but only about 7 per cent of the current budget deficit of approximately US$300 billion and a much smaller percentage of total government expenditures. Thus, in terms of addressing the serious budget deficit problems confronting governments in the US, Canada and elsewhere, 'reinventing government' is a 7 per cent solution. Even for governments without serious deficit problems (such as New Zealand currently, though it still faces a major public debt burden), the potential savings from 'reinventing' government as a percentage of total government expenditures are likely to be quite small. This is to argue not that im- proving the performance of government should not be taken seriously, but rather that it should be done mostly for its own sake, and only incidentally because of its potential contribution to deficit or debt reduction.[64]

Third, in adopting more technically efficient instruments, governments need to be especially sensitive to the transition costs entailed for various classes of citizens. They need to seek ways of moderating these costs, if a sense of fairness and compassion in spreading the costs of change is to be preserved and if political resistance to change is to be overcome, even if transition policies somewhat attenuate the efficiency gains from choice of superior policy instruments.

Fourth, it would be inconsistent with the Hayekian critique[65] of central planning as being unable to acquire, process and apply the vast volume of information required to make welfare-enhancing collective decisions to advocate massive system-wide changes, even changes favouring more individual and institutional autonomy and more market-type forms of competitive discipline, when often we cannot know all the efficiency, distributional and social effects of these changes in advance. A sense of modesty in this respect would place a significant policy premium on incrementalism, experimentation and pilot programmes, rather than convulsive paradigm shifts. As Dilulio, Garvey and Kettl argue:

> One of the basic concepts of contemporary social science, that of bounded rationality, supports the evolutionary approach to institutional reform. According to the bounded rationality hypothesis, policy-makers mostly delude themselves when they think that 'comprehensive study' or 'bold inventive action' can produce useful, enduring change. The world of politics is too rich in both information and uncertainty; once-and-for-all efforts at structural reform must fail. When used as an evocative symbol, the metaphor of invention can help concentrate the mind, charge the imagination, perhaps inspire a certain willing suspension of disbelief. But the inventive approach has its limits as a guide to practical action.[66]

Finally, as the American writer H. L. Mencken once remarked, for every complex problem there is a solution that is neat, plausible and wrong. My conclusions attempt to take seriously this cautionary wisdom.

Notes

1 Quoted in US National Performance Review, *From Red Tape to Results: Creating a Government that Works Better and Costs Less* (September 7, 1993); published as *The Gore Report on Reinventing Government* (New York, Times Books, Random House, 1993) (henceforth the *Gore Report*), p.i and p.1.

2 David Osborne and Ted Gaebler, *Reinventing Government* (New York, Plume, 1993).

3 John Dilulio, Gerald Garvey and Donald Kettl, *Improving Government Performance* (Washington, DC, Brookings Institution, 1993), p.4.

4 *Gore Report.*

5 *Public Service 2000: The Renewal of the Public Service of Canada* (Ottawa, Supply and Services, 1990).

6 Task Force on Program Review (Neilsen Task Force), 1986.

7 Economic Council of Canada, *Responsible Regulation* (Ottawa, Supply and Services, 1979); *Reforming Regulation* (Ottawa, Supply and Services, 1981).

8 Royal Commission on Financial Management and Accountability (Ottawa, 1979).

9 *Gore Report*, p.5, p.8; see also Dilulio *et al.*, pp.6–9.

10 See Richard French, *How Ottawa Decides* (Toronto, James Lorimer, 1980).

11 For a masterful and comprehensive review of this literature, see Paul Milgrom and John Roberts, *Economics, Organization and Management* (New Jersey, Prentice Hall, 1992).

12 See Michael Jensen and William Meckling, 'Theory of the Firm: Managerial Behavior, Agency Costs, and Ownership Structure', *Journal of Financial Economics* 3 (1976), p.305; Michael Jensen and Clifford Smith, 'Stockholder, Manager, and Creditor Interests: Applications of Agency Theory', in Edward Altman and Martin Subrahmanyan (eds), *Recent Advances in Corporate Finance* (Homewood, Illinois, Richard D. Irwin, 1985), p.38.

13 Jensen and Smith, *ibid.*

14 This includes monitoring costs (actions taken by the principal to ensure that the terms of the contract are adhered to) and bonding costs (actions taken by the agent to restrict his or her ability to act against the principal's interest).

15 There will always be some residual loss by the principal when the contracting, monitoring and bonding costs do not ensure that the agent acts as a perfect proxy for the principal.

16 This was the central thesis of Adolf Berle and Gardiner Means in their famous book, *The Modern Corporation and Private Property* (New York, Macmillan Publishing Co., 1932). Most shareholders hold only a small number of shares and therefore have little influence over managers. (See Eugene Fama, 'Agency Problems and the Theory of the Firm', *Journal of Political Economy* 88 (1980), p.288.) While shareholders with large blocks of shares (such as institutional investors) are quite common, the control they exert over management is tempered by the fact that they find it difficult to acquire needed information about most issues facing management.

17 Fama, *ibid.*, pp.292–93.

18 *Ibid.*

19 *Ibid.*, p.241.

20 See Henry Manne, 'Mergers and the Market for Corporate Control', *Journal of Political Economy* 73 (1965), p.110; Manne, 'Our Two Corporate Systems: Law and Economics', *Virginia Law Review* 53 (1967), p.259.

21 Obviously, however, the professionally managed firm has offsetting advantages over the owner-managed firm: it may be better able to raise large amounts of capital, to take advantage of scale and of managerial expertise available through the use of professional managers. According to Easterbrook and Fischel: 'Those who have wealth can employ it productively, even if they are not good managers; those who can manage but lack wealth can hire capital in the market; and the existence of claims that can be traded separately from employment allows investors to diversify their own investment interests.' (Frank Easterbrook and Daniel Fischel, *The Economic Structure of Corporate Law* (Cambridge, Mass., Harvard University Press, 1991), p.11).

22 John Donahue, *The Privatization Decision: Public Ends, Private Means* (New York, Basic Books, 1989), pp.49–51.

23 See Winston Bush and Arthur Denzau, 'The Voting Behaviour of Bureaucrats and Public Sector Growth', in Thomas Borcherding (ed.), *Budgets and Bureaucrats:*

The Sources of Government Growth (Durham, NC, Duke University Press, 1977).

24 Ronald Coase, 'The Nature of the Firm', *Economica* 4 (1937), p.386.

25 See, for example, Oliver Williamson, 'Hierarchical Control and Optimal Firm Size', *Journal of Political Economy* 75 (1967), p.123.

26 See, for example, Armen Alchian and Harold Demsetz, 'Production, Information Costs, and Economic Organization', *American Economic Review* 62 (1972), p.777; John McManus, 'The Costs of Alternative Economic Organization', *Canadian Journal of Economics* 8 (1975), p.334; Oliver Williamson, *Markets and Hierarchies* (New York, Free Press, 1975); Williamson, 'Transaction Cost Economics: The Governance of Contractual Relations', *Journal of Law and Economics* 22 (1979), p.3.

27 See Easterbrook and Fischel, *The Economic Structure of Corporate Law;* 'Symposium, Contractual Freedom in Corporate Law', (1988/89) *Columbia Law Review*, p.1395.

28 See Michael J. Trebilcock and J. Robert S. Prichard, 'Crown Corporations in Canada: The Calculus of Instrument Choice', in J. Robert S. Prichard (ed.), *Crown Corporations in Canada* (Toronto, Butterworth, 1983).

29 See Donald Dewees, Michael Trebilcock, Ian Freedman and Brent Snell, *The Regulation of Solid Waste Management in Ontario: A Policy Perspective* (University of Toronto, April 1993), ch. 5.

30 *Public Service 2000.*

31 *Managing Change in the Public Service: A Guide for the Perplexed* (Task Force on Workforce Adaptiveness, Public Service 2000, 1990); *Public Service 2000: A Report on Progress* (Paul Tellier, 1992). See also Donald Kettl, *Reinventing Government? Appraising the National Performance Review* (Washington, DC, Brookings Institution, 1994).

32 See Sir Roger Douglas, *Towards Prosperity* (Auckland, David Bateman, 1987), ch. 19; Roderick Deane, 'Reforming the Public Sector', in Simon Walker (ed.), *Rogernomics* (Auckland, GP Books, 1989); Peter McKinlay (ed.), *Redistribution of Power? Devolution in New Zealand* (Wellington, Victoria University Press, 1990).

33 *Gore Report.*

34 See Economic Council of Canada, *Education and Training in Canada* (Ottawa, Supply Services, 1992), ch. 2.

35 *Wall Street Journal*, October 28, 1993.

36 Harold Demsetz, 'Why Regulate Utilities?', *Journal of Law and Economics* 11 (1968), p.55.

37 Oliver Williamson, *The Economic Institutions of Capitalism: Firms, Markets, Relational Contracting* (New York, Free Press, 1985), ch. 13.

38 Oliver Williamson, 'The Logic of Economic Organization', *Journal of Law, Economics and Organization* 4 (1988), p.77.

39 Oliver Williamson, *The Economic Institutions of Capitalism*, p.350; see also Victor Goldberg, 'Regulation and Administered Contracts', *Bell Journal of Economics* 7 (1976), p.426; and Ronald Hirshhorn, 'Government Enterprise and Organization Efficiency' (Ottawa, Economic Council of Canada, 1987).

40 See Gordon Cassidy, *Contracting Out* (Discussion Paper 94–06, School of Policy Studies, Queen's University, Kingston, Ontario, 1994).

41 Henry Hansmann, 'The Role of Non-Profit Enterprise', *Yale Law Journal* 89 (1980), p.835; Hansmann, 'Ownership of the Firm', *Journal of Law, Economics and Organization* 4 (1988), p.267.

42 Richard A. Posner, 'What Do Judges and Justices Maximize? (The Same Thing Everybody Else Does)', *Supreme Court Review* (forthcoming).

43 For example, in the social welfare field, Lisbeth Schorr in her book, *Within Our Reach* (New York, Doubleday, 1988), documents numerous case studies in the US of government financed but locally or community provided services, such as pre-natal and post-natal care, pre-school education, family planning services and special school programmes for disadvantaged children, which have proven highly effective in reducing the incidence of negative outcomes for high-risk children. For a more critical view, see Steven Smith and Michael Lipsky, *Non-Profits for Hire: The Welfare State in the Age of Contracting* (Cambridge, Mass., Harvard University Press, 1993).

44 See Donahue, *The Privatization Decision*, pp.150–78; B. R. Johnson and P. P. Ross, 'The Privatization of Correctional Management: A Review', *Journal of Criminal Justice* 18 (1990), p.351; D. F. Linowes, Report of the President's Commission on Privatization, *Privatization: Toward More Effective Government* (University of Illinois Press, 1988), pp.146–55; Kenneth Avio, 'Remuneration Regimes for Private Prisons', *International Review of Law and Economics* 13 (1993), p.35.

45 As exemplified in the nineteenth century in contracts to ship convicts from Britain to Australia: see Robert Hughes, *The Fatal Shore* (New York, Knopf, 1987).

46 For a review of these studies, see Harry Kitchen, 'Efficient Delivery of Local Government Services', School of Policy Studies, Queen's University Discussion Paper No. 93–15 (1993); Dewees *et al.*, *The Regulation of Solid Waste Management in Ontario*, ch. 6.

47 These studies cover a wide range of services: fire protection, urban transport, airlines, postal service, water supply, debt collection, electric utilities, national park management, residential waste collection, street cleaning, janitorial services, traffic signal maintenance, asphalt overlay construction, turf maintenance and street tree maintenance.

48 Thomas Borcherding, 'Towards a Positive Theory of Public Sector Supply Arrangements', in Prichard (ed.), *Crown Corporations in Canada*, p.136; Donahue, *The Privatization Decision*, p.82.

49 Stephen Breyer, 'Analyzing Regulatory Failure: Mismatches, Less Restrictive Alternatives, and Reform', *Harvard Law Review* 92 (1979), p.594; Breyer, *Regulation and Its Reform* (Cambridge, Mass., Harvard University Press, 1982); Charles Schultze, *The Public Use of Private Interest* (Washington, DC, Brookings Institution, 1977).

50 See John Rawls, *A Theory of Justice* (Cambridge, Mass., Harvard University Press, 1971).

51 See generally Dennis Mueller, *Public Choice II* (Cambridge, Cambridge University Press, 1989).

52 See, for example, Breyer, *Regulation and Its Reform*; Schultze, *The Public Use of Private Interest*; George Stigler, 'Law or Economics?', *Journal of Law and Economics* 35 (1992), p.455, pp.458-59.

53 Michael Trebilcock, Douglas Hartle, Don Dewees and Robert Prichard, *The Choice of Governing Instrument* (Economic Council of Canada, 1982), ch. 2; Michael Trebilcock and Douglas Hartle, 'The Choice of Governing Instrument', *International Review of Law and Economics* 2 (1982), p.29.

54 See Herbert Simon, *Administrative Behaviour* (New York, Free Press, 1976), p.65.

55 Charles Lindblom, 'The Science of "Muddling Through" ', *Public Administration Review* 19 (1959), p.79, pp.82-83.

56 Schultze, *The Public Use of the Private Interest*, pp.89-90.

57 Trebilcock *et al.*, *The Choice of Governing Instrument*, pp.33-34.

58 See Robert Howse, Robert Prichard and Michael Trebilcock, 'Smaller or Smarter Government?', *University of Toronto Law Journal* 40 (1990), p.498.

59 See OECD Survey, *Regulatory Reform, Privatization, and Competition Policy* (Paris, 1992).

60 Steven Kelman, *Making Public Policy: A Hopeful View of American Government* (1987); see also Jerry Mashaw, 'The Economics of Politics and the Understanding of Public Law', *Chicago-Kent Law Review* 65 (1990), p.123; Daniel Farber, 'Democracy and Disgust: Reflections on Public Choice', *Chicago-Kent Law Review* 65 (1990), p.161; Daniel Farber and Philip Frickey, *Law and Public Choice* (Chicago, University of Chicago Press, 1991).

61 See J. M. Keynes, *The General Theory of Employment, Interest, and Money* (London, Macmillan & Co.,1936), pp.383-84.

62 Joseph Schumpeter, *Capitalism, Socialism and Democracy* (Cambridge, Mass., Harvard University Press, 1975), p.87.

63 Gary Becker, 'Comment', *Journal of Law and Economics* 19 (1976), p.245; see also Becker, 'A Theory of Competition Among Pressure Groups for Political Influence', *Quarterly Journal of Economics* 98 (1983), p.371; Stigler, 'Law or Economics?', pp.458-59.

64 See Dilulio *et al.*, *Improving Government Performance*, pp.10-11, pp.79-82.

65 Friedrich Hayek, *The Road to Serfdom* (Chicago, University of Chicago Press, 1944).

66 Dilulio *et al.*, *Improving Government Performance*, p.2.

CHAPTER TWO

Contracting and Accountability

JOHN MARTIN

Government cannot be reduced to a series of contracts.[1]

John Stewart

Introduction

The respected British commentator John Stewart observed recently:

> Carried too far, government may become a series of separate units, some external, others normally internal, which conduct their relationships through a series of contracts. The consultant of the future called in to examine, let us say, a local authority constituted on this basis will surely say: 'This is a strange organization, that has lost its capacity to learn and to adapt, and above all, to see problems and issues that do not fit into the boxes into which it has divided itself, or the contracts it has drawn up . . . A capacity for government is required.'[2]

Stewart's vision of the future is already with us in New Zealand. Over the past decade the government of New Zealand has been fragmented — by the lateral division of the former sectoral departments, by the creation of Crown entities, and by the decentralization of activities to the periphery or outside the boundaries of government completely. To the extent that there has been any 'grand design' to this deconstruction of the state it was perhaps encapsulated in Bill Birch's 'idea of a three-tier state sector'.[3] The three tiers were:

1. [T]hose activities closest to Ministers . . . [Departments'] role would be to provide advice, decide how to implement decisions and then to review the implementation of those decisions.
2. [T]he agencies that for various reasons should still be owned by the state, but which have much clearer incentives than departments; and which can be organised to meet more explicit targets.
3. The third tier is where the private sector delivers services on behalf of the Government and its agencies.

Central to this model is the idea of 'contract', which replaces hierarchy and command as the mechanism by which the parts are linked together and, we must presume, are to achieve the purposes of government.

I do not propose to recall the series of structural reforms which, under two governments, have given effect to this model. Nor do I necessarily reject its utility. Indeed, as I hope to demonstrate, it has unquestionably assisted the achievement of considerable *efficiency* gains — if for no other reason than to require agencies to attempt to articulate the purpose for which they exist. I do, however, question its universal applicability and, in particular, suggest that we have perhaps — despite the rhetoric — given insufficient attention to the implications for political *accountability*.

The issue is timely. The received wisdom in places of influence in Wellington is that the 'one right way' forward in public-sector reform is through tighter specification of objectives throughout government and greater resort to contracting. There is, for example, considerable interest in the work of Australian consultant Gary Sturgess, whose minimalist views on the role of government are summed up in the projected working title of a forthcoming book, *Virtual Government*.[4] And recently, the Minister of Finance indicated that further restructuring was in prospect: 'There is room for . . . separating out delivery of services from policy advice . . . where the private sector was a better supplier there would be privatisation.'[5]

I propose to reflect on these trends by considering what we might mean by 'contract' in the governmental context. I will then examine briefly two case studies: one in which the government has long had a purchasing relationship with the voluntary sector (Plunket), and the other a relationship *within* the structure of government (the Civil Aviation Authority). After this, I will outline some criteria by which we might judge the adequacy of accountability procedures in contractual relationships. In particular, I want to direct some attention to the rights of citizens in respect of contracts entered into by the Crown or its agents.

My interest in this area was stimulated some years ago by the writings of American scholars on 'third party' government and 'government by proxy' — notably contributions by Donald Kettl[6] and Lester Salamon.[7] The insights I derived from these writings explained some of the phenomena that I had been observing in New Zealand government even before 'the revolution'. They also provided for me a healthy counterweight to the emphasis on agency theory in the reforms of the past decade. Given Kettl's contribution to the present book it would be, I think, an act of supererogation to draw too heavily on his work in this chapter; but I do wish to acknowledge the benefits I have gained from it. The case studies considered here are examined within Salamon's conceptual framework.

If there is a theme to this chapter it is that the more we fragment the structure of government by replacing command hierarchies with networks of contracts, the more we call in question the nature of responsible government by attenuating the responsibility of elected representatives. This is, of course, not a particularly profound or novel observation; indeed, some readers may regard it as trivial. The aim of systems in government, they may say, is to play the same role as the price system does in the private sector.[8] The pursuit of efficiency and the delivery of preferred outcomes must, accordingly, take priority over questions of responsibility and accountability.

A final preliminary observation. Not surprisingly, the nature of contract is principally the property of lawyers and economists. In New Zealand our new-model systems of government have been designed by economists; on the ground the lawyers have had a major part to play. This chapter is the product of some reflection by a retired practitioner with a background in political science who is also an occasional bush lawyer but has no more than a passing acquaintance with economics.

The Nature of Contract in Government

It is probably useful to examine in a preliminary way some of the connotations of 'contract' for lawyers and economists. Sir Kenneth Keith (to whom I often turn with gratitude in these matters) refers to contract in these terms:

> In principle [contracts] are agreements concluded on an equal footing by two or more parties who freely consent and who freely settle the terms of the

agreement. The parties usually are concerned only with protecting and advancing their reciprocal private interests, and not with serving a public policy.[9]

This is, I am assured, a complex area of the law. Nonetheless, there are, it seems, three key aspects to the private law of contract:[10]

1. There are at least two parties to every contract; and those parties must possess contractual capacity. [*In respect of the public sector we are immediately alerted to the question: can we define the parties to a relationship described as 'contractual'?*]

2. Contracts create rights and duties for the parties only — the principle of privity. [*In respect of the public sector it is often presumed that a contract between A and B confers rights and duties on a third party — sometimes the public.*]

3. 'Consideration' is an essential of contract — 'a reciprocal transaction between the parties, involving mutual benefit and detriment. A mere promise is not a contract'. [*To what extent are 'contractual' arrangements in government such a reciprocal transaction; are they not sometimes directions?*]

Let us turn, again briefly, to the contribution of the economists. Perhaps most important is the distinction between *spot*, *classical* and *relational* contracts.[11] The market model — on which so much of the critique of traditional systems of government has been based — is predicated on myriad *spot* transactions between willing buyers and willing sellers. 'I sell, you buy, and that is that.'[12] These are 'off the shelf' transactions which do not require lengthy negotiations or formal documentation, but in the event of dispute a contract is inferred.

Important relationships are not, however, the subject of spot contracts. The purchase of major assets, notably those specific to a particular business, or sale and purchase transactions over time, are usually the subject of formal, binding legal arrangements — the *classical* contract.

Many long-term relationships are, however, in the form of *relational* (or implicit) contracts — understandings which endure not because of legal sanctions enforceable in the courts but because of 'the shared needs of the parties to go on doing business with each other'.[13] Trust is of the essence. Strictly speaking, such arrangements are not contracts at all. Many relationships within 'the Government' (loosely defined) described as contracts seem to me to be of the nature of relational contracts. Even where, as in the case of employment, there may be a legal contract, this may simply be the starting-point. The employment relationship, particularly at senior levels, may not be assisted by too specific a listing of responsibilities and expectations. Indeed, 'working to rule' would be to deny the ethos of any professional public service of which I am aware.

Flexibility and duty have priority over precision of job specification. But a classical contract aims to limit flexibility. Similarly, a relational contract facilitates an easy flow of information while a classical contract inhibits it (it might be used against you).

Of course, the notion of 'opportunism' argues against the use of relational contracts. How can the parties protect themselves against the self-regarding behaviour of the other? The crucial consideration is whether both parties believe that 'they are playing a repeated game'.[14]

In New Zealand the answer has been seen as straightforward: set clear objectives; appoint the right people; put in place appropriate incentives and disincentives; and ensure that there are effective monitoring processes. All this can be tied together in a 'contract' — whether we call it a statement of corporate intent (in respect of SOEs), a performance agreement (in respect of chief executives in the 'core' public service) or a charter (in the education service). This prescription has some obvious attractions when set against the 'fudging' of the traditional bureaucracy — over-done though this criticism sometimes seems. It focuses attention on the different interests of the various parties in the governmental process; it attempts to clarify the different roles; and by specifying performance (rather than simply compliance) it seeks to engender both greater efficiency and enhanced accountability. The mire of confusion about both the objectives of government and the contribution of the various actors is to be replaced by the transparency of contract. But is this not a shade facile? And is it not conceivable that such a system may create new problems?

A number of general questions can be raised. First, and most obviously, there is the problem of specifying objectives. Oliver Williamson[15] has reminded us of the relevance of *bounded rationality* and *uncertainty* in considering whether activities should be undertaken in-house or contracted out. In practice, we might observe the difficulties of specifying the outcomes sought by ministers — see, for example, the National Government's strategic document *The Next Three Years*. Equally, the complexity of social behaviour, and especially the difficulty of ascribing effect to cause, should engender a sense of humility in specifying performance. The seductiveness of the quantifiable needs to be guarded against.

The provision of information can also be a rather more complex exercise than is sometimes assumed. First, there is the sheer difficulty and cost of developing adequate information systems. The choices between 'bespoke' and 'off-the-peg', or 'penury' and 'profligacy', in determining performance indicators illustrate the point.[16] There is, second, the issue raised earlier about the interests of the parties in being 'free and frank' when exposed to sanctions. Indeed, a third area of legitimate questioning concerns sanctions. The usual contractual sanction is *ex post*: if there is inadequate performance the contract is terminated (or the employee dismissed). But that is too late — especially for ministers whose concern with political risk is well documented in the Logan Report.[17]

Fourth, in terms of political responsibility, the separation of functions — funder/purchaser/provider and so on — and the allocation of tasks does not resolve the accountability issue. When things go wrong, is it the principal or the agent who is held publicly to account? Or are there still multiple accountabilities (remembering that dual accountability in the health service was deemed to be a fatal flaw)? Such questions are of particular salience when we are dealing with 'contracts' between bodies *within* the public sector. Put bluntly, where in the chain of contracts — in the SOE sector, the 'core' public service, or the health[18] or education sectors — does the minister's political responsibility end? The answer will, I suggest, be found in the political process, not in black-letter law of statute or contract.

Fifth, as Stewart[19] again reminds us, questions of *values* arise. If fairness, justice and due process are the hallmarks of best practice in public organizations, can that necessarily be said of bodies with which the government contracts? Because the implementation of such values can be costly, contracting is perhaps seen as an avenue by which their dominance can be side-stepped. The issue is captured by the familiar contrasting of 'citizens' with 'customers' or 'clients'. To what extent can the public be guaranteed fundamental rights (see the New Zealand Bill of Rights Act 1990) when services are contracted out?

Sixth, there is something to be said for the flexibility which hier-archical arrangements *can* facilitate. This point is connected to the earlier comments about uncertainty and information. Much of government is concerned with reacting to the unexpected, and learning from the experience. Policies evolve; so too do processes. 'Government by contract carried too far sets boundaries to the political process, limiting it to defined points in time and to defined terms.'[20] I can think of many situations in government where the constraint of a specified contract — and the time-consuming need for renegotiation — would not, in my judgement, have been in the public interest.

Finally, we should acknowledge that the purpose of much contracting in the New Zealand public sector has been to 'depoliticize' activities of government (the State Owned Enterprises Act 1986, the Reserve Bank Act 1989, the Health and Disability Services Act 1993). It is, I suggest, still legitimate to question whether it is beyond doubt that all 'political' decisions are less than optimal.

Rethinking Public Management: Third-Party Government and the Changing Form of Government Action

Salamon's ten hypotheses in his 1981 article are set out at the end of this chapter in Annex 1. Much water has, of course, flowed under the bridge since − in terms of both the literature and the resort to contracting by most governments, including the US and New Zealand. I want to use just two pairs of Salamon's hypotheses:

1. The more indirect the form of government action . . . the more difficult will be the implementation of the resulting program and the less likely will the program be to achieve its goals.
2. The more direct the form of government action, the more likely it is to encounter political opposition.

and

9. The more a form of government action uses performance standards instead of design regulations, the less cumbersome it is administratively and the more efficient is its use of resources.
10. The more a tool involves reliance on federally determined performance standards, the more likely it is to encounter political opposition and resistance from its administrators.

The first pair raises for consideration the issues of control and accountability. The second pair directs attention to the widespread shift from inputs to outputs and outcomes as the focus of contractual systems. Together they highlight the advantages and disadvantages of contracting.

Whatever the reasons for contracting functions of government away from the centre most examples involve placing discretionary authority in the hands of organizations other than that which conceived of and is probably funding the activity. Depending on the specific administrative arrangements, this may or may not lead to structures of such complexity that the implementation of programmes becomes distorted. But beyond questions of administrative efficiency, as Salamon notes 'of equal or greater importance is the incongruence that can arise between the goals of the . . . government — as articulated, however imperfectly, in legislation, report language, or regulations — and the goals of the . . . implementing agents'.[21] In my case studies I want to suggest that there is, at the very least, potential for this lack of congruence to emerge. Conversely, in attempting to remove this possibility, contracting authorities are likely to tighten specifications and reporting procedures. In the process they risk losing the gains from conferring discretion upon the contracted agents.

Salamon's second hypothesis is set within the US federal context. It does, however, raise for discussion a variation which in New Zealand has some salience. This is the proposition that contracting functions to third parties shifts opprobrium from the centre to the periphery. In short, governments can divert the blame to those to whom they have devolved by contract the delivery of services — even though the nature and extent of those services is shaped by direction from the centre. That proposition could certainly be advanced in respect of health and education in New Zealand.

Hypotheses 9 and 10 contrast design standards — input controls — with performance standards. The argument is familiar. Regimes which specify the means by which contracted services are to be provided stultify initiative and perpetuate misallocation of resources. Salamon helpfully raises a number of reasons why 'attractive as performance indicators are . . . they are not without their problems'.[22] Of particular interest is his point that

> the use of performance standards involves greater uncertainty since results are not apparent for a considerable time and great opportunity exists for mistakes along the way. Those responsible for program oversight can therefore be expected to find such uncertainty exceedingly unattractive.[23]

My position is that the establishment of clear performance indicators may not always be an adequate substitute for hands-on management.

Two Case Studies

1. Plunket

The government's relationship with the Plunket Society provides some useful insights into changes in the basis of contracting by government for services. Plunket is an incorporated voluntary society with a tradition extending back to 1908. Its principal function has been to provide 'well-baby services'. It has long received government funding but in the last few years this relationship has undergone two substantial changes: from a grant for inputs to a contract for outputs; and from a national relationship with central government to four contracts with Regional Health Authorities (RHAs) from July 1, 1993.

Under a 1979 Cabinet decision, Plunket was provided with a 'subsidy equal to the Society's actual expenditure on the salaries and employer's superannuation contributions of approved Plunket nurses (district and family support units), headquarters staff, Karitane nurses and paediatricians'. Limits were set by reference to salary rates paid in comparable public service employment and a maximum staff establishment. A subsidy was also provided for 40 per cent of the net cost of motor vehicles purchased by Plunket 'provided that replacements of vehicles shall be purchased at intervals determined in accordance with the rulings of the Departmental Motor Vehicles Committee administered by the Ministry of Transport'.[24]

In essence, this was the basis of the government's expenditure, approaching $20 million, on the services of Plunket until 1989–90. Accounting information was required by the Department of Health in justification; but, despite continual discussion about 'evaluation', there was no formal accountability by the Plunket Society for the *effectiveness* of the expenditure of this significant sum of public money. (I leave aside a separate 'contract' for services in South Auckland.)

In 1990 the Minister of Health signed a contract with the society for specific services for the 1990–91 year. This shifted the government's contribution from specific inputs to *services* 'but in a broad all encompassing fashion'[25] — parent support and education, well-child screening and surveillance, child-safety projects, advocacy on behalf of children and their families. For the year to June 30, 1992, the contract was modified to translate Plunket's obligation into specific *outputs* — nine contacts by Plunket with children from birth to age five, and a series of preparation for parenthood programmes. The society, which had welcomed the move to service funding (which, it claimed, enabled efficiencies to be initiated), argued in its 1992 annual report that output specification 'stymies innovation and the development of efficiencies and suggests that all clients experience common needs'.

Administration of the contract passed to the four RHAs from July 1, 1993 — and the national contract was rolled over at the preceding year's expenditure level. The specified outputs were modified to four home visits during a child's first three months and up to eight subsequent contacts in the pre-school years. From July 1, 1994 separate regional contracts have been negotiated with the four RHAs within the *Government's Policy Guidelines for RHAs 1994–95*, namely:

- While RHAs are required to purchase a well child service that is free to the user, they should not extend the transitional arrangement for 1993–94 for continuity of service provider where it would be now more appropriate for them to contract with a range of service providers in order to improve the coverage, effectiveness and acceptability of the service.
- RHAs should purchase culturally appropriate well child services for Maori.

Several interesting points emerge from even this superficial examination of the Plunket case:

(i) The inadequacy on all counts — effectiveness, efficiency and accountability — of grants for *inputs* to a 'third party'.

(ii) The paucity of information provided to Parliament throughout the period examined: a one-line item in Vote: Health later absorbed into a global figure, 'Payments to Boards and Organisations on Behalf of the Crown'; and for the year ended June 30, 1994 an item for Children's Health Care Services ($28.014 million) under the heading 'Outputs to be Supplied by Other Parties — including RHAs'.

(iii) The decline in narrative information provided by the new style of annual reports to Parliament in terms of the Public Finance Act.

(iv) The impact on the providing organization of being required to contract with the Crown (or the Crown's agents) in terms of outputs. Plunket, which valued a direct relationship with the Minister of Health, has now reorganized on a regional basis; but more effort has been required to develop an appropriate information system.

(v) A degree of contestability now exists: there is, for example, a contract with a Rotorua trust to provide well-baby services to Maori.

To sum up, the notion of contracting is particularly appropriate for the delivery of a service which a government wishes to see provided free of charge to the appropriate members of the public and where there is an established organization capable of providing it. The principal sanction available to the government (or to an RHA) lies in its discretion to continue the contract: there is no obligation to do so (although under the grant arrangement there was never any expectation that Plunket would not continue to be funded to the extent of around 90 per cent of expenditure from the public purse). To the extent, however, that other independent service-providers enter the game, the question of accountability becomes even more important. To what extent is the Minister of Health prepared to take responsibility for the actions of the RHA, let alone Plunket or other providers? What information will be provided to Parliament, or indeed to the interested public? There is no certainty that details of the RHA's purchase arrangements will be made available by either the funder or the provider.

The Plunket case is a *classical* contract. There are, nonetheless, large elements of a *relational* contracting arrangement: the reality is that Plunket certainly needs public funding for its continued existence in anything like its present form; and that given the National Government's declared 'well baby' policy the RHAs need Plunket. The contractual form has, however, been a potent vehicle for enhancing 'value for money'.

In terms of Salomon's hypotheses, all we can say under the first — that implementation becomes more difficult as it becomes less direct — is that the funder had little but anecdotal knowledge of effectiveness under a grant arrangement; and that it is too early to comment on the effectiveness of a contractual arrangement two stages removed from the responsible minister. On the second — that opposition is less with indirect administration of programmes — arrangements with Plunket have never, to the best of my knowledge, been the subject of party-political controversy, despite (or because of?) the lack of detailed information made available to Parliament. Performance standards clearly have advantages over design standards; but there is some anecdotal evidence of support for Salomon's contention that performance standards are a point of contention between the funders and the providers, Plunket believing that its flexibility is unduly constrained.

2. Civil Aviation Authority

The reduction in the size of the Ministry of Transport from around 5000 staff in 1986 to less than 50 at present is among the most dramatic representations of the new-model public service (see Figure 2.1). The ministry is now a small 'policy ministry' with its former delivery and

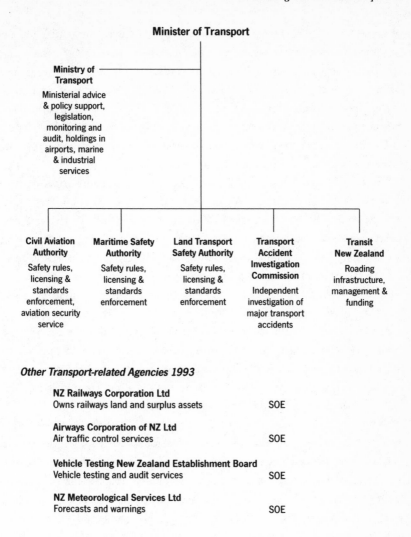

Minister of Transport

Ministry of Transport
Ministerial advice & policy support, legislation, monitoring and audit, holdings in airports, marine & industrial services

Civil Aviation Authority
Safety rules, licensing & standards enforcement, aviation security service

Maritime Safety Authority
Safety rules, licensing & standards enforcement

Land Transport Safety Authority
Safety rules, licensing & standards enforcement

Transport Accident Investigation Commission
Independent investigation of major transport accidents

Transit New Zealand
Roading infrastructure, management & funding

Other Transport-related Agencies 1993

NZ Railways Corporation Ltd
Owns railways land and surplus assets　　　　SOE

Airways Corporation of NZ Ltd
Air traffic control services　　　　SOE

Vehicle Testing New Zealand Establishment Board
Vehicle testing and audit services　　　　SOE

NZ Meteorological Services Ltd
Forecasts and warnings　　　　SOE

Figure 2:1 *Government Transport Sector Structure 1993*

regulatory activities contracted to statutory bodies, including the Civil Aviation Authority (CAA). The CAA is a body corporate — with contractual capacity — established by the Civil Aviation Amendment Act 1990. It is a Crown entity, in terms of the Public Finance Act 1989, headed by a five-member board of business and aviation industry representatives. It is charged with representing the 'public interest' in civil aviation and reports directly to the Minister of Transport, for whom the ministry acts as monitoring agent. The CAA's functions include: providing advice to the minister on civil aviation safety and security; establishing safety and security standards; controlling entry and exit to the industry; and promoting safety and security. Its funding comes from a mix of 'user-pays' and general taxation (for the purchase of policy advice). Underlining the proposition that 'contractualism' is dominant is the invitation (in Section 72E of the Act) for the CAA to contract out its activities after appropriate procedures.

Section 72F of the Civil Aviation Act requires the authority to enter into an annual Performance Agreement with the Minister of Transport. The Act requires the agreement to include the objectives for the year, the CAA's methods of assessing whether the objectives are being achieved, and the estimated impact and consequences the authority's actions will have on the safety of the civil aviation system in the current and future years. This is, in effect, 'the contract', which is a document of some forty pages and very 'legal' in form. Outputs, output performance targets and measures are set out in a schedule to the agreement. So too is the authority's best estimate of the impacts on, and consequences for, a safe aviation system in New Zealand of the CAA's output. The definition of these measures is clearly not an easy task; I suspect that there is a tendency to focus first on the financial performance of the authority.

The authority is also required (by Section 72G of the Act) to issue a Service Charter which will cover 'standards of services which the public may expect', procedures for redress and remedy, and provision for the appointment of an independent person to resolve disputes about alleged failures to meet the standards. The service standards are very general (see Annex 2); the authority's vision, mission, strategic goals and values are set out; and there is an office directory.

There are some considerations special to the New Zealand civil aviation industry which have influenced the present structure.[26] I want to direct attention only to those which impinge on the issue of accountability.

(i) The CAA derives its authority from legislation that speaks frequently of 'the public interest'. At the same time it is funded essentially by 'user pays' — levies on the aviation industry. Leading members of the industry have been appointed by the minister to the CAA board ('user pays, user says'?).

(ii) There are two statutory accountability documents: the Performance Agreement and the Service Charter. One is public, the other is available in the registry of the CAA subject to the provisions of the Official Information Act 1982.

(iii) Under the Public Finance Act, the CAA is required to provide to Parliament annual accounts and a report.

(iv) Certain licensing and other powers are vested in the CAA and its director.

(v) Monitoring the contract is the function of a 'contracts division' in the ministry. The skills and expertise of 'contracting' are increasingly seen as a generic employment category in the public service; there is a recognised need to work with those who have the subject knowledge and who need to look laterally across the 'decoupled' authorities (including the SOE, Airways Corporation of New Zealand) so that the minister has 'the big picture'.

(vi) Conflict between the parties is to be resolved, desirably by discussion, but in the event that agreement cannot be reached the minister has absolute discretion to direct.

In sum, the Performance Agreement between the CAA and the minister represents an increasingly common form of 'contract' between agencies of government. Reform of the education sector following *Tomorrow's Schools* in 1989 has provided evidence of the uncertainties in relationships based on 'contract' between ministers and statutory agencies. Sandra Beatie discusses 'accountability relationships in crisis', including the action by one agency to commence court proceedings when it considered its contract was not being honoured.[27] The outcome was a Cabinet decision (and amending legislation) to attempt to put beyond doubt that the minister could ensure the implementation of government policy. The areas of interest are: the ability of the minister to direct, in this case, the CAA; the circumstances in which the board may be dismissed and the procedures by which the board's budget is determined (i.e. the sanctions available); and the extent to which the CAA's performance can be adequately specified and therefore adequately monitored by and on behalf of the minister.

Above all, the question must be asked: to what extent is this a 'contract' freely entered into? What gains are there that could not have been achieved by a rearrangement within the Ministry of Transport with clear hierarchical lines of accountability reaching back to the minister (except for those regulatory functions properly vested in statutory officers)? What advantages and disadvantages are there in having appointed boards interposed between the Minister of Transport and the various regulatory and delivery agencies in the transport field? What is the potential for 'gridlock' between a board with decided views and the minister? There is, it seems to me, scope for rewarding and ongoing research as this and similar 'contractual' and 'quasi-contractual' arrangements develop.

Conclusion — Accountability for Third-party Government

The Plunket case illustrates the advantages, in terms of 'contracting', for the delivery of services. The parties are clear; the services — as outputs — can be defined; and effective processes for monitoring can be developed. Procedures for the resolution of differences, short of resort to the courts, are readily available, as are the sanctions of non-payment and ultimately non-renewal of contract. To a large extent this is the stuff of classical contracts. There is, however, still a strong element of relational contracting. As already noted, Plunket and the RHAs need each other, although some degree of contestability in provision (but not purchasing) is likely to emerge. The modalities of accountability are less reassuring: who is responsible for what and how much information is available to the public? Not necessarily the purchase agreements between RHAs and Plunket.

The case of the CAA is an example of 'contractualism' *within* the machinery of government — a governance arrangement at the heart of the New Zealand reforms. A regulatory activity is placed at arm's length from the minister; but the tasks of the authority are to be specified in a Performance Agreement with the minister. This statutory arrangement must be seen to be a continuing one — a relational contract. Again, who is responsible for what and how much information is available to the public? Given the availability of the Service Charter, does the public require the Performance Agreement too? On the face of it, the answer is yes.

Let me generalise these observations about 'public services', defined as:[28] (i) services provided by a public body directly; (ii) services purchased by a public body through contract; and (iii) services which a private body has a public law duty to provide.

The first point to be made is that arrangements for 'third party' provision of public services always involve more than one 'contract', namely, (a) between the individual 'client' or 'customer' and the provider; (b) between the 'client' and the public body which is the funder; and (c) between that public body and the provider.

Second, the avenue available to clients to express their preferences is through the political process — either to the minister or to the funder directly (or both). Even when the user pays there are no effective 'market signals' — the extent of the services is defined by *authority* (the law, the minister or the statutory body involved). For that reason ministers must be ultimately responsible for 'third party' government, including the performance standards.

Third, as a continuation of this 'political' point it can be asserted that all *citizens* have a right (which goes beyond any claims they may have as actual or potential *clients*) to know details of the services being purchased with public money (Plunket) or being provided under statutory powers (CAA). This implies the publication by the funder or the provider (or both) of the services available to the public.

Fourth, as a corollary of the preceding point, citizens have a right to receive the promised service; if they do not, some form of compensation would seem to be appropriate (although this has not been a necessary concomitant, for example, of the British Citizens' Charter).

There is, I suggest, a case for recognising that there are indeed at least *three* parties to any provision of public services by a 'third party'; and that the primary contract between the public body and the provider (or the minister and the statutory body in the CAA case) should be supplemented by a 'contract' between citizens and the provider (ultimately backed by statute or by the responsible minister). The CAA Service Charter and the various British charters provide us with precedents here. Similarly, all primary contracts should be transparent (although a case *might* be made for withholding commercially sensitive pricing data). Moreover, governments need to ensure that there are adequate procedures for complaint and redress. In all these areas there is a significant literature and ample precedent.[29] New Zealand is behind the play, and if 'contractualism' is at the heart of public-sector reform we need to devote some attention to these aspects of accountability for 'third party' government.

Annex 1. *Rethinking Public Management: Third-party Government and the Changing Forms of Government Action*

Five Dimensions

1. The Directness/Indirectness Dimension

Hypothesis 1: The more indirect the form of government action — i.e., the more it places important discretionary authority in the hands of non-federal actors and the more the interests and goals of these actors diverge from those of the federal government — the more difficult will be the implementation of the resulting program and the less likely will the program be to achieve its goals.

Hypothesis 2: The more direct the form of government action, the more likely it is to encounter political opposition.

2. The Automatic/Administered Dimension

Hypothesis 3: The more automatic the tool of government action, the easier to manage, the fairer the operation, and the less disruptive the side effects.

Hypothesis 4: The more automatic the tool of government, the less certain the achievement of program purposes, the greater the leakage of program benefits, and the more problematic the generation of needed political support.

3. The Cash Versus In-Kind Dimension

Hypothesis 5: Programs that utilize cash are easier to manage and more highly valued than programs that provide assistance in kind.

Hypothesis 6: The greater the reliance on in-kind tools of action, the greater the prospects for political support.

4. The Visibility/Invisibility Dimension

Hypothesis 7: The less visible a tool of government action is in the regular budget process, the less subject it will be to overall management and control.

Hypothesis 8: The less visible the costs of a tool, the more attractive the tool will be to those who benefit from it. The more powerful the beneficiaries, therefore, the more likely they will be to receive whatever benefits they secure through less visible tools.

5. Design Standards versus Performance Standards for Program Control

Hypothesis 9: The more a form of government action uses performance standards instead of design regulations, the less cumbersome it is administratively and the more efficient is its use of resources.

Hypothesis 10: The more a tool involves reliance on federally determined performance standards, the more likely it is to encounter political opposition and resistance from its administrators.

Source: Lester M. Salamon, 'Rethinking Public Management' (see note 7).

Annex 2. *Service Standards: Our Commitments and Your Rights*

We are committed to treating you — our customer — as we would want to be treated. This means you have the right to expect us to be courteous, helpful and treat your concern as ours. In carrying out this commitment, we will strive to:

- Listen.
- Treat the information you give us as confidential where appropriate, and use it for lawful purposes only.
- Be fair and consistent.
- Provide timely and accurate responses.
- Be open and transparent.
- Do what we say we will do, do it when we say we will do it, and do it right.
- Remedy the situation or make amends, as appropriate, where we have failed to meet these standards.

In addition, when contacting us by telephone, you may expect to be put through to the person best able and available to deal with your enquiry, and that person to:

- Answer the phone promptly.
- Identify himself or herself by name.
- Record your enquiry.
- Act promptly where a response is required.

When you choose to write to us, whether a general enquiry or an application for an aviation document, you may expect:

- Acknowledgment of your letter within 10 working days of receipt.
- Identification of the person replying to your letter.
- A response which addresses your needs and respects your opinion.
- Accurate information provided to you in clear simple language.
- Progress reports where matters proceed over a period of time.

In face-to-face situations, you may expect:

* Access to the person or persons best able and available to assist you.
* Such person or persons to identify themselves by name and to provide evidence of their employment with the Authority if so requested.
* Such persons to act in a helpful, co-operative and professional manner.
* The provision of the information which you seek as quickly as possible and within the legal requirements or limitations applicable to the provision of that information.

Source: Service Charter and Directory *(CAA, 1993, p.10).*

Notes

1   John Stewart, 'The Limitations of Government by Contract', *Public Money and Management*, 13 (1993), pp.7–12.

2   *Ibid.*

3   Hon. W. F. Birch, 'Speech to Master of Public Policy Students', Victoria University of Wellington, February 21, 1991.

4   Gary Sturgess, 'Why Is Government in Business Anyway?', address to conference hosted by Government Pricing Tribunal of NSW and Centre for Applied Economic Research, Sydney, February 28, 1994.

5   Quoted in 'Justice First for Efficiency Shakeup', *Dominion*, July 2, 1994.

6   Donald Kettl, *Government by Proxy: (Mis?)Managing Federal Programs* (Washington, DC, Congressional Quarterly Press, 1988).

7   Lester M. Salamon, 'Rethinking Public Management: Third-Party Government and the Changing Forms of Government Action', *Public Policy* 29 (1981), pp.255–75.

8   The Treasury, *Economic Management* (Wellington, Government Printer, 1984), p.210.

9   Sir Kenneth Keith, 'Medicine and the Law: An Era of Change', address to National Medico-Legal Conference Auckland, August 18–19, 1992.

10   Ian Harden, *The Contracting State* (Buckingham, Open University Press, 1992), p.38.

11   John Kay, *Foundations of Corporate Success: How Business Strategies Add Value* (Oxford, Oxford University Press, 1993).

12   *Ibid.*, p.30.

13   *Ibid.*, p.31.

14   *Ibid.*, p.59.

15   Oliver Williamson, *The Economic Institutions of Capitalism* (New York, Free Press, 1985).

16 Neil Carter, 'Learning to Measure Performance: the Use of Indicators in Organizations', *Public Administration* 69 (1991), pp.85–101.

17 Steering Group, Review of State Sector Reforms (Wellington, 1991).

18 For a discussion of contracting in the health service, see Philippa Howden-Chapman, 'Doing the Splits: Contracting in the New Zealand Health Service', *Health Policy* 24 (1993), pp.273–86.

19 Stewart, 'The Limitations of Government by Contract', p.11.

20 *Ibid.*, p.12.

21 Salamon, 'Rethinking Public Management', p.268.

22 *Ibid.*, p.271.

23 *Ibid.*, p.272.

24 Department of Health, *Notes to the Estimates for Year ended 31 March 1990* (Wellington).

25 Plunket, *Annual Report* (Wellington, 1992).

26 See Peter J. Davey, 'The Civil Aviation Authority of New Zealand: A Case Study in Organisational Change and Development', unpublished MPP research paper, Victoria University of Wellington, 1993; and Owen Batchelor, 'Cost Recovery in Civil Aviation: The Theory, the Need and the Consequences', unpublished MPP research paper, Victoria University of Wellington, 1994.

27 Sandra J. Beatie, 'The Constitutional and Accountability Arrangements of Education Crown Agencies', unpublished MPP research paper, Victoria University of Wellington, 1993.

28 Following Harden, *The Contracting State*, p.9.

29 See, for example, Jenny Potter, 'Consumerism and the Public Sector: How Well Does the Coat Fit?', *Public Administration* 66 (1988), pp.149–64); Harden, *The Contracting State*; and Michael Connolly, Penny McKeown and Grainne M. Byrne, 'Making the Public Sector More User Friendly? A Critical Examination of the Citizen's Charter', *Parliamentary Affairs* 47 (1994), pp.23–36.

CHAPTER THREE

Accountability, Responsibility and Corruption: Managing the 'Public Production Process'

ROBERT GREGORY

Differing Managerial Cultures

A central proposition of this chapter is that those responsible for consolidating, evaluating and enhancing the New Zealand state-sector reforms should draw on a broader range of scholarly inquiry than was used in designing the new 'public production process', which has been shaped by insights drawn almost exclusively from organizational economics.[1] A more multi-disciplinary, experientially based — and more commonsensical? — approach should better ensure that some aspects of the reforms do not ultimately exacerbate rather than overcome the problems they were originally intended to address.

I have outlined elsewhere[2] the reasons why the reforms might introduce new varieties of 'goal displacement', a contradiction common to virtually all large bureaucratic organizations, and one which the changes were explicitly designed to overcome. In similar vein, this chapter will discuss the possibility that, unless a broader range of theory and experience is drawn upon, other unintended and undesirable consequences might follow. Of central concern in this discussion are the consequences that may flow from an exaggerated preoccupation with managerial accountability at the expense of administrative responsibility.

A basic conceptual framework that is central to both discussions is outlined by James Q. Wilson in his major work on American public bureaucracy.[3] In summary, Wilson deploys a four-way matrix (see Figure 3.1) to differentiate among public agencies according to (i) the observability of an agency's *outputs*, and (ii) the observability of its *outcomes.* The former comprise the work the agency does, and the latter the effects of that work on the community. To quote Wilson:

> The outputs (or work) of police officers are the radio calls answered, beats walked, tickets written, accidents investigated, and arrests made. The outcomes (or results) are the changes, if any, in the level of safety, security, order, and amenity in the community.[4]

It should be noted that Wilson uses the two terms in almost the same way as New Zealand's Public Finance Act 1990, which is one of the three main statutory foundations of the state-sector reforms (the others being the State Owned Enterprises Act 1986, and the State Sector Act 1988).

Managers of *production* organizations — or of production tasks — can evaluate workers 'on the basis of their contribution to efficiency', measured clearly as a ratio between outputs and outcomes. In *procedural* organizations workers are much more likely to be assessed according to their compliance with rules and procedures, given that processes can be observed while outcomes cannot. In a *craft* environment compliance must be assessed against the outcomes produced rather than the means of doing so. In a *coping* culture 'effective management is almost impossible' since neither work nor outcomes are readily observable.[5]

In Wilson's view, managers in the four different types of organization — production, procedural, craft and coping — will need to use different mixes of incentives to encourage operators to comply with agency rules.[6] Hence, each type of organization will be characterised by a different type of management culture, and the critical factor in determining the type of organization and the appropriate management culture will be the particular task being carried out. In practice, many large public organizations will be carrying out a range of different tasks — for example, New Zealand's 'big three': the departments of Justice, Social Welfare and Inland Revenue — and thus may encompass a mix of managerial cultures.

Wilson's own warning should be heeded: 'My classification is a crude effort to sort out some important differences. It is hardly a theory and many agencies do not fit its categories. Use with caution.'[7] Moreover, some tasks, under differing circumstances (to outline these would need a stronger attempt at theory building than can be offered here), may straddle categories or shift from one to another.

Figure 3.2 provides an indicative categorization of some of the tasks carried out within the New Zealand state services. The main thrust of the

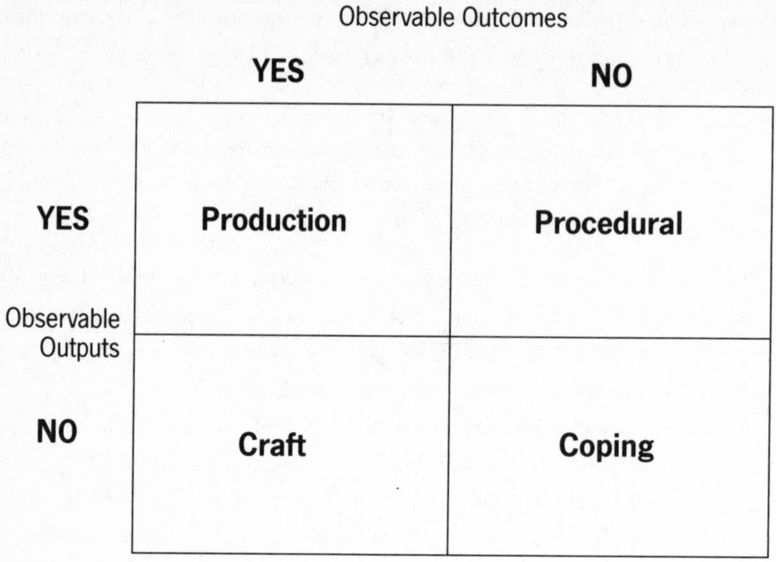

Observable Outcomes

	YES	**NO**
YES	Production	Procedural
NO	Craft	Coping

Observable Outputs

Figure 3:1 *Wilson Matrix*

state-sector reforms has been to encourage all public agencies in New Zealand to treat all their tasks as if they were or could be made into *production* ones. In the context of this discussion, this is the idea behind the pejorative interpretation of 'managerialism'. For, as Wilson's matrix indicates, such an aspiration seems insufficiently sensitive to differences among the sorts of tasks that public organizations are required to carry out. While it may be quite appropriate for production agencies, especially state-owned enterprises, it is much less so for the other three types of organization. Treating all tasks as if they were amenable to a production culture not only is likely to have counter-productive effects with regard to goal-displacement,[8] but may also encourage official behaviour which, while accountable, is less responsible, even corrupt.

No detailed analysis can be provided here of the various managerial modes that might be considered appropriate for differing public-sector tasks. Instead, the discussion will identify several interconnected variables that need to be considered in relation to differing tasks if state-sector organizations are to be both accountable *and* responsible. Three general propositions will be advanced: first, that the concept of accountability may generally be sufficient for the management of production and procedural

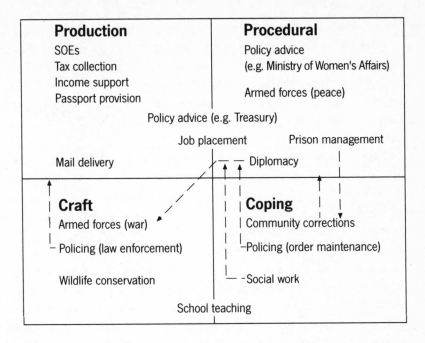

Figure 3:2 *The Different Tasks of Public Agencies*

organizations; second, that the notion of responsibility is much more appropriate for the management of craft and coping organizations; and third, that corrupt official practices may be more likely to occur when a concern for accountability displaces the need for responsibility, especially in craft and coping organizations.

Accountability and Responsibility

In the state-sector reforms there has emerged a huge contrast between the fulsome attention paid to accountability and the very sparse consideration of responsibility. Perhaps the two words are considered synonymous. But they are not, as they represent two concepts which, while related, embody different ideas about the behaviour of public officials.

Accountability, as the word itself suggests, is about the need to give an *account* of one's actions. In an organizational context, the primary duty of obligation is to provide such an account to one's superiors in the hierarchical chain of bureaucratic command. Ralph Hummel captures the essence of bureaucratic accountability in pointing out that managerial control is based on the attempt to render all work 'visible', through reporting systems and procedures.[9] Managers must *know* what their subordinates are doing, and their subordinates must tell them. Work that is hidden is potentially threatening to the organization, understood as a control system. Information about the work carried out is the *sine qua non* of effective management. In this view, if work (outputs) cannot be seen it cannot be properly supervised.

What is responsibility, as distinct from accountability? Frederick Mosher distinguished between what he termed 'objective' and 'subjective' responsibility.[10] The former is really the equivalent of accountability as outlined above: it is the formal obligation to give an account of one's actions to those in superordinate positions of authority. Lines of accountability are depicted in the traditional organization chart. Subjective responsibility, on the other hand, is to be understood not as a formal, externally imposed duty but as a felt sense of obligation. It is not only 'upward-looking', in a hierarchical sense, but may be experienced as a pull in other directions, to a number of 'significant others'. Subjective responsibility, unlike objective responsibility (accountability), is the stuff of moral dilemmas.

The main difference goes beyond this idea of multiple directions. Whereas accountability is expressed *to* another party or other parties, responsibility is accepted *for* the actions of oneself or others. Also, responsible as distinct from (merely) accountable action implies some degree of prudence, good judgement or moral probity. For this reason, of course, public officials can be called to account for irresponsible (including morally reprehensible) actions taken by themselves or others; but their accountability does not necessarily say anything about their willingness to accept responsibility — in a causal sense — for those actions. These distinctions have been well canvassed in public administration literature (and in other scholarly traditions) since the Nuremberg trials, when accountable German officials disclaimed responsibility on the ground that they were only following the orders of their superiors.[11] Broadly speaking, therefore, accountability may best be understood as a necessary but insufficient component of responsibility.

A lot has already been written about the impact of the New Zealand state-sector reforms on the status and workability of the conventional doctrine of ministerial responsibility,[12] but little has been said about the idea of individual responsibility in the day-to-day activities of public officials.

Accountability for Production and Procedural Tasks

As Wilson indicates, the work involved in carrying out some tasks is relatively easy to observe, while in other cases it is much more difficult. Accountability, therefore, understood as the need to make work visible, is more easily fostered in tasks which lend themselves to a production or procedural managerial mode than in those tasks which are more consistent with craft and coping modes. In the two former categories, work is observable as it happens; in other words it is *directly* (or simultaneously) controllable. There is little scope for rendering misleading, or downright untrue, accounts of what is going on. In the latter two categories, however, work can often be made visible only after it happens. It is *indirectly* (or retrospectively) controllable, since it depends heavily on accounts given — stories told — by operators whose actual conduct is not observable by their managerial superiors.

In these cases managers may be told by their operators only what they want or expect to hear. The 'reality' reported to managers in craft and coping contexts may indeed be 'socially constructed', and their knowledge of what operators are actually up to must often be based on information gleaned from other sources, such as 'clients' or members of the public. This is what Herbert Kaufman calls 'unplanned feedback'.[13] These operators are the 'street-level bureaucrats' discussed by Michael Lipsky — police officers, social workers, corrections officers, school teachers, and so on.[14]

Especially in coping situations, managers find themselves handling 'crises' once they have occurred rather than, in the case of production and procedural situations, preventing them from happening. Regulatory manuals will nevertheless be voluminous in all four cases, but for two different reasons: either because *discretion* is not necessary since work is readily prescribable (as in the production and procedural contexts), or because it is necessary and work must be rendered proscribable (as in craft and coping situations).

Clearly, if accountability is wanted, then it is much better to have production and procedural organizations than craft and coping ones. And if problems of goal displacement are to be overcome, then it is better to have production rather than procedural modes of management. The difficulty is that accountability, which is a function of the observability — or visibility — of work, is simply not an adequate means of fostering managerial compliance and purposeful action in craft and coping contexts.

Responsibility for Craft and Coping Tasks

The need for accountability often becomes a source of frustration for many officials who are required to carry out tasks that are highly dependent on the discretionary exercise of specialised knowledge. They are often professionals working in craft organizations. In these cases, as with professionals and other workers in coping organizations, there may be greater scope for 'morally hazardous' behaviour since their work is less observable than that of workers in production or procedural organizations. And in production organizations there may be less non-compliant behaviour simply because outcomes are clearly achievable without it. In procedural organizations all actions will be watched, as Wilson points out, because they can be watched, whereas outcomes remain elusive (and sometimes illusory). Agency theory has been invoked by architects of the state-sector reforms to curb the likelihood of 'morally hazardous' behaviour.[15]

However, while there may be greater scope for such behaviour in a craft context, there may be no greater propensity for it, and perhaps even less. This is because compliance in craft organizations depends much less on formal, legalistic constraints, which are intended to keep activities visible and accountable, and much more on such qualities as a strong sense of shared mission, commitment to professional norms, standards and values, and above all on maintaining high levels of mutual trust and respect.

Coping organizations have professionals, too — or often aspiring professionals[16] — but because neither their work nor the outcomes they produce are readily observable there will be much less willingness by managers to rely primarily on mission, professional values and trust (indeed, there is likely to be a lack of trust). So in both craft and coping contexts the managerial prerogative may often be experienced in a strongly negative sense by those being 'managed'. In the former it is felt to undermine trust; and in the latter, as Wilson observes, it is often seen to be exercised unfairly: 'Teachers do not like principals who fail to back them up in conflicts with pupils or parents. Police officers do not like [superiors] who fail to back them up in conflicts with citizens and lawyers'.[17]

Especially in craft and coping situations, therefore, because work cannot be made visible — unless the nature of the task is transformed in the process[18] — accountability must be broadened to become responsibility. Public administration scholarship has long recognized and understood this dimension of official compliance. So too has organization theory in general.

It was a central component of Chester Barnard's classical theory of organization as a willingly co-operative system designed to achieve a common purpose. He spoke, among many other things, of 'the establishment of the morality of standards of workmanship'.[19]

A preoccupation with accountability creates strong incentives for managers and operators to collaborate in constructing a body of 'artifactual' knowledge, which is a crafted product of dubious veracity. This is a consequence of the drive to maximize measurable outputs and so enhance the appearance of organizational effectiveness. This knowledge becomes, in effect, the agency's own officially constructed 'reality', self-sustaining and largely beyond intelligent, reflective revision.

For such reasons officially determined rates — crime figures, un-employment numbers and estimates of the incidence of child abuse, alcoholism, domestic violence and so on — may say almost as much about the organizations and professionals who generate them as about the 'realities' they purport to measure. Indeed, one need not move beyond the political sociology of official statistics to find a scholarly tradition which raises more pertinent questions about the sort of positivist assumptions that underpin New Zealand's state-sector reforms, and which may diminish rather than enhance governmental learning capacity.[20] These assumptions include the idea that 'efficiency' can be measured objectively, that resources can always be allocated 'rationally' rather than politically, and that policy and administration (now called management) ought to be readily separable. Although Wilson's work falls squarely within a 'mainstream' tradition of public administration scholarship, which itself has long since challenged such beliefs, his own account of the 'statistics game' played by the FBI under J. Edgar Hoover shows how a strong incentive to measure organizational success has a direct effect on administrative behaviour, not necessarily for the better.[21]

In New Zealand, the growing production ethos of public management is likely to render such theoretical insights even more appropriate in attempts to interpret and explain the activities of public agencies, particularly the production of outputs which take the form of officially sanctioned rates, and which are instrumental in shaping public perceptions of, and attitudes towards, social problems. For example, F. Goodyear-Smith's critical analysis of what she calls the 'sexual abuse industry' alludes to this phenomenon.[22] And no doubt criminologists (and civil libertarians) in New Zealand will be keeping a sharp eye on how the police go about achieving their publicly announced plan to 'reduc[e] the incidence and effects of crime' by 1998,[23] and how crime-prevention strategies are implemented to identify and support so-called 'at risk' families and young people.[24] Definitions and responses to the road-toll problem are, arguably, also locked into dominant political and professional perceptions.

The indiscriminate pursuit of measurable accountability is likely to have the greatest impact on coping tasks, insofar as they come to be regarded as production ones. There is a real dilemma here. Neither outputs nor outcomes are measurable, so managerial control is problematic, and there is thus greater scope for official and personal corruption. But tighter control-systems which measure only what can most readily be measured may enhance accountability at the expense of an effectiveness more attuned to the complex circumstances that coping tasks must address. In other words, a distinction needs to be made between accountability as control *per se* and accountability as *controlled effectiveness*. The former, when control becomes an end in itself, may be apparent in the form of a counter-productive obsession, whereas the latter recognises the importance of control — notably perhaps in financial management — but remains sensitive to the politically tendentious and technologically uncertain nature of the operating context.

If prisons, for example, are to be required by society to meet simultaneously the conflicting objectives of containment, (re)habilitation and punishment (to name only three), then it does not seem sensible to manage them as if they were production organizations. Much of the work of prison officers is directly controllable, but much of it is only indirectly so, as they seek to cope with the 'situational imperatives' that confront them in their day-to-day work.[25] The actions of some Mangaroa Prison officers led to public controversy when it was later disclosed that in December 1993 an inmate, who was awaiting sentence for stabbing a police constable, was allowed to visit his *de facto* wife while being transferred to Auckland. A Justice Department report criticised the officers 'for allowing themselves to be "bullied" into the visit', which 'was made so the officers escorting [the prisoner] would not have to fight him all the way to Auckland'. The Minister of Justice was reported as saying that 'he was being driven insane and crazy by events at the prison' which had seen 20 escapes in two years.[26] While the judgement and competence of prison staff in responding to 'situational imperatives' are proper concerns for management — and Ministers of Justice — such imperatives are in themselves unavoidable given the nature of the task. When operators' responses prove to be politically controversial they usually result in procedures being 'tightened'.

A similar observation can be made with regard to those coping tasks carried out by the Children and Young Persons Service of the Department of Social Welfare. The management of the service has been the subject of considerable public controversy, much of it relating to funding and budgeting, training, management support, staff morale, and criticism levelled by the Commissioner for Children.[27] In August 1994 a youth was killed in a stolen car after he had absconded from a home run by the service. Public comment highlighted the difficult nature of coping tasks: for example, a central question was whether these homes should be run more like prisons with a higher priority given to security, as readily measured by the absconding rate, which reportedly was 58 per cent lower in 1993–94 than in the previous year.[28]

Increased Corruption in Public Agencies?

Requiring all tasks to be managed as if they were amenable to a production culture may increase rather than diminish the possibility of non-compliance, even corruption. A summary depiction of the following arguments is provided in Figure 3.3.

To begin, let us consider Edward Banfield's application of agency theory to public and private organizations. He identifies two forms of corruption:

> An agent is *personally corrupt* if he [*sic*] knowingly sacrifices his principal's interest to his own, that is, he betrays his trust. He is *officially corrupt* if, in serving his principal's interest, he knowingly violates a rule, that is, acts illegally or unethically albeit in his principal's interest.[29]

Perhaps paradoxically, official corruption (as defined above) is often necessary if public bureaucracies are to do anything at all consistent with achieving their espoused purposes. Rules have to be bent, and 'misplaced initiative' has to occur if operators are to respond with common sense to the needs of their 'clients'.[30] However, an over-blown commitment to a production culture may make a virtue of procedural and legal corner-cutting, enhancing a 'can-do' mentality and so increasing a less benign incidence of official corruption taken in (what are thought to be) the principal's interests.

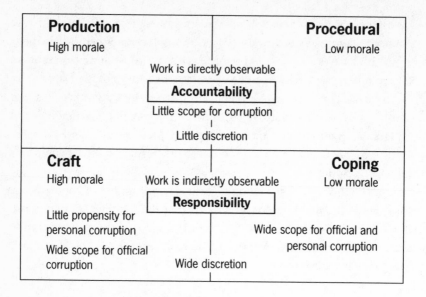

Figure 3:3 *Conceptual Summary*

This may be especially so when the production ethos is overlaid with strong expectations of commercial enterprise on the part of officials. A private 'keyholder' security service operated by a police officer might be a case in point. In 1993 it was publicly revealed that the police hierarchy had sanctioned a Wellington detective running a profit-making emergency telephone-number service in his spare time. The Commissioner of Police is reported to have said that 'police were in a "win win" situation, having a system it would not otherwise have had, at absolutely no cost'. The commissioner later 'admitted police were mistaken to have entered into the contract', serving officers were banned from running such services, and new rules were to be drawn up covering potential conflicts of interest arising from police officers having outside jobs.[31] It appeared that unfavourable news media attention brought about this reconsideration, which would seem to confirm David Bradshaw's point:

> I believe that the public still expects very high ethical standards from its public servants . . . notwithstanding the changes that have occurred. You only need to look at the attention that the media gives to indiscretions by public officials to realise that this is so. Very often the same conduct that is criticized when it occurs in the Public Service would be rewarded as an exercise of initiative in the private sector.[32]

Barnard claimed that falsifying the books 'for the good of the organization' — official corruption — was more common in public than in private organizations;[33] and Banfield has ascribed this to the fact that government executives are more likely than their business counterparts to be motivated by non-pecuniary values (involvement in 'affairs of state', proximity to political power, commitment to 'the public interest').[34] Government departments in New Zealand, and of course elsewhere, have in the past been disposed to eliminate personal corruption virtually at *all* costs. But, as Banfield points out, this situation differs markedly from that prevailing in business organizations, which 'will incur costs to prevent corruption insofar — but *only* insofar — as it expects them to yield marginal returns equal to those that could be had from other investments.'[35]

On the face of it, therefore, requiring public agencies to behave as if they were private ones may be expected to result in less official corruption but more personal corruption. In January 1994, Robert Sheldon, Chairman of the House of Commons Public Accounts Committee, reported that public standards of probity and integrity had fallen to their lowest level since the creation of the modern civil service last century. He argued that increased mismanagement, inefficiency and outright fraud were threatening the long-standing incorruptibility of Britain's public services. He also claimed that the decline in standards had been exacerbated by government attempts to bring private-sector expertise into public-sector management. In his view these managers were not imbued with the public-sector ethos of probity associated with public servants.[36] These arguments suggest that official corruption, too, is more likely to increase as a result of the narrow preoccupation with accountability.

A more telling factor, however, is *morale*. Generally speaking, organizational morale is likely to be higher in production and craft contexts than in procedural and coping ones, because clear outcomes can be readily observed (produced). There will be a stronger sense of achievement, relevance and purpose. Yet morale is high in production and craft contexts for different reasons: in the former because there is a clear and unambiguous relationship between work done and results produced; in the latter because professionals are given the operational autonomy that they so highly value.

A consequence of treating craft tasks as if they were production ones effectively undermines this autonomy. Individual self-esteem may be lowered, general morale may drop, and an air of cynical obedience may result. Professionals would be inclined to tell managers what they wanted to hear (often with an absurdly contrived conscientiousness) in the demeaning knowledge that their own commitment to solidary norms and values was no longer regarded as being a guarantor of responsible action. Trust, in other words, is down-graded, particularly the 'goodwill trust' that ensures honest commitment beyond the terms of a legal contract.[37] As Banfield argues, with words that have particular relevance for craft and coping management cultures:

> *[I]n certain circumstances* it may be impossible to substitute monitoring for dependability ... similarly, *in certain circumstances* it may be impossible to substitute a narrowing of discretion for dependability (the work may require the exercise of a very broad discretion).[38]

Such trust, for example, has traditionally been regarded as essential to a healthy working relationship between ministers and their officials under the doctrine of ministerial responsibility. It cannot be secured simply by the signing of a written contract, if at the same time other important factors in sustaining it are becoming attenuated — say, the willingness of ministers to accept responsibility for the actions of their officials. According to a former Chairman of the State Services Commission (1975–81), Robin Williams:

> The idea of the minister always supporting the department and accepting at least nominal responsibility for all the events that occurred in it has gone. Now he [sic] really can't accept nominal responsibility because the chief executive is more clearly accountable for the overall operation. The rules have changed, by no means clearly for the better, and I'm not at all sure that the public today can hold ministers as accountable for what happens as they could in the old days.[39]

Other commentators and events provide evidence to support the view that the conventions of ministerial responsibility have come under increasing strain.[40] The State Services Commissioner, Don Hunn, for example, was reported to be concerned by 'the increasing involvement of government officials in election campaigns' following parliamentary opposition claims that before the Selwyn by-election, in August 1994, the Minister of Education had asked his officials to cost Alliance policies without telling them what they were doing.[41] And after the 1993 general election the State Services Commission rebuked the Treasury for its costings of Labour Party policies before the election.

Moreover, some empirical research has indicated that the new managerialist ethos may be weakening understanding of, and commitment to, some of the traditional tenets of ministerial and administrative responsibility, as it gives rise to 'technocrats' who are committed to policy programmes but tend to be impatient with political processes.[42] Technocracy generates its own threats to open politics and responsible government, as John Ralston Saul indicates:

> The technocrats suffer from character defects which have to do with their inability to maintain any links between reason, common sense and morality . . . That is to say they don't seem to understand the historical process. Instead they seem actually to believe that their definitions of the world will become both real and permanent simply because they are the result of applied logic . . . Their talents have become the modern definition of intelligence. It is an extremely narrow definition and it eliminates a large part of both the human experience and the human character.[43]

This chapter does not seek to dwell on the issue of ministerial responsibility *per se*; but its attenuation would seem to reflect the demise of a coherent public-service ethos. Rather than a 'public service' as such, there are now individual agencies enjoying considerable autonomy, and with a view of themselves as production organizations modelled on the lines of corporate business. In 1993, the Minister of Internal Affairs requested an inquiry into the appointment procedures for Lottery Grants staff, following a police investigation into allegations that about $200,000 had been diverted into bogus charities. (Four people were later charged with defrauding the Internal Affairs Department.) The Secretary of Internal Affairs wrote to the minister setting out constitutional arrangements that define the information that may be supplied to ministers: 'I've given him advice on what the parameters are and he has accepted that advice'.[44]

If the new production culture does encourage official corruption, or 'creative accounting' designed to demonstrate the organization's effectiveness in meeting measurable targets, then the crucial question is: under what circumstances does official corruption carried out for the principal's gain degenerate into personal corruption whereby the books are 'cooked' for individual gain, not necessarily or even mainly financial? Or, at a more empirical level, to what extent has this in fact been occurring?

Clearly, these two questions beg a considerable amount of further research, and even then answers are likely to remain inconclusive. Before the state-sector reforms the State Services Commission, as the central personnel agency, had a clear responsibility for the conduct and performance of public servants. Figures on disciplinary proceedings brought against public servants were recorded in the commission's annual reports to Parliament. That responsibility lapsed with the reforms of 1988, which left individual chief executives responsible for the conduct of their staff. It is questionable whether chief executives have a strong incentive to record disciplinary matters publicly in the way that the commission, as a central agency, once did. And the establishment of state-owned enterprises has undoubtedly worked to inhibit disclosure under the Official Information Act, on the ground of commercial sensitivity.

In any case, it is impossible to know conclusively whether there would have been more corruption had the reforms *not* been implemented. In 1989, a few years after the corporatization and commercialization programme began, the Audit Office had already expressed its concern at 'the increasing number of reported frauds being perpetrated from within public sector organizations', pointing out:

> Whereas until recently recorded instances of [public sector] frauds were reasonably few and far between, there has been a dramatic increase in the past twelve months with some 45 cases being known to us. The amounts involved range from relatively small sums to two instances each involving nearly $2 million.[45]

Since then there have been a number of well-publicized instances of personally corrupt practice, allegations of it, financial mismanagement or exorbitant personal spending within the public sector. Probably the most startling was the resignation in October 1994 of none other than the then Controller and Auditor-General himself, because of 'personal financial difficulties'. An independent investigation later claimed that he owed the Audit Office nearly $157,000 for personal expenses, incurred mostly while travelling overseas. (At the time of writing the former chief executive was contesting this amount.)[46] Apart from the Lottery Grants affair mentioned above, other instances include: a power project commercial manager charged with defrauding the Electricity Corporation of more than $4 million;[47] a railways consultant jailed for twelve months after being found guilty of dishonesty offences relating to a railways scrap-metal operation;[48] a former Inland Revenue Department officer convicted of forgery charges involving attempts to divert IRD cheques to personal use;[49] a 1992 audit which found that a co-ordinating committee administered by the

Department of Social Welfare had engaged in 'grandiose' spending and wrong accounting practices;[50] the sacking of a senior air force officer after it was revealed that renovations to his official residence ended up costing about $500,000 more than was authorised, and the later dismissal of another officer who was found to have 'systematically bypassed the Defence orders and instructions governing works activities over a period of at least three years';[51] a Department of Social Welfare staff member dismissed after an internal investigation into the passing-on of confidential client information to an Invercargill debt-collection agency;[52] and the resignation and sacking, respectively, of two senior defence officials after theft and dishonesty charges involving about $60,000.[53]

Any increase in personal corruption in the state services would surely have no single, or even predominant, cause, and might simply reflect a rise in corporate dishonesty offences generally.[54] And any possible increase in the incidence of corrupt practices would have to be weighed against the benefits that are judged to have accrued from the reforms, including the possibility that more incidents are brought to light now because of more effective control systems. Pending more rigorous research into these questions, assessments must remain tentative and impressionistic.

Conclusion

The preceding analysis suggests that instances of corruption — both official and personal — in the New Zealand state services will probably increase significantly in the years ahead. It is speculated, necessarily tentatively, that this will be in part because the state-sector reforms, promulgated with the aim of enhancing accountability, are based on a narrow, essentially economistic, view of human behaviour in organizations. There may be something of a self-fulfilling prophecy at work: to the extent that officials, no matter what type of tasks they are engaged in, are regarded as 'morally hazardous', then that is what they will increasingly become. In short, more public officials may be expected to behave as if they were untrustworthy, self-seeking, opportunistic, morally hazardous and adversely selected neo-Taylorites.[55] Interestingly, in quite a different context, where he explores the existence of an innate moral sense in human beings, Wilson notes research showing that 'only one group of subjects clearly preferred to be free riders . . . graduate students in economics'.[56] (Any 'causal' relationship, of course, remains ambiguous.)

Moreover, we may consider the increasing use of contracting out, in order to enhance efficiency, as another major factor in the equation. This issue is examined in other chapters in this book, but clearly the rise of a 'transactional bureaucracy' (a category not provided for in Wilson's matrix) will place more and more public officials in critical brokerage positions where their competencies will need to be measured in ethical and not just technical terms.

Finally, from a broader perspective, and at the risk of some polemical indulgence, it can plausibly be suggested that the international emergence of an exorbitantly paid, plushly cosseted and mystically competent managerial class is itself a manifestation of a third type of organizational corruption, with more insidious consequences than the other two variations discussed here.[57] Organizational executives, public and private, may be increasingly seduced by material rewards which are felt to be justly appropriate for the life-style to which they have grown accustomed. In New Zealand, a hardened cynic might be forgiven for thinking that the state-sector reforms were designed by the people who stood to gain most from them.

Whatever the case, we do know that complex issues should not be subject to oversimplified responses. It is hardly possible to construct elegant theoretical models which will predict and explain relationships among the variables identified in Figure 3.3. But Wilson's typology forms the basis of a more inclusive conceptual framework which can be used to better organize our thinking about some strengths and weaknesses of the 'public production process'. It would require a massive research agenda to determine the optimal managerial qualities for the four types outlined by Wilson, and even that may really be unnecessary. Perhaps the best managers have innate skill and perception, and an intuitive understanding of the work they have to manage; and these attributes would be honed on the job. In the many decades since Frederick Winslow Taylor articulated his ideas,[58] little has occurred to suggest that the term 'scientific management' is not oxymoronic. Such narrowly based theoretical prescriptions will not serve in the search to consolidate a state-sector ethos which values responsible pro-active commitment as highly as accountable reactive control.

Notes

1   The term 'public production process' was coined by John Alford in 'Towards a New Public Management Model: Beyond "Managerialism" and Its Critics', *Australian Journal of Public Administration* 52 (1993), pp.135–48.

2   Robert Gregory, 'Consolidating the Reforms: Can the Production Model Be Counter-Productive?', *Public Sector* 17 (1994), pp.18–21.

3   James Q. Wilson, *Bureaucracy: What Government Agencies Do and Why They Do It* (New York, Basic Books, 1989).

4   *Ibid.*, pp.158–59.

5   *Ibid.*, pp.174–75.

6   *Ibid.*, pp.174–75.

7   *Ibid.*, p.159. A university, for example, does not fit readily since the concept of collegiality is central to its management. This might be changing as universities, too, become increasingly subject to managerialist nostrums that may help turn them into 'degree factories'. But that is another story.

8   Gregory, *op. cit.*

9   Ralph P. Hummel, *The Bureaucratic Experience: The Critique of Life in the Modern Organization* 4th edn (New York, St Martin's Press, 1994).

10   Frederick C. Mosher, *Democracy and the Public Service* (New York, Oxford University Press, 1968).

11   See, for example, Hannah Arendt, *Eichmann in Jerusalem: A Report on the Banality of Evil* (London, Faber, 1963); Barry Clarke, 'Beyond the "Banality of Evil"', *British Journal of Political Science* 10 (1980), pp.417–39; Michael Jackson, 'The Eye of Doubt: Neutrality, Responsibility and Morality', *Australian Journal of Public Administration* 46 (1987), pp.280–92; Michael Jackson, 'The Public Interest, Public Service and Democracy', *Australian Journal of Public Administration* 47 (1988), pp.241–51; H. C. Kelman and L. H. Lawrence, 'Assignment of Responsibility in the Case of Lt. Calley: Preliminary Report on a National Survey', *Journal of Social Issues* 28 (1972), pp.177–212; K. Kernaghan and J. Langford, *The Responsible Public Servant* (Halifax, NS, Institute for Research on Public Policy and Institute of Public Administration of Canada, 1990).

12   David Bradshaw, 'Standards of Professionalism: The Community and the Public Interest', paper presented at the Public Service Senior Management Conference, Wellington, September 10, 1993; John Martin, 'Ethos and Ethics', in Jonathan Boston *et al.* (eds), *Reshaping the State: New Zealand's Bureaucratic Revolution* (Auckland, Oxford University Press, 1991); John Martin, 'Ethics in Public Service: The New Zealand Experience', in N. Preston (ed.), *Educating for Public Service Ethics* (Brisbane, Federation Press, 1994); John Roberts, 'Ministers, the Cabinet, and Public Servants', in Jonathan Boston and Martin Holland (eds.), *The Fourth Labour Government: Radical Politics in New Zealand* (Auckland, Oxford University Press, 1987).

13   Herbert Kaufman, *Administrative Feedback: Monitoring Subordinates' Behavior,*

(Washington, DC, Brookings Institution, 1973).

14 Michael Lipsky, *Street-Level Bureaucracy* (New York, Russell Sage Foundation, 1980).

15 Agency theory sees social and political life as a series of contracts in which a *principal* enters into exchanges with an *agent*. Strong emphasis is placed on the legalistic dimensions of such contracts.

16 The principal defining characteristic of a professional occupation is regulated entry on the basis of appropriate theoretical knowledge acquired through several years of tertiary-level education. See Mosher, *op. cit.*, chapter 4.

17 Wilson, *op. cit.*, p.170.

18 Gregory, *op. cit.*

19 Chester Barnard, *The Functions of the Executive* 30th edn (Cambridge, Mass., Harvard University Press, 1968), p.279.

20 For the sociology of official statistics, see, for example, W. Alonso and P. Starr (eds), *The Politics of Numbers* (New York, Russell Sage Foundation, 1987); R. Bogdan and M. Ksander, 'Policy Data as a Social Process: A Qualitative Approach to Quantitative Data', *Human Organization* 39 (1980), pp.302–9; and J. Kitsuse and A. Cicourel, 'A Note on the Uses of Official Statistics', *Social Problems* 12 (1963), pp.131–247. On governmental learning, see D. Schon, *The Reflective Practitioner* (New York, Basic Books, 1983).

21 Wilson, *op. cit.*, p.162.

22 F. Goodyear-Smith, *First Do No Harm: The Sexual Abuse Industry* (Auckland, Benton-Guy, 1993).

23 New Zealand Police, *Strategic Plan 1993–1998: Reference Version* (Wellington, 1992), p.2. See, for example, a public exchange between the police and Victoria University criminologist Prof. Warren Young (*Dominion*, October 29, 1993). Young is reported as saying that under the current system of tallying crime statistics false complaints were counted as cleared crimes. This distorted the picture of the level of offending and clearance rates. The *Dominion* reported that the police rejected the claims.

24 Crime Prevention Unit, Department of the Prime Minister and Cabinet, *The Crime Prevention Unit — A Fact Sheet* (Wellington, circa 1994).

25 The term 'situational imperatives' is Wilson's (*op. cit.*, pp.52–53, 75, 169). For an examination of performance indicators in New Zealand prisons, see Robert Brown, 'Managerialism and Attainable Objectives in the New Zealand Prison System', unpublished MPP thesis, Victoria University of Wellington, 1994.

26 See *Dominion*, March 22, 1994 and August 24, 1994; and *Evening Post*, August 23, 1994.

27 See, for example, reports in *Dominion*, March 29, 1994; and *Evening Post*, July 4, 1994.

28 *Dominion*, August 12, 1994.

29 Edward C. Banfield, 'Corruption as a Feature of Governmental Organisation',

Journal of Law and Economics, 18 (1975), pp.587–88.

30 See E. Katz and B. Danet, *Bureaucracy and the Public: Reader in Official–Client Relations* (New York, Basic Books, 1973); and Lipsky, *op cit.*

31 See *Dominion*, September 8, 1993; and *Evening Post*, September 10, 1993.

32 Bradshaw, *op. cit.*

33 Barnard, *op. cit.*, p.277.

34 Banfield, *op. cit.*, p.601.

35 *Ibid.*, p.593.

36 Reported in *Transparency International Newsletter*, March 1994, pp.5–6.

37 The term 'goodwill trust' is M. Sako's. For a discussion of Sako's ideas in relation to contracting out in the New Zealand public sector, see Jonathan Boston, 'Purchasing Policy Advice: The Limits to Contracting Out', *Governance* 7 (1994), pp.1–30. Max Weber described the modern bureaucratic organization as 'formally the most rational known means of carrying out imperative control over human beings' — Max Weber, *The Theory of Social and Economic Organisation*, ed. T. Parsons (New York, Free Press, 1964), p.337. Essentially, bureaucracy is predicated on the assumption that people — functionaries — cannot be trusted and 'ideally' must be rendered mindless automatons if the organization's productive capacity is to be maximized.

38 Banfield, *op. cit.*, pp.590–91 (emphasis added).

39 *Dominion*, April 27, 1994.

40 For example, John Martin cites three major cases in 'Ethics in Public Service'. See also observations by the Chief Ombudsman, (now Sir) John Robertson, 'Ethics in the Public Sector: The Role of Parliament and Officers of Parliament (A New Zealand Viewpoint)', paper presented to the National Conference of the Royal Australian Institute of Public Administration, Brisbane, 1990; and Catriona MacLennan, 'Where Does the Buck Stop for New Zealand Departmental Blunders?' *Dominion*, April 29, 1994.

41 *Evening Post*, August 11, 1994.

42 R. J. Gregory, 'The Attitudes of Senior Public Servants in Australia and New Zealand: Administrative Reform and Technocratic Consequence?', *Governance* 4 (1991), pp.295–331; Robin Gauld, 'Technocratic Theory: A Study of New Zealand Health Policy-Making, 1990–1993', unpublished MA thesis, Victoria University of Wellington, 1993.

43 John Ralston Saul, *Voltaire's Bastards: The Dictatorship of Reason in the West* (New York, Free Press, 1992), pp.106–7. On technocracy theory generally, see: J. Ellul, *The Technological Society* (London, Jonathan Cape, 1965); F. Fischer, *Technocracy and the Politics of Expertise* (London, Sage Publications, 1990); J. Meynaud, *Technocracy* (London, Faber, 1964); and L. Winner, *Autonomous Technology: Technics-Out-of-Control as a Theme in Political Thought* (Cambridge, Mass., MIT Press, 1977).

44 *Dominion*, September 10 and 23, 1993. About a year later this chief executive's

contract became the first to be terminated, before its due expiry, since the introduction of the State Sector Act in 1988. This action followed a succeeding minister's disapproval of the chief executive's decision to appoint to a civil defence job a former senior air force officer who had earlier been sacked following overspending on his official residence (see footnote 51). According to State Services Commissioner, Don Hunn, the relationship between the minister and the chief executive had been 'uneasy and therefore not fully effective' for some time. See *Dominion*, October 15, 1994.

45 *Report on the Public Accounts for the Year Ended 31 March 1989* (Wellington, Government Printer, 1989), p.27.

46 *Dominion*, October 12, 1994; *Dominion*, November 18, 1994.

47 *Dominion*, May 6, 1994.

48 *Dominion*, September 10, 1993.

49 *Dominion*, April 5, 1994.

50 *Dominion*, April 6, 1994.

51 *Dominion*, February 1, 1994; and *Dominion*, September 29, 1994.

52 *Dominion*, September 7, 1993.

53 *Dominion*, September 22, 1994.

54 See Penny Teutenberg, 'The Fraud Epidemic', *NZ Business*, September (1994), pp.14–21. She attributes to Deputy Police Commissioner, Peter Doone, the belief that 'the heady days of the early 1980s economic boom saw a deterioration in professionally accepted standards of commercial behaviour by those at the helm of some major companies and, by implication, their financial and legal advisers.'

55 Around the turn of the century, American engineer Frederick Winslow Taylor developed 'scientific management', an ideology designed to maximize worker productivity through the manipulation of economic incentives and the precise measurement and ordering of work. See F. W. Taylor, *Scientific Management* (New York, Harper, 1947).

56 James Q. Wilson, *The Moral Sense* (New York, Free Press, 1993), p.117. Wilson cites the work of G. Marwell and R. E. Ames, 'Economists Free Ride, Does Anyone Else?', *Journal of Public Economics* 15 (1981), pp.295–310, who sought to discover how common it is for people to invest money in some group enterprise when they could get a higher return by investing in an individual one.

57 See, for example, Saul, *op. cit.*, chapter 16; and John Kenneth Galbraith, *The Culture of Contentment* (Boston, Houghton Mifflin, 1992). A report in the *Evening Post*, August 15, 1994, headed 'Fat Salaries Reignite UK Privatisation Debate', notes that: 'Apparently, there is an enormous gravy train just waiting to be boarded if you are an executive with a public utility company. Public anger was simmering after revelations last month that chiefs in the water supply industry . . . had received enormous salaries since privatisation. In many cases, those receiving the huge pay packets were working for the same companies for much less before they were privatised.' There has been public controversy in New

Zealand on similar matters. The Audit Office has been investigating $95.6 million of public money paid to consultants used by the Treasury in selling state assets between 1989 and 1991. The practice of paying performance bonuses to state servants has also come in for critical comment, notably in its application to the Treasury (see *Evening Post*, editorial, July 28, 1994), and the Accident Compensation and Rehabilitation Insurance Corporation. In regard to the latter, the *Dominion*, September 23, 1993, editorialized that, 'Once senior public servants did their job for a fair salary: now they expect huge top-ups for doing no more than what they were employed to do.'

58 See note 55.

CHAPTER FOUR

Inherently Governmental Functions and the Limits to Contracting Out

Jonathan Boston

It is one thing to hire outside concerns to supply goods and services. It is quite another to hire outside concerns to judge what the government ought to buy, how much it ought to pay, and how good the goods and services actually are. The more the government has contracted out its core functions, the more the government worsens its problem of building capacity.

Donald Kettl[1]

Introduction

Contracting out is very much in vogue, both within the OECD and beyond. Increasingly, as Donald Kettl puts it, governments are 'relying on *private* partners to do *public* work'.[2] Traditional, career-oriented public bureaucracies are being gradually transformed into so-called 'transactional bureaucracies'. That is to say, government departments are shedding many of their delivery functions to private contractors, non-profit organizations and quasi-governmental bodies. As a consequence, a growing number of public servants are spending their time managing contracts rather than delivering services. Correspondingly, control by administrative hierarchy is being replaced with control by contract. Such is the extent of contracting out and so widespread is the use of formal contractual mechanisms *within* the public sector that there is increasing talk, most notably in the United States, of the 'contracting state', the 'hollow state', the 'shadow state' and even the 'virtual state'.[3] While it is exaggerated to suggest that the state — and more particularly the permanent bureaucracy — has become little more than a hollow shell, the range of services contracted out cannot be extended indefinitely without at some point undermining the state's core capability.

In New Zealand, as described in chapter 2, the new model of public management has placed a heavy emphasis on the separation of funders/ purchasers and providers, and the separation of policy advice from policy implementation. It has also led to an extensive use of 'contracts' of various kinds to govern relationships, not merely between public- and private- sector organizations but also between (and within) public-sector organizations. In accordance with this 'new contractualism', some government departments now employ a significant proportion of their 'permanent' staff on fixed-term contracts and regularly draw on the services of consultants to undertake short-term assignments. This means that there are proportionately fewer people providing contracts *of* service and a correspondingly greater number providing contracts *for* service. What is more, consultants are being used increasingly to formulate policy advice, to serve on inter- departmental advisory bodies, and to evaluate the implementation of government programmes. Nor is it unknown for employees of private organizations to serve as senior departmental managers, albeit on a short- term basis. Meanwhile, some ministers are employing consultants to advise them on their strategies for purchasing (departmental) outputs.

Among the issues posed by such trends is whether the role of the state can and should be reduced to that of a mere contractor for services or whether there are certain public functions which only government employees should carry out. Does the integrity, legitimacy and even perhaps the sovereignty of the state necessitate that certain distinctively *public* functions should never be contracted out to private providers? Further, are there functions where the state should retain an in-house capacity to provide a good or service, even if it is not the sole provider? And are there cases where 'inherently governmental functions' (somehow defined) have already been contracted out? These are important issues and they deserve close scrutiny. After all, the hollowing-out of the state, the government's increasing dependence on the private sector, and the growing interpenetration of public and private organizations raise serious questions about the location of public power within society, the legitimacy of governmental action, the accountability of the executive, the scope for judicial review, and the design, implementation, evaluation and democratic control of public policy.

To date, such matters have generated relatively little public debate in New Zealand. They have, however, been the subject of growing attention in a number of other countries, especially the United States. In the early 1990s, the General Accounting Office (GAO) prepared a report examining whether government contractors at the federal level were undertaking functions which might be regarded as 'inherently governmental' in nature.[4] While recognizing the difficulty of defining such functions, the GAO nonetheless concluded that portions of 28 out of the 108 departmental service contracts examined appeared to involve functions of an inherently governmental nature.[5] Examples included arrangements which gave contractors a significant influence over the development of departmental policy, or entailed contractors preparing testimony and questions for departmental witnesses to use before regulatory bodies. The GAO expressed grave reservations about such contracts, and urged federal agencies to develop more precise guidelines on the kinds of governmental functions which should not be contracted out. In addition, it suggested the need for a short generic list of governmental functions which should never, as a matter of policy and irrespective of circumstances, be contracted out.

So far no similar analysis has been done in New Zealand. Nor, to my knowledge, are there any comprehensive guidelines — whether at the level of individual departments or covering the whole public sector — which specify the kinds of functions which should be undertaken primarily or solely in-house. To encourage debate on whether such guidelines are needed, and, if so, of what they might consist, this chapter begins by exploring the proposition that there are certain public tasks or activities which can be regarded as the 'defining functions' of the state or as 'inherently governmental functions'. In so doing, extensive reference is made to the GAO report mentioned above. Having considered some of the broader issues, the chapter then assesses several arguments that have been advanced in New Zealand in recent years for increasing the extent to which the policy outputs of government departments are subject to contestable bidding. My argument, in short, is that there are considerable risks for the state associated with the extensive contracting-out of policy advice. It is thus in the public interest for governments to have at their disposal in-house, non-partisan policy advisers capable of providing expert advice across the broad range of policy issues that typically confront elected officials.[6]

Some Preliminary Matters of Clarification

Since the late 1980s, the language of contract in New Zealand has been applied to a growing number of relationships within the public sector, including those of an interpersonal, intra-organizational and inter-organizational nature. Thus, ministers now have signed contracts (or, strictly speaking, performance agreements) with their departmental chief executives, and purchase agreements with their departments. In health care, for instance, there is a cascading series of contracts between funders, purchasers and providers (e.g. between the Minister of Health and the chief executive of the Ministry of Health, between the minister and the four Regional Health Authorities, between the ministry and the Public Health Commission (soon to be abolished), between Regional Health Authorities and Crown Health Enterprises and other health-care providers, and between Crown Health Enterprises and private suppliers). The nature, significance and legal status of such 'contracts' is beyond the scope of this chapter. Note, however, that many of the 'agreements' now commonly referred to as 'contracts' are not legally binding; they are more in the nature of mutual undertakings, and one of the instruments through which hierarchical control is exercised within the state apparatus.

The application of the language of contract to relationships within the public sector might suggest that it is no longer valid to draw a sharp distinction between 'in-house' (i.e. public) providers and external (i.e. private) providers. After all, it might be contended that ministers are always, in a sense, involved in a contractual relationship with service providers, whether they choose to purchase their desired outputs from a government department, a Crown entity, a private firm or a non-profit organization. From this standpoint, 'contracting out' is an inherent and unavoidable feature of governance; the only difference is that, whereas ministers have an ownership interest in public organizations, they have no such interest in private organizations.

In my view, such an approach is not very satisfactory. The differences between public and private provision are not limited solely to issues of ownership, though of course these are important. My examination of the provision of policy advice later in the chapter will, I trust, highlight the existence of other important differences. Likewise, although the language of contract has been extended to the relationships between ministers and public organizations, it is still meaningful to distinguish between in-house

	Public funding	**Private funding**
Public provision	Non-commercial & non-contracted, 'core' public functions	Commercial functions undertaken by public organizations
Private provision	State-funded goods & services provided by private organizations	Commercial functions undertaken by private organizations

Figure 4:1 *Options for Funding and Provision*

(or departmental) provision and contracting out. Hence, for the purposes of this chapter, the term 'contracting out' will be used to refer to situations where publicly funded services are purchased from private organizations (whether the purchaser is a government agency or a minister). As depicted in Figure 4.1, the relevant category is the lower-left quadrant. By contrast, 'in-house' provision will be taken to refer to the supply of publicly funded services by public organizations, in particular government departments.

Let me emphasize that I have absolutely no quarrel with the idea of public agencies or ministers purchasing various goods and services from private providers. Contracting out is undoubtedly a vital and cost-effective strategy in a great many cases. Governments simply could not operate effectively or efficiently if they were unable to purchase goods and services from external suppliers. Consequently, I have no intention of reviewing here the long-standing debate over the relative merits of contracting out (about which there is an extensive academic literature[7]). Instead, my concern is with the criteria which should guide policy-makers in evaluating whether the provision of certain goods and services should be contracted out. Particularly useful here are the insights which can be drawn from the literature on the economics of organizations, especially agency theory and transaction cost analysis.[8] These theories are described in chapter 1.

Governments have always relied on the private sector, to some degree, for the provision of various goods and services, and have frequently delegated their powers and functions to intermediary organizations — some public, some private, and some located in the murky borderlands between.[9] There is nothing novel, therefore, about contracting out. What is new about the current situation is, first, the extent to which goods and services are being contracted out and, second, the fact that a growing number of services which were previously provided solely by public organizations are being considered as legitimate candidates for external contracting. Hence, whereas contracting out was once limited to the more peripheral or secondary functions of the state and those activities which can be readily quantified and measured (such as cleaning, garbage collection, payroll services, building and construction), it is increasingly being used to supply goods and services which lie at the core of the state's responsibilities (such as policy advice, planning, regulation, law enforcement and emergency services). In New Zealand, for example, contracting out has recently been applied to debt collection, and has been significantly extended in areas like community care, education, training and health care. Further, at the time of writing there was legislation before Parliament which, if enacted, will facilitate the contracting-out of prison management. Consideration has also been given to external contracting in areas like fire-fighting, the collection of taxes, and the provision of agricultural regulatory services (e.g. the control of imports and border inspection to prevent unwanted introduction of pests and disease, the inspection of export products, and so on).[10] In short, private organizations of various kinds are increasingly performing functions traditionally undertaken by governmental organizations, and this trend seems likely to continue.

The momentum for contracting out was given an added boost by the Public Finance Act 1989 and the resultant introduction of an output-based system of appropriations. Under this system, all the goods and services provided by government departments, including policy advice, are categorized as 'outputs'.[11] These outputs, in turn, are now more clearly specified and more accurately priced, and their quality more rigorously assessed. As a result, many previously vague departmental activities have been 'commodified'. This means, among other things, that it is now much easier for policy-makers to consider whether particular departmental outputs are really necessary and, if they are, whether they might be produced more cheaply and effectively by private organizations.

Inherently Governmental Functions

The issue as to what are the proper or legitimate functions of the state raises important philosophical questions over which there is never likely to be complete agreement. On the one hand, libertarians maintain that the functions of the state should be limited to the protection of life and property. This includes the provision of defence forces and a police force, together with the collection of taxes necessary to fund such services, but little else. On the other hand, those who reject libertarianism — including conservatives, liberals, social democrats and socialists — maintain that the state has responsibilities which extend well beyond matters of external and internal security and the protection of property rights. Equally vital are the administration of justice, environmental protection, the regulation of commerce, and the provision of income support and various social services. In a parliamentary democracy like New Zealand, the responsibility for determining the proper limits to the role of the state lies with the elected government. Thus, the task of deciding what is and what is not a governmental function is the prerogative of politicians; public servants and others may offer advice but should not make the final decisions.

Once it has been determined that the government should undertake a particular task (e.g. to defend the country's borders or ensure that its citizens have access to good health-care services), the issue arises as to whether the task should be undertaken in-house (by government employees) or by private contractors. For example, is it acceptable for the employees of private organizations to obtain security clearances, or even perhaps to be awarded a contract which gives them the power to determine the eligibility of departmental staff for such clearances? Is it appropriate for consultants to represent government departments in public forums and give evidence on their behalf at hearings before parliamentary select committees? Is it in the public interest to contract out prison management or the core policy functions of government departments, or for private contractors to undertake regulatory or enforcement functions, such as the inspection of workplaces, the control of people entering the country, the direction of traffic flows in cities, or the investigation of complaints by citizens against those undertaking public functions? Is it appropriate for consultants who are the employees of private organizations to perform management functions within a government department, such as the recruitment or supervision of staff? Finally, while it may be acceptable for private contractors to collect fines or debts owed to public agencies, is it appropriate for them to exercise discretion, such as resolving disputes, terminating collection actions or initiating legal action?

Bear in mind that even the most basic or core functions of the state can, at least in principle, be contracted out. Mercenaries can be recruited to fight a nation's wars. Taxes can be collected by private organizations. Contractors can be employed to provide customs, immigration and diplomatic services. Whether the contracting-out of such services is in the public interest, however, is quite another matter.

As noted, the issues surrounding the proper limits to external contracting were examined in a report by the GAO in the early 1990s. The report observes that, while the issue of what constitutes 'inherently governmental functions' has been debated in the US since at least the Declaration of Independence, it has never been fully resolved. Surprisingly, perhaps, there are few constitutional or statutory limitations on the kinds of activities which may be contracted out by government agencies.[12] Nor have policy analysts, political theorists or constitutional experts devoted much attention to such matters. To provide guidance to federal employees, a number of agencies, most notably the Office of Management and Budget (OMB), have issued circulars from time to time addressing the matter of governmental functions, but none of these documents, in the view of the GAO, has 'clearly defined inherently governmental functions'.[13] The general principle applied by the OMB is that consultants 'shall not be used in . . . performing work of a policy, decisionmaking, or management nature, which is the direct responsibility of agency officials'.[14] Further, the OMB defines a governmental function, at least in the administration of commercial activities, as

> a function which is so intimately related to the public interest as to mandate administration by government employees. These functions include those activities which require either the exercise of discretion in applying government authority or the use of value judgment in making decisions for the government.[15]

The OMB has classified governmental functions into two categories: those involving the act of governing, and those pertaining to monetary transactions and entitlements. The various functions in each category are listed in Table 4.1. In all likelihood, few people would dispute that most, if not all, of the functions listed here are rightly the responsibility of a government to perform. However, most of the functions are defined in relatively broad terms.

---

1. Functions Relating to the Act of Governing

1. Criminal investigations, prosecutions and other judicial functions.
2. Management of government programmes requiring value judgements, as in the direction of national defence.
3. Management and direction of the armed services.
4. Activities performed exclusively by military personnel who are subject to deployment in a combat, combat support or combat service role.
5. Conduct of foreign relations.
6. Selection of programme priorities.
7. Direction of federal employees.
8. Regulation of the use of space, oceans, navigable rivers and other natural resources.
9. Direction of intelligence and counter-intelligence operations.
10. Regulation of industry and commerce, including food and drugs.

2. Functions Related to Monetary Transactions and Entitlements

1. Tax collection and revenue disbursements.
2. Control of the Treasury accounts and money supply.
3. Administration of public trusts.

Source: General Accounting Office, Government Contractors, *p. 20*

Table 4.1: *Categorization of Governmental Functions*

To illustrate, most people would agree that the 'conduct of foreign affairs' is an inherently governmental function; only nation states, after all, can have foreign policies. But the conduct of foreign affairs embraces a large number of separate activities, such as securing policy advice, determining foreign policy, negotiating with foreign governments, reporting on and interpreting the significance of international events, contributing to the operations of international organizations, and so forth. Some of these activities are without doubt 'inherently governmental' and should be undertaken only by the elected government (e.g. determining foreign policy). Some activities which are currently undertaken partly by ministers and partly by government officials, such as negotiating with foreign governments, may be possible to contract out, at least to a degree. However, the desirability of doing so is open to serious question (e.g. foreign governments may be unwilling to negotiate with private-sector consultants). Then again there may be functions which could readily be contracted out but where it may also be desirable to retain an in-house capacity (e.g. reporting on international events). Finally, there may be functions which might best be contracted out and where there is no need to retain an in-house capacity. Precisely where the line should be drawn between these various categories is likely to be disputed. Much will depend on the criteria deemed relevant for guiding the use of contractors. I will return to this matter shortly.

In evaluating the OMB's guidelines, the GAO acknowledges repeatedly that the concept of 'inherently governmental functions' is difficult to define, and that the matter is complex and contentious.[16] The question is essentially of an ideological or judgemental nature; it is not amenable to a technical solution. The GAO also notes that other federal agencies have sought to develop criteria for determining whether a particular function should be contracted out. For instance, in keeping with OMB instructions, the Department of Energy (DOE) has taken the view that government management functions ought not to be contracted out, and has defined such functions as those which are 'so intimately connected with government operations that they must be administered by government employees in order for the government to retain essential control and responsibility'.[17] According to this definition, examples of government management functions would include:

- determining the success or failure of DOE internal management and program management activites;
- determining environmental impacts of energy policies and projects; and
- establishing administration goals, priorities and schedules.[18]

The Environmental Protection Agency (EPA) issued a directive in October 1990 on the agency's policies with respect to contracting. This stated that certain activities should not be administered by contractors, including preparing congressional testimony, responding to congressional correspondence, determining the EPA's policy, conducting administrative hearings, and representing the EPA to outside parties.[19] Previously, in April 1990, the EPA's Administrator had drawn attention to other agency activities where contracting out might pose unacceptable risks. These activities included:

- support services, such as analyses and feasibility studies, in developing EPA policy;
- specialized expertise in developing statements of work, work assignments,

and other contract-ordered tasks; and

- any situation in which a contractor has access to confidential business information and/or any sensitive information.[20]

The GAO points out that, despite such guidelines and directives, it has not been uncommon for agencies to employ contractors to undertake functions that could be classified as inherently governmental in nature. Among the reasons for doing so were staff shortages, the lack of staff with the relevant technical or professional expertise, and the fact that in some cases it was easier to secure funding for contract work than to employ new staff.[21] It is likely that similar reasons have contributed to the growing use of consultants by government departments in New Zealand.

In formulating principles to determine whether certain governmental functions should be carried out only by public officials, the GAO — correctly, in my view — invokes the criterion of 'the public interest'.[22] Accordingly, the question which should be posed in any particular situation is whether contracting out by a government agency might in some way infringe, undermine or jeopardize the public interest. This, of course, begs the question as to what 'the public interest' means. Unless this concept can be given a reasonably precise meaning, it will be of little use to policy-makers. The problem, however, is that there is no agreement on the meaning of 'the public interest'.[23] Nor, for that matter, is there agreement on the meaning of related aggregative concepts like 'the public good', 'the common good', 'the general interest', 'the national interest' and 'the general welfare'. They are all essentially contested concepts. In my view, this lack of consensus does not mean that we should abandon such concepts. Rather, as Brian Barry argues, we need to develop criteria which can be used to give 'the public interest' meaning in particular contexts (e.g. what is in the interest of the taxpaying public, or the voting public, or the travelling public).[24] Depending on the context, such criteria could include public health and safety, maintaining the legitimacy of the democratic order, preserving the integrity of the tax system, the efficient and effective use of resources, and so forth. Doubtless, such criteria will provoke dissent and will be open to conflicting interpretations, but this is unavoidable.

The methodology employed by the GAO is broadly in line with the approach I have just sketched. Hence, in applying the concept of the public interest to the issue of whether certain functions, in particular consulting services, should be contracted out, the GAO proposes various guidelines.

These are set out in Annex 1. Underpinning these guidelines, two main tests or criteria can be identified. If a proposal for contracting out fails one or other of these tests, the public interest might be compromised.

First, the GAO argues that governments must always *retain control* over the policy process (including both policy formulation and implementation) and the management of public agencies.

> A key criterion in determining whether service contracts are appropriate is whether the government maintains sufficient in-house capability to be thoroughly in control of the policy and management functions of the agency.[25] ... This includes the capacity to adequately direct, supervise, and monitor contracts.[26]

In the GAO's view, retaining control of the decision-making process requires more than a government 'simply being a final authority or signatory to a document. Government officials should be active throughout the decisionmaking process'.[27] Likewise, public officials need to guard against the possibility of losing control as a result of their agency becoming unduly dependent on a single external supplier of a particular good or service. Further, the GAO argues that 'agencies should keep in mind that regardless of whether the government carries out activities with its own employees or by contract, it must have the core capability — a sufficient number of trained and experienced staff — to properly manage and be accountable for its work'.[28] Agencies must also ensure that they retain the 'ability to develop and consider options other than those provided by the contractor'.[29] In this regard, 'the government must be a "smart buyer" when purchasing assistance service and be able to make independent judgements about policy recommendations'.[30] In other words, a department must not become so dependent on the expertise and information held by a contractor that it is unable to challenge, or offer informed comment on, the merits of the contractor's policy advice. Moreover, it must always know precisely what it is buying, from whom, and whether it is getting exactly what it intended to purchase.

In case it is not self-evident why governments need to retain control over the system of policy advice and the management of public agencies, the answer is simple: if the government loses control, then that control will pass to private contractors. Such people are not democratically elected or politically accountable and may use their power to pursue goals that are contrary to the will of the people. In particular, they may pursue their own interests, and in many, if not most, cases these will conflict with the public interest. When a government loses control over the process of policy-making and implementation, therefore, it exposes itself and its citizens to serious risks. These include the possibility of nepotism, favouritism and other forms of corruption, the likelihood that private organizations will exploit their power at the expense of the public purse, a loss of public trust in the political system, and ultimately the loss of sovereignty.

The second criterion advanced by the GAO is that only government officials should have the authority in the decision-making process to *exercise discretion or make value judgements*.[31] Unfortunately, the GAO does not elaborate on this matter. It is not clear, therefore, whether the GAO is suggesting that contractors should be precluded from exercising *any* form of discretion, or only certain forms of discretion. Likewise, it is unclear whether the bar on consultants making value judgements should apply universally or only in certain contexts. Plainly, the whole rationale for contracting out would be undermined if contractors were prevented from exercising *any* form of discretion. Similarly, many matters concerning the formulation and implementation of policy involve value judgements, and it is hard to see how contractors could operate efficiently and effectively unless they were, at times, able to make such judgements. This is not to suggest, of course, that contractors should have the authority to determine a government's policies or priorities, but then neither should non-elected public officials have such authority.

While the GAO's proposed guidelines and criteria can certainly be refined, in my view they offer a useful starting-point for thinking about the limits which should apply to contracting out publicly funded goods and services. Moreover, in the absence of such guidelines in New Zealand, they provide a helpful policy framework for departments to embrace. They are also relevant to the current debate over proposals to change the system by which ministers secure advice and purchase policy outputs. Let me explore this matter further.

The Limits to the Contracting-out of Policy Advice

Current Arrangements for the Provision of Policy Advice

In New Zealand, as in most OECD countries, in-house departmental advisers supply the bulk of the policy advice sought by governments.[32]

In 1992–93, the government purchased around $386 million of policy advice from 32 departments.[33] If the cost of diplomatic services, including advice, supplied by the Ministry of Foreign Affairs and Trade is excluded, the figure is reduced to around $245 million, or about 1,220 person/equivalents.[34] Of this total, departments spent about $48.5 million on advice contracted out to third parties.[35] Hence, expenditure on consultants was roughly a fifth of government spending on policy advice. To put these figures in context, expenditure on policy advice is about 1 per cent of total public expenditure and less than 0.4 per cent of GDP. Of course, governments secure advice from a wide range of non-departmental sources: royal commissions, commissions of inquiry, advisory committees, independent statutory bodies, academics, interest groups, political parties and members of the public. In many cases, the advice is provided free of charge.

For the purpose of appropriating public funds under the Public Finance Act 1989, the policy advice provided by government departments in New Zealand is categorized into various output classes.[36] Departments with relatively limited advisory responsibilities may supply only one policy output class (which is simply referred to in the Estimates as 'policy advice' or 'policy advice and ministerial servicing'). Departments with substantial advisory responsibilities, like the Treasury, may have up to three policy output classes. In 1991–92 there was a total of 67 policy output classes across the public sector. Within each output class, there are usually many specific policy outputs. These are specified in departmental corporate plans.

While there has been a substantial increase in expenditure on consultants during the past decade, the precise magnitude of this increase is uncertain, owing to a lack of longitudinal data. It is clear, however, that the use of consultants has been more extensive in some areas of public policy than others. For instance, National's health-care reforms have generated a strong demand for consultants. In the period from late 1990 to mid-1993, the Ministry of Health engaged 377 consultants at a cost of $11.3 million.[37] Other departments also made extensive use of consultants to provide advice on health policy during the same period, including the Treasury, the Department of Prime Minister and Cabinet, and the Ministry of Maori Development. Another feature of the current environment is the growing number of middle-level, and even senior, public servants resigning from their departments to become private-sector consultants. In some cases, such individuals have ended up as consultants to the departments where they were most recently employed.

Other features of the current arrangements for the supply of policy advice in New Zealand are worth highlighting. First, there has been a tendency since the mid-1980s for policy advice functions to be decoupled, in organizational terms, from the delivery of services. Second, the Treasury is without doubt the largest and most influential supplier of policy advice. It employs almost 200 policy analysts and managers, and absorbs around 15 per cent of the government's total expenditure on policy advice.[38] Third, as in other countries, government departments supply policy advice to a single client (e.g. a Cabinet minister or a number of portfolio ministers). They are prohibited from selling their advisory services to non-governmental clients. The government is the sole purchaser of departmental policy outputs. It is also the owner of the public organizations supplying advice.

Fourth, there is nothing to prevent governments from purchasing advice from non-departmental sources. Indeed, it has become relatively common for ministers to seek advice from private sources and committees of inquiry, and many employ outside policy advisers in their ministerial offices. In a number of cases (e.g. health policy and science policy) outside experts referred to as 'purchase advisers' have been recruited to advise ministers on their strategy for purchasing outputs, including policy outputs. Such advisers also assist ministers in monitoring and assessing the performance of providers. It is important to emphasize that, under current arrangements, individual ministers can determine the quantity of advice (at least in dollar terms) they wish to purchase from their departments. They are also at liberty, subject to the approval of their Cabinet colleagues, to reduce the quantity of policy outputs purchased from their departments and to secure advice from other sources. In other words, there are no constitutional or statutory requirements for the government to purchase advice from departments or to maintain a critical mass of policy expertise on a particular issue within the public sector.

Fifth, just as departments are unable to sell their advisory services to the highest bidder, so too they are limited in the range of matters on which they can tender advice. That is to say, the provision of policy advice is disaggregated, with each department having responsibility for a specific set of policy issues. Of course, it is impossible in practice to draw the policy boundaries between departments with precision, and typically there is a substantial overlap. Sometimes the overlap is deliberate. This, together with the fact that departments generally develop a distinctive policy line, facilitates inter-departmental rivalry and conflict. Consequently, despite the absence of formal, competitive bidding for contracts to supply policy advice, there is no lack of struggle between departments for influence over government policy. Multiple advocacy and the competition of ideas is very much alive.

Notwithstanding the relative flexibility and contestability of the current arrangements for purchasing policy advice, critics maintain that the system is flawed. One of the problems, it is argued, is the lack of reliable information on what particular pieces of policy advice ought to cost. As a result, it is not clear whether the government is getting value for money. As the State Services Commission puts it, there is no market for policy advice

> in which prices are continuously being set, no comparisons being made with the price (or cost) of outputs from competing departments, nor any other benchmark by which to measure their relative value.[39]

The absence of a competitive market for policy advice, it is claimed, limits the incentives for productive efficiency and enhances the opportunities for rent-seeking and slackness. Admittedly, the policy bench-marking exercise undertaken by the Treasury in 1993 has enabled the government to identify which departments are the most costly. Of the 32 departments surveyed, the cost of producing policy advice per person ranged from an average of $466 per day in the cheapest department to over $3,500 per day in the most expensive department; the average across all departments was around $950 per day.[40] But of course there may well be legitimate reasons why policy advice in certain areas is more expensive to produce than in others. Some departments are required to consult more extensively than others, and some need to employ a proportionately larger number of specialists or senior analysts.

Another claimed weakness with the current purchase arrangements is that departments often have a virtual monopoly on the technical expertise in their particular field of policy. This both limits the capacity of ministers to secure expert advice from other sources and gives the departments an unhealthy influence on the policy-making process.

Proposals for Increasing the Extent to Which Policy Advice Is Contracted Out

Concerns of this kind have prompted various suggestions in recent years for reforming the system by which ministers secure advice. It is regularly argued, for instance, that more of the policy work of government departments should be contracted out to the private sector. Several radical proposals for making the purchase of policy advice more contestable were canvassed (but not supported) by the State Services Commission (SSC) in 1991–92.[41] The first of these involved the creation of an internal market within the public service for the provision of policy advice. Under this approach, government departments and agencies would compete for contracts to supply particular policy outputs. A second option was to create an external market whereby both public and private organizations would compete on equal terms for contracts to supply policy outputs. Under this scenario, there could be no guarantee that a government would retain an in-house advisory capacity in particular policy areas.

How such arrangements would operate in practice was not spelt out by the SSC. Presumably, however, the government would need to establish an independent agency to advise ministers on their contracting strategy and to handle the bidding process. Such an agency would be responsible for maintaining the integrity of the bidding process, ensuring that bids were properly co-ordinated, monitoring the performance of successful bidders, and enforcing government contracts. Needless to say, if ministers were to choose the organizations from which the government purchased its advice, there is a significant risk that advisers would be chosen more on their ideological acceptability than on their policy competence. To make matters worse, advisers would have incentives to fashion their advice to suit the policy preferences of the government in power.

Proposals of a similarly radical nature were advanced more recently by Dr Andrew West, a senior adviser in the Crown Company Monitoring Advisory Unit.[42] At a policy seminar in February 1994, West questioned the need for governments to rely so heavily on the public service for their policy advice. In fact, he asked whether there is a need for governments to have *any* public service advisers. Rather than continuing with the existing advisory structures, a better approach, he argued, would be for governments to purchase their advice from private suppliers. Trans-action costs under this model would be reduced because 'compliance with the Public Finance Act . . . would be removed and the relationship between purchaser and provider reformatted around *bona fide* contractual law'.[43] Moreover, he maintains that 'provisions for compliance with ethical codes of conduct and the Official Information Act' could be covered within the relevant contracts.[44]

West envisages that a deregulated market for the provision of policy advice would operate as follows:

> . . . each Minister might employ a highly capable resource of personal advisors within their Office to develop purchase contracts and tender them out on a contestable basis. The Minister would seek to contract the best skills available so as to purchase the most effective and efficient outputs. To lower transaction costs and secure continuity of supply these contracts would probably be let for the term of the Government. Each would have clear performance measures for quality of output. The Minister's Office would monitor the performance of the contracted agents. The advisors in Ministerial Offices would most probably prepare the final policy papers for their Ministers, based on information purchased by contract . . . Initially departments would compete with any other provider in the market for public policy advice. Private sector providers would seek to employ public servants with key advisory skills (already occurring). Some individuals would resign to establish their own consultancies (already occurring). Ultimately, the Government would review its need to own departments.[45]

West accepts that it may be neither feasible nor desirable to contract out all the functions of the control agencies, especially the Treasury. For example, he acknowledges that it may be difficult to preserve the integrity of the Budget process if the outputs of the Treasury were all undertaken by private-sector providers.[46] Likewise, he recognizes that extensive external contracting of policy outputs presupposes that governments would develop co-ordinated annual strategic plans and would co-ordinate their purchasing strategies across portfolios.[47] Governments would also need to fashion protocols to guarantee public access to information gathered by private-sector advisers. However, in his view none of these problems is likely to prove 'insurmountable'.[48] Nor is he particularly concerned about the possibility that his proposals would politicize the provision of advice or reduce the extent to which governments receive impartial advice. As he puts it, 'the notion of impartiality being the exclusive domain of Government employees seems quaint'.[49]

Without question, West's proposals would entail a major departure from the existing arrangements for the provision of policy advice. To my knowledge, no system of this nature has ever been attempted anywhere in the world, let alone successfully implemented. Nevertheless, given the increasing reliance by departments on outside consultants, the growing use by ministers of purchase advisers, and the continuing criticisms of the current arrangements for producing policy advice, West's proposals deserve careful scrutiny.

The Case for Maintaining In-House Policy-Related Expertise

A useful starting-point for assessing the various approaches to the prouction of policy outputs is the literature on agency theory and transaction cost analysis. A central concern of this literature is with the comparative advantages — in terms of minimizing production costs and transaction costs — of alternative structures of governance. What institutional arrangements, in other words, are best for carrying out particular functions? In brief, the literature suggests that contracting out or the use of market-type arrangements is preferable, in terms of minimizing the costs of specifying, negotiating, monitoring and enforcing contracts, in certain conditions, whereas in-house production via hierarchical or rule-governed organizations, like government departments, is better in the opposite conditions.[50] In-house provision or direct employment is said to be preferable when the following conditions apply:

(i) there is a high degree of general and/or behavioural uncertainty, and in particular a high risk of adverse selection of agents by the principal;

(ii) there is only limited contestability (or small numbers bargaining) owing to the existence of specific assets (e.g. durable transaction-specific sunk investments);

(iii) there is a high likelihood of opportunism by at least one of the parties to the contract: opportunistic behaviour is more likely in the context of asset specificity, small numbers bargaining, substantial information asymmetries, and significant conflicts of interest; and

(iv) the relevant transactions are frequent and complex.

Hence, as John Bryson and Peter Smith-Ring put it, 'when transactions occur frequently, are associated with a great deal of uncertainty, and involve high asset specificity, hierarchical governance structures tend to be more efficient than markets, *ceteris paribus*'.[51] One of the reasons why in-house provision is likely to be preferable in such conditions is that it facilitates the use of more open-ended or incomplete contracts, thereby reducing the requirement to specify in advance all the possible, often complex, contingencies that might arise during the course of a contract.[52] This in turn reduces the transaction costs. Another advantage is that it enables the problems of behavioural uncertainty and opportunism to be managed and controlled, at least to some extent, through the use of hierarchical authority, ethical codes, institutional routines, rules and norms, and the building of long-term relationships.[53]

By contrast, market arrangements are said to be better when the opposite conditions apply (i.e. when there is low uncertainty, a low risk of adverse selection, a high degree of contestability, an absence of specific assets, a low risk of opportunism, and a low number of relatively simple transactions). In such circumstances it is likely that the contractor 'types' — in terms of trustworthiness, reliability, competency and expertise — will be known to the principal, and the number of potential suppliers will be large (both at the time of the initial contract and during subsequent tendering rounds). Further, where it is easy to measure the quality and quantity of the goods or services being purchased, monitoring of the contractor by the principal will be correspondingly straightforward.

What implications do such considerations have for the way public policy advice is purchased by governments? Broadly speaking, there are likely to be significant advantages, in terms of minimizing both production and transaction costs, in placing a heavy reliance on in-house provision.[54] This certainly does not mean that all advice should be produced in-house, but it suggests that there are likely to be benefits in having an in-house advisory capacity across the broad spectrum of policy issues. Hence, if a government were to adopt the kind of purchasing model proposed by West (or the two options canvassed by the SSC), it would run significant risks. In particular, there is a strong likelihood that the production of policy advice under such a model will be more expensive and its quality more variable and less reliable. Worse, governments could well end up with diminished control over their advisers and find themselves increasingly at the mercy of opportunistic suppliers.

From the perspective of transaction cost analysis, there are at least four problems with West's approach:

(i) The degree of contestability between suppliers in many policy domains is likely to be limited.

(ii) There are bound to be major difficulties specifying and monitoring contracts.

(iii) Political uncertainties, such as unexpected changes of ministers or governments, will increase the costs of external contracting.

(iv) There is likely to be an increased risk of opportunistic behaviour, with consequent difficulties for maintaining trust between ministers and advisers, and between competing advisory agencies.

More generally, West's proposals are bound to exacerbate existing problems of vertical co-ordination between ministers and their advisers, and horizontal co-ordination both at the Cabinet level and between the various teams of advisers. Let me elaborate briefly on each of these points.

(i) The Limits to Contestability

Various factors are likely to limit contestability for the supply of policy advice in a deregulated market. To start with, contestability will be limited in many policy domains by asset specificity in the form of specialist knowledge and task-specific labour skills. In many fields of public policy in New Zealand, there are only a few experts. At present, most of them are employed in government departments. The lack of non-departmental policy expertise, of course, reflects the relatively limited size of the policy community in a country with a small population like New Zealand. To be sure, there is a growing body of policy expertise in various private-sector firms (such as share-brokers, chartered accountants and merchant banks). But such expertise is concentrated primarily in economic policy and does not extend across the whole sweep of public policy. Moreover, few non-departmental organizations would be able to supply a full advisory service for a minister. Such a service would include: the preparation of discussion papers, option papers, strategic assessments, draft legislation and ministerial speeches; the drafting of replies to parliamentary questions; the day-to-day provision of oral advice for ministers and Cabinet committees; advice on the implementation of policy; advice on how to respond to unanticipated problems; assistance in negotiations with third parties (including foreign governments, sub-national governments and public interest groups); and help with formulating the government's strategic objectives.

Consequently, if competitive tendering for policy output classes (or even disaggregated outputs) were introduced, in many cases there are likely to be few credible bidders. Furthermore, given the need for reasonably long-term contracts (in the interests of recruiting quality teams and developing an institutional memory), successful contractors will enjoy significant advantages over potential rivals when the contract is renegotiated. This would raise the usual problems associated with small numbers bargaining, including the possibility that incumbent advisers would seek to exploit the lack of credible rival bidders.

The small pool of policy expertise is only one of the factors limiting the degree of contestability. At least four other constraints are likely to be important. First, there is the key issue of trust. As M. Sako argues, in a world characterized by uncertainty, imperfect information and bounded rationality, trust can be regarded as an intangible capital asset which 'economizes on the costs of bargaining, monitoring, insurance and dispute settlement'.[55] It does so by reducing behavioural uncertainty, increasing the prospects that promises will be honoured, and assists the parties in handling unforeseen contingencies. Given the highly political nature of much governmental policy-making, ministers naturally place a high premium on the integrity, loyalty, reliability and trustworthiness of their advisers; they want people who are not only competent but also fully trustworthy. In Sako's terms, they want people who display 'goodwill trust'.[56] This involves a willingness to go beyond the mere fulfilment of the terms of a contract and to have the interests of the other party always at heart. In all likelihood, some potential suppliers of policy advice will not be trusted by ministers, and hence will be unsuccessful in any bid to secure a contract to provide advice.

Second, if a government wishes to secure advice from a range of theoretical and ideological perspectives, it will want to avoid giving a single organization too many contracts. Likewise, because policy advisers are able to exercise significant influence on policy decisions, a government will wish to maintain multiple advocacy on important policy matters. Such factors will limit the range of organizations able to bid for certain policy output classes.

Third, contestability will be limited by the need for advisers and advisory agencies to avoid potential conflicts of interest. Because of the sensitivity of many policy issues and the need for confidentiality during the policy-making process, governments will wish to avoid situations in which their advisers are advising other clients, whether domestic or foreign, on similar issues. This means that those wishing to bid for contracts to supply policy outputs will be severely constrained, if not

Murrell Library
Missouri Valley College
Marshall, Missouri 65340

prohibited, from selling some of their services to other clients. Such constraints are likely to limit the field of suppliers, since many firms will not wish to become too heavily dependent on a single client (i.e. the government) — or at least not in the absence of long-term contractual arrangements (or an agreement by the government to award compensation in the event of their contract being altered significantly or terminated early).

Fourth, if a minister were to cease purchasing policy outputs from his or her department, there would inevitably be redundancies, with resultant fiscal costs. Such costs are likely to be an extra constraint on the willingness of ministers to make major changes in their purchasing strategies.

(ii) The Difficulties of Specifying and Monitoring Contracts

The business of purchasing policy advice by governments supplies a classic example of the problems of contract specification, monitoring and enforcement. One of the central difficulties is that many of the outputs of the policy process are very difficult to quantify. Equally, if not more, important is the problem of assessing quality. There is no agreement, for instance, on what constitutes good advice. Moreover, all the measures employed in New Zealand to assess quality — such as the timeliness of the advice, the qualifications of the advisers, and compliance with quality-assurance procedures — are only proxies; they may provide an *indication* of the quality of the advice, but little more.

A further problem is contract specification. The difficulties here are caused primarily by uncertainty and bounded rationality. Ministers never know precisely on what subjects they are likely to require advice during the next month, let alone the next year. Their policy needs are in a constant state of flux. Problems can arise suddenly and unexpectedly. Nor do ministers know how much advice they will need. As a result, the work programme of policy advisers cannot be fashioned systematically according to some pre-ordained, well-planned strategic design, but must be constantly altered in response to events, crises and the changing balance of political opinion.[57] Given this situation, any contract covering a policy output class (or even a significant policy output) will need to be relatively open-ended. This is likely to make it more difficult to monitor a supplier's performance and ensure compliance.

For such reasons, the provision of policy advice offers many opportunities for self-interested behaviour by suppliers. For example, advisers can readily cut corners in the interests of maximizing their profits or making their lives easier; they can choose to ignore certain arguments or particular information; and they can deliberately advocate policies that are in their interests (e.g. policies that can be expected to generate continuing work). Such behaviour may be difficult to detect.

(iii) The Problems of Political Uncertainty

Political uncertainties are likely to make proposals of the kind advanced by West very difficult to implement. Suppose contracts were let, as he suggests, for the duration of a government's term. An immediate problem is that the term cannot be predicted accurately, even under a stable, first-past-the-post electoral system. Under the forthcoming system of proportional representation in New Zealand, uncertainties over the term of a government will almost certainly increase.[58]

Another problem is that the turnover of ministers is usually much higher than that of governments. If contracts are negotiated by purchase advisers working to particular ministers, difficulties are bound to arise. For example, if a minister is shifted to another portfolio or resigns, this would have significant implications for the minister's staff since the new minister may wish to install his or her own purchase advisers. Such advisers are likely, in turn, to want to alter the purchase contracts to accommodate the new minister's policy interests and priorities. Indeed, the new minister may have little confidence in the existing supplier of advice and wish to terminate the contract. It requires little imagination to work out the complexities and difficulties that such situations could create, not to mention the potentially high costs of contract termination.

(iv) The Risks of Opportunism

Under all methods of purchasing policy advice there will be incentives for suppliers to protect their reputations in order to secure and then maintain their contracts. Likewise, as noted above, under all purchasing options ministers are likely to find it difficult to monitor the activities of their advisers and exercise effective control over them. Nevertheless, under West's proposals there are likely to be greater incentives and opportunities for advisers to act out of self-interest. For one thing, the literature suggests that profit-maximizing firms tend to behave more opportunistically than non-profit organizations like government departments (see chapter 1).[59] This is because any surplus generated by a firm accrues directly to the owners (and/or managers). Hence, a greater reliance on firms for the provision of advice runs added risks, which increase if contestability is limited.

The opportunities for self-interested behaviour by contractors will be enhanced if the experience or competence of those making purchasing decisions and monitoring contract performance is reduced. Under West's proposals, much will depend on the quality of the people chosen as contract managers by ministers, and their capacity to assess the advice being supplied. There is certainly a risk that some purchase advisers will be chosen more for their political skills and personal loyalty to a minister than for their competency as contract managers or policy advisers. In these circumstances, some contractors will not be subject to stringent monitoring, and there may be a decline in the quality of advice received by ministers.

A further complication is that, under a purchasing model based on competitive bidding, contractors will have an added incentive to criticize the advice provided by other contractors, partly to protect their own patch and partly in the hope of securing further contracts. This situation may generate additional inter-organizational conflict, intensify the problems of horizontal co-ordination, and render it more difficult for ministers to ascertain the best course of action.

If there is a risk of greater opportunism by contractors under West's proposals, there is also a risk of more opportunistic behaviour by purchasers (i.e. ministers and their purchase advisers). The nature of this risk will depend, at least in part, on the rules governing the tendering process. Clearly, if ministers are directly involved in choosing the organizations from which they will secure the bulk of their advice, it is reasonable to suppose that political or ideological considerations will influence their choice. This in turn will increase the dangers of cronyism, nepotism and other forms of corruption. Such outcomes will not only reduce the quality of the policy advice received but undermine the integrity of the whole political system.

(v) Problems of Co-ordination

West's proposals are bound to increase the problems of co-ordination in government at all levels. More organizations will be competing to supply policy advice. Some of these may possess only limited institutional memory. The degree of trust, co-operation and information-sharing between competing contractors is likely to be lower than under the current institutional arrangements. And contracts for policy output classes will, in effect, be of a shorter duration than at present. Particular difficulties under West's model are likely to include:

(a) managing the system of collective policy-making by Cabinet, including the flow of papers between contractors and purchase advisers, and the servicing of Cabinet committees;

(b) the formulation and implementation of policies that have inter-organizational or cross-sectoral dimensions;

(c) managing the process of developing policy options and action plans in response to crises or national emergencies; and

(d) handling significant ministerial reshuffles or changes in government (with the resultant need to appoint new purchase advisers and secure new policy contractors).

In short, under West's proposals the inter-departmental teamwork which is so essential for efficient and effective policy-making within a Cabinet system of government is likely to be extremely difficult, complex and taxing for all concerned.

Summary

If the preceding analysis is correct, there are likely to be significant risks associated with the purchasing model proposed by West. Severe difficulties co-ordinating the process of policy development are probable, especially following changes of government or changes in the suppliers of policy outputs. Problems of adverse selection and opportunism could well be exacerbated. Guaranteeing the quality of policy advice is likely to be harder, as is ensuring that advice is 'free and frank'. And the problems of maintaining trust between the various suppliers of advice, as well as between suppliers and purchasers, are bound to be aggravated. Rather than reducing production and transaction costs, West's proposals can be expected to have the opposite effect. Quite apart from this, if private firms were to become the sole, or even primary, repository of knowledge and expertise on certain policy matters, it would enable them to exercise considerable political influence. As Kettl puts it:

> It is one thing for . . . administrators to delegate the delivery of goods and services to private partners. It is quite another for those private partners to have such an advantage in expertise over government officials that they, not government, are, in effect, the authors of public policy.[60]

For such reasons, West's model has little to commend it. Requiring departments to compete on a regular basis with each other and outside parties for the right to supply policy outputs would be very risky and almost certainly counter-productive.

In criticizing West's model, I do not wish to suggest that departments should never contract out the provision of policy advice. Nor am I arguing that ministers should avoid seeking advice from non-departmental sources. On the contrary, there are likely to be many occasions when contracting is desirable, in terms of both cost and quality. And it will often be sensible for ministers to seek advice from expert panels, commissions of inquiry and other independent sources. At the same time, there are significant risks if departments lose their capacity to evaluate critically and impartially the nature of the advice being tendered by external contractors (or other suppliers). Consequently, in deciding whether or not to contract out particular policy tasks, departmental managers need to consider the longer-term impact of their decisions on their capacity to maintain adequate in-house expertise across the broad range of policy issues for which they are responsible. What is deemed to be 'adequate' will obviously be a matter for departmental managers to judge, and such judgements are likely to vary according to the nature and complexity of the policy issues in question. The key point, however, is that the greater the proportion of a department's policy work that is contracted out, and the more heavily senior managers rely on short-term appointees to prepare key policy papers, the greater the chances of them losing control over the nature and quality of their department's policy outputs.

Individual ministers, too, must be mindful of the risks of purchasing a significant proportion of their advice from non-departmental sources. In particular, they should consider how their decisions will affect their department's ability to retain a critical mass of policy expertise, maintain an adequate institutional memory, and provide a satisfactory and comprehensive ministerial servicing capacity. Further, ministers have a responsibility to ensure that their purchasing decisions do not compromise the integrity of the policy process (e.g. by giving a private firm undue influence over policy formulation), foreclose the purchasing options available to their successors in office, or undermine the conventions of the Westminster system of government (especially the non-partisan role of public servants).

Returning to an earlier theme of this chapter, the question arises as to whether the provision of policy advice to ministers should be regarded as an 'inherently governmental function'. Any answer here will clearly depend on how this term is defined. If it means something which only an elected government (i.e. in New Zealand the Cabinet) should decide or undertake, then plainly policy *advice* is not inherently governmental. Policy *making*, on the other hand, certainly is. If the term means something which only government employees should undertake, then again policy advice cannot be regarded as inherently governmental. After all, as argued above, it is perfectly proper for ministers to seek advice from non-departmental sources. However, if the term refers to a function where an in-house or governmental capacity is in the public interest, then in my view policy advice is inherently governmental. Undoubtedly, this function can be, and often is, contracted out. But it should never be contracted out to such an extent that governments lose their professional, non-partisan, in-house advisory capacity.

Conclusions

This chapter has considered some of the issues surrounding the limits to the contracting-out of publicly funded goods and services. If nothing else, I trust that the preceding analysis has highlighted the complexity of the issues at stake. Plainly, in many cases the question is not simply the relative merits of in-house provision versus contracting out, but equally whether it is in the public interest to retain a permanent, in-house capacity and, if so, whether such a requirement is compatible with external contracting. Further, if an in-house capacity is considered desirable, then other issues arise concerning what this capacity should consist of and how it should be organized.

Where the provision of publicly funded goods and services is contracted out, it is essential for the relevant public agencies to retain adequate control over their suppliers. This, of course, requires them to maintain sufficient in-house expertise to oversee the process of contract management, including the capacity to monitor and assess each contractor's performance. The American experience in this respect is salutary.[61] Too often in recent years, federal agencies have not retained adequate in-house expertise, thereby placing themselves at the mercy of potentially opportunistic contractors. It is important that New Zealand (and other) policy-makers learn from this experience and put in place proper safe-guards. Indeed, this will be all the more important if future governments become increasingly 'hollow' — i.e. most major delivery functions are undertaken on contract by private firms or quasi-governmental organizations. For, if the core machinery of the state is significantly weakened, the capacity of governments to act as 'smart buyers' will be put in jeopardy. This will not merely increase the risks of policy failure, but also threaten democratic control of public expenditure and public policy.

More generally, there is the question of whether the new contractualism and the trend towards a hollow state will prove to be a durable form of governance. In my view, there is little prospect that the current emphasis on markets, contestability and contracting out will be a passing fad. But I strongly suspect that the pendulum will swing back in favour of bureaucracy and hierarchy at some time in the future. Traditional bureaucracies, to be sure, have their weaknesses; but they also have many strengths, 'including reliability, predictability, probity, cohesion and continuity'.[62] And while administrative hierarchies have their defects, they have the virtue of enabling governments to maintain a firm grip on the levers of power. Moreover, relational contracts (see chapter 2), which are, of course, a central feature of traditional bureaucracies, have in many cases significant advantages over classical contracts in terms of flexibility, adaptability, the fostering of 'goodwill trust', the capacity for learning, and so forth. The case for bureaucracy is not, perhaps, conclusive. But it is often persuasive — and waiting to be rediscovered.

Annex 1. *Guidelines for Determining Whether Contracting Out for Consulting Services Would Be Appropriate*

1. The work to be done must be specific enough that a detailed contract can be written regarding the work assignments, responsibilities, and products expected.

2. The agency must retain the technical capability to prescribe, monitor, and evaluate the work of the contractor. In addition, the agency should consider the impact of contracting on the future technical capacity of the agency. Technical capacity should not be eroded over time through the use of contracts to the degree that future contracts could not be effectively monitored and evaluated.

3. The institutional memory must reside with the agency, not with the contractor.

4. Maintain competition at the time of the initial award and when renewal is being considered. Avoid situations in which the contractor, by virtue of its work for the agency, develops exclusive expertise to the degree that a monopoly is established.

5. Only government officials are to make policy decisions. Government officials must be involved in the decisionmaking process to a greater degree than merely making the final policy decision on the basis of analysis and/or advice by a contractor. They must approve the analytical process leading to the decision options and use discretion and make the value judgements throughout the process.

6. Government officials must set a definite time period for the use of the contractor. If the need is for a long or indefinite period, government employees should do the work. Also, the contract should require a finite or deliverable product, such as a report, analysis or opinion, which is different from the normal, routine work products of the agency.

7. Attention should be paid to possible individual or organizational conflicts of interest. To the extent possible, take steps to ensure that the advice or service to be received is impartial and that the contract will not result in an unfair competitive advantage to the contractor.

8. Compare the costs and benefits, both long- and short-term, of using a contractor or government employee. However, in situations in which governmental functions are identified, most functions should more appropriately be done by government employees, and cost may not be a relevant consideration.

Source: General Accounting Office, Government Contractors, *p.32.*

Notes

1   Donald Kettl, *Sharing Power: Public Governance and Private Markets* (Washington, DC, Brookings Institution, 1993), p.19.

2   *Ibid.*, p.21.

3   See Ian Harden, *The Contracting State* (Buckingham, Open University Press, 1992); Martin Laffin, 'Recent Changes in US and Australian Bureaucracies', paper prepared for the 'New Ideas, Better Government' Fulbright Symposium on Public Sector Reform, June 23–24, 1994, p.15; H. Brinton Milward, 'Nonprofit

Contracting and the Hollow State', *Public Administration Review* 54 (1994), pp.73–77. For a critique of the trend to 'hollow government', see R. A. W. Rhodes, 'The Hollowing Out of the State', *Political Quarterly* (1994), pp.138–51. For a helpful overview and analysis of the contractual approach to public management, see OECD, *Performance Management in Government: Performance Measurement and Results-Oriented Management* (Paris, Occasional Papers No. 3, 1994), pp.67–77.

4   United States General Accounting Office, *Government Contractors: Are Service Contractors Performing Inherently Governmental Functions?*, GGD–92–11 (Washington, November 1991). A more detailed specification of 'inherently governmental functions' is set out in *Federal Register* 57, 190 (September 30, 1992), pp.45096–103.

5   *Ibid.*, p.5. These contracts were randomly selected and had a total value of about US$241 million.

6   For a fuller analysis of the issues surrounding the contracting–out of policy advice, see Jonathan Boston, 'Purchasing Policy Advice: The Limits to Contracting Out', *Governance* 7 (1994), pp.1–30.

7   See, for example, John Donahue, *The Privatization Decision: Public Ends, Private Means* (New York, Basic Books, 1989); Donald Kettl, *Sharing Power*; Steve Hanke (ed.), *Prospects for Privatization* (New York, Academy of Political Science, 1987); E. S. Savas, *Privatization: The Key to Better Government* (Chatham, NJ, Chatham House Publishers, 1987); Lester Salamon, *Beyond Privatization — The Tools of Government Action* (Washington, Urban Institute, 1989); Ira Sharkansky, 'Policy Making and Service Delivery on the Margins of Government: The Case of Contractors', *Public Administration Review* 40 (1980), pp.116–23; John Stewart, 'The Limitations of Government by Contract', *Public Money and Management* 13 (1993), pp.7–12.

8   See John Bryson and Peter Smith-Ring, 'A Transaction-based Approach to Policy Intervention', *Policy Sciences* 23 (1990), pp.205–29; Aidan Vining and David Weimar, 'Government Supply and Government Production Failure: A Framework Based on Contestability', *Journal of Public Policy* 10 (1990), pp.1–22; Oliver Williamson, *The Economic Institutions of Capitalism: Firms, Markets, Relational Contracting* (New York, Free Press, 1985).

9   See, for instance, Dietmar Braun, 'Who Governs Intermediary Agencies? Principal Agent Relations in Research Policy-Making', *Journal of Public Policy* 13 (1993), pp.135–62; David Coursey and Barry Bozeman, 'Decision Making in Public and Private Organizations: A Test of Alternative Concepts of "Public-ness" ', *Public Administration Review* 50 (1990), pp.525–34; Mark Emmert and Michael Crow, 'Public, Private and Hybrid Organizations: An Empirical Examination of the Role of Publicness', *Administration and Society* 20 (1988), pp.216–44; Donald Kettl, *Government by Proxy: (Mis?)Managing Federal Programs* (Washington, DC, Congressional Quarterly Press, 1988); Ronald Moe,

'Exploring the Limits to Privatization', *Public Administration Review* 47 (1987), pp.453–60; Lloyd Musolf and Harold Seidman, 'The Blurred Boundaries of Public Administration', *Public Administration Review* 40 (1980), pp.124–30; Lester Salamon, 'Rethinking Public Management: Third-Party Government and the Changing Forms of Government Action', *Public Policy* 29 (1981), pp.255–75.

10 See Jeremy Corban, 'Contracting Out Inland Revenue', paper prepared for MAPP 508, Master of Public Policy Programme, Victoria University of Wellington, 1990; Caroline Peren, 'Achieving the Benefits of Corporatisation within the Bureaucracy: A Case Study of MAF Quality Management', paper prepared for MAPP 510, Master of Public Policy Programme, Victoria University of Wellington, 1993; Susan Redward, 'The Delivery of Agricultural Regulatory Services: In What Circumstances Is Contracting Out Preferable to Direct Provision?', paper prepared for MAPP 510, Master of Public Policy Programme, Victoria University of Wellington, 1993.

11 For details of this system see June Pallot, 'Financial Management Reform', in Jonathan Boston *et al.* (eds), *Reshaping the State: New Zealand's Bureaucratic Revolution* (Auckland, Oxford University Press, 1991).

12 General Accounting Office, *Government Contractors*, p.53.

13 *Ibid.*, p.3.

14 OMB, Circular A–120, quoted in *ibid.*, p.19.

15 *Ibid.*

16 General Accounting Office, *Government Contractors*, p.18.

17 *Ibid.*, p.21.

18 *Ibid.*

19 *Ibid.*, p.22.

20 *Ibid.*, p.21.

21 *Ibid.*, p.6.

22 *Ibid.*, p.3.

23 The literature on 'the public interest' is extensive. See particularly Brian Barry, *Political Argument* (London, Routledge and Kegan Paul, 1965); Carl J. Friedrich (ed.), *The Public Interest* (New York, Atherton Press, 1966).

24 Brian Barry, *Political Argument*, pp.207–25.

25 General Accounting Office, *Government Contractors*, p.3. There is a growing number of US studies which highlight the problems that can arise when governmental systems are so 'hollow' that there is very little institutional capability left for maintaining proper oversight and control, and indeed when private contractors constitute the institutional memory in the policy-making system. See H. Brinton Milward, 'Nonprofit Contracting and the Hollow State'.

26 General Accounting Office, *Government Contractors*, p.30.

27 *Ibid.*, p.3.

28 *Ibid.*

29 *Ibid.*, p.5.

30 *Ibid.*, p.30. For a more detailed consideration of what it means to be a 'smart buyer', see Kettl, *Sharing Power*, p.180.

31 General Accounting Office, *Government Contractors*, p.30.

32 For analyses of the current system of policy advice in New Zealand, see Jonathan Boston, 'Purchasing Policy Advice'; Max Bradford, 'The Purchase of Policy Advice: The New Zealand Model — Observations from a Parliamentary Perspective', paper presented to an AIC conference on 'Efficient and Effective Policy', June 29-30, 1993, Wellington; Jeremy Corban, 'The Provision of Strategic Advice to Government', MPP thesis, Victoria University of Wellington, 1994; Gary Hawke, *Improving Policy Advice* (Wellington: Victoria University Press, 1993); Don Hunn, 'Measuring Performance in Policy Advice: The New Zealand Perspective', paper presented to an OECD conference on 'Performance Measures and Target Setting', April 25-26, 1994, Paris; Richard Morris, 'The Pricing of Policy Advice: The Proposed Cabinet Benchmark', paper presented to an AIC Conference on 'Managing Quality Policy', March 7-8, 1994, Wellington; Claudia Scott, 'Review of the Purchase of Policy Advice from Government Departments', *Public Sector* 15, 2, 1992, pp.19-24; State Services Commission, *Review of the Purchase of Policy Advice from Government Departments* (Wellington, 1991); State Services Commission, *The Policy Advice Initiative: Opportunities for Management* (Wellington, 1992).

33 Richard Morris, 'The Pricing of Policy Advice', p.5.

34 *Ibid.*

35 *Ibid.* For an analysis and critique of the current use of consultants by government departments, see Audit Office, *Report of the Controller and Auditor-General: Third Report for 1994* (Wellington, 1994), pp.15-41.

36 For details of this system see State Services Commission, *Review of the Purchase of Policy Advice from Government Departments*.

37 *Dominion*, June 22, 1993.

38 Max Bradford, 'The Purchase of Policy Advice: The New Zealand Model — Observations from a Parliamentary Perspective', Appendix 2.

39 State Services Commission, *Review of the Purchase of Policy Advice from Government Departments*, p.24.

40 Richard Morris, 'The Pricing of Policy Advice', p.4.

41 State Services Commission, *Review of the Purchase of Policy Advice from Government Departments*, pp.28-33.

42 Andrew West, 'Public Service Is Independent of Public Servants', paper presented to an AIC Conference on 'Managing Quality Policy', March 7-8, 1994, Wellington. See also Andrew West, 'Public Service Is Independent of Public Servants', *Public Sector* 17 (1994), pp.26-28.

43 Andrew West, 'Public Service Is Independent of Public Servants', paper presented to an AIC Conference, p.3.

44 *Ibid.*

45 *Ibid.*

46 *Ibid.*, p.4.

47 *Ibid.*

48 *Ibid.*

49 *Ibid.*, p.3.

50 See especially Oliver Williamson, *Markets and Hierarchies* (New York, Free Press, 1975); Oliver Williamson, *The Economic Institutions of Capitalism*.

51 John Bryson and Peter Smith-Ring, 'A Transaction-Based Approach', p.217.

52 Oliver Williamson, *The Economic Institutions of Capitalism*, p.72.

53 See Christopher Hood and Michael Jackson, *Administrative Argument* (Aldershot, Dartmouth, 1991), p.86; and T. Moe, 'The New Economics of Organizations', *American Journal of Political Science* 28 (1984), p.753.

54 For a fuller treatment of these issues see Jonathan Boston, 'Purchasing Policy Advice', pp.14–28.

55 M. Sako, 'The Role of "Trust" in Japanese Buyer–Supplier Relationships', *Ricerche Economiche* 45 (1991), p.451. See also Aidan Vining and David Weimar, 'Government Supply and Government Production Failure', pp.6–7.

56 M. Sako, 'The Role of "Trust" in Japanese Buyer–Supplier Relationships', p.453.

57 Timothy Plumptre, *Beyond the Bottom Line: Management in Government* (Halifax, Institute for Research on Public Policy, 1988), p.294.

58 See Jonathan Boston, 'The Future for Cabinet Government in New Zealand: The Implications of MMP for the Formation, Organization and Operations of the Cabinet', Graduate School of Business and Government Management, Victoria University of Wellington, Working Paper Series 3/94, p.12.

59 James Ferris, 'Contracting and Higher Education', *Journal of Higher Education* 62 (1991), p.11.

60 See Donald Kettl, *Sharing Power*, p. 204.

61 *Ibid.*, pp.41–177.

62 R. A. W. Rhodes, 'The Hollowing Out of the State', p.151.

CHAPTER FIVE

The Reconfiguration of the State and the Appropriate Scope of Judicial Review

Mai Chen

Introduction

Those disgruntled with the actions of various governments to recon-figure the state over the last ten years have sometimes looked to the courts to undermine its effects. They have not liked the profit-making orientation of Crown-owned companies (CROCs) in general, and state-owned enterprises (SOEs) in particular, which were created to perform previous state trading functions. They argue that courts should endeavour, via judicial review challenges, to ensure that such bodies make decisions consistent with their public nature despite being private companies in form. After all, CROCs and SOEs are comprised wholly of public assets and they are entrusted with making decisions in the public interest.[1]

The problem is that many of the significant commercial decisions CROCs and SOEs make, such as entering or terminating contracts, are not exercises of statutory powers. The power to contract arises from their status as companies formed under the Companies Act. Section 4 of the Judicature Amendment Act 1972 (JAA) requires that decisions be the exercise of statutory powers before courts can subject them to judicial review.

Proponents of expansive judicial review have argued for a modified gloss on, or an amendment to, the definition of 'statutory power' to allow judicial review of decisions by 'public bodies' with public effect. Some have even argued that, as long as the decision has public effect, it does not matter that the body making it is private.[2] Then, despite the government's reconfiguration of the state, the line where the distinction between public and private falls for the purpose of judicial review does not change. Moving solely to a 'public effect' test for judicial review would even increase the dimensions of the public sphere, as more decisions would be capable of being subjected to judicial review and thus required to meet a higher standard of decision-making.

Through the back door, then, those opposed to the government 'abdicating responsibility to the market', as they see it, want the courts to ensure that CROCs and SOEs are making decisions in the public interest. The problems with this approach are:

(i) the presumption that courts are up to the job; and

(ii) the thwarting of Parliament's intention that commercial decisions be left in the hands of CROC and SOE board members selected for their commercial expertise. Accountability for such decisions is to be exacted by a range of non-judicial accountability mechanisms on SOEs and CROCs that private companies are not subject to.[3]

The Courts' Response to Corporatization

The courts have been divided over whether commercial decisions such as the exercise of contractual powers by SOEs should be subject to judicial review. Earlier High Court precedents had subjected the exercise of contractual powers by SOEs such as Telecom (as it then was) to judicial review, by reason of the continued public ownership of the SOE and the social responsibility provision in s.4(1)(c) of the SOE Act.[4] However, this approach was reversed by the Court of Appeal in the recent decision of *Auckland Electric Power Board* v. *Electricity Corporation of New Zealand (AEPB)*.[5] The Court of Appeal found that the power to terminate the contract, the decision challenged in *AEPB*, arose from the Companies Act 1955. Thus, as with the termination of a contract by any other private company, the corporation's decision was not the exercise of a 'statutory power' and thus not subject to judicial review.

On appeal, the Privy Council appeared to reverse the Court of Appeal's approach. In *Mercury Energy Ltd* v. *Electricity Corporation of New Zealand Ltd (Mercury Energy)*,[6] the Judicial Committee stated:

A state-owned enterprise is a *public body*; its shares are held by Ministers who are responsible to the House of Representatives and accountable to the electorate. The Corporation carries on its business in the *interests of the public*. Decisions made in the public interest by the Corporation, a body established by statute, may adversely affect the rights and liabilities of private individuals without affording them any redress. Their Lordships take the view that in these circumstances the decisions of the Corporation are in principle amenable to judicial review both under the Act of 1972 as amended and under the common law ... (Emphasis added.)[7]

However, the Privy Council went on to state that:

It does not seem likely that a decision by a state-owned enterprise to enter into or to determine a commercial contract to supply goods or services will ever be the subject of judicial review in the absence of fraud, corruption or bad faith.[8]

The reality is that fraud and bad faith are very difficult grounds on which to base a judicial review challenge since they are notoriously hard to prove, and corruption is a very severe abuse of process which only rarely occurs, and brings with it criminal sanctions when it does. Thus, judicial review is merely one of the tools available when corruption occurs.

Bad faith is a commission by the decision-maker of a reviewable error knowing that an error is being committed, while fraud is the deliberate misleading of the decision-maker by others in a position of influence over him or her. Proving bad faith is so difficult that there seems to have been no case where judicial review on this ground has succeeded. Similarly, proving fraud requires the establishment, to a very high level, of all the ingredients of perjury other than the formality of oath or affirmation.

Consequently, it is questionable whether the Privy Council decision is really different in effect from that of the Court of Appeal. The reason for the limited scope the Privy Council gave to the judicial review of SOEs appears to be the presence of non-judicial accountability mechanisms to check excessive price increases by SOEs. The Privy Council stated:

Where a state-owned enterprise is concerned, the shareholding Ministers may exercise powers to ensure directly or indirectly that there are no price increases which the Ministers regard as excessive. Retribution for excessive prices is liable to be exacted on the *directors* of the state-owned enterprises at the hands of the *Ministers*. Retribution is liable to be exacted on the Ministers at the hands of the House of Representatives and on the elected members of the *House of Representatives* at the hands of the *electorate*. Industrial disputes over prices and other related matters can only be solved by industry or by Government interference and not by judicial interference in the absence of a breach of the law. (Emphasis added.)[9]

Nevertheless, the approach of the Privy Council in *Mercury Energy* differed in two main respects from that of the New Zealand Court of Appeal. These differences of approach provide scope for judges wanting to undertake expansive judicial review to do so. Whether that is warranted is a separate issue discussed at the end of this chapter.

Scope of Actions Subject to Judicial Review Under S.4 of the JAA

The first major difference between the Privy Council's approach and that of the New Zealand Court of Appeal is the *test* the Privy Council applied to determine the scope of actions subject to judicial review under s.4 of the JAA. Unlike the Court of Appeal, who concluded that the Electricity Corporation's power to determine the contractual arrangements was derived from contract and not the SOE Act, the Privy Council concluded:

> *By and pursuant to the Act of 1986*, the Corporation is empowered to operate the business of generating and distributing bulk electricity and for that purpose to enter into and determine contracts with customers and others. (Emphasis added.)[10]

Thus, the exercise of contractual powers is subject to the SOE Act and can be subject to judicial review under s.4 of the JAA. In fact, all decisions, whether of a commercial or non-commercial nature, would be caught under such an analysis, contrary to the statements of the Court of Appeal in the *New Zealand Stock Exchange* v. *Listed Companies Association Incorporated* case:[11]

> Parliament could never have intended that any corporate body recognised by statute or owing its existence to a specific or general statute such as the Companies Act could have all its commercial operations subject to constant judicial review.[12]

This underscores the wider significance of the Privy Council's statement for the test of what actions are caught under s.4 of the JAA. The approach adopted by the Court of Appeal in *AEPB* to determine the scope of judicial review appears to be consistent with these precedents. The court focused on the source of power for the decision and found it to be the Companies Act, not the SOE Act.

In contrast, the impact of the Privy Council statement is to broaden the scope of actions subject to judicial review under s.4 of the JAA to those where the statute merely confers a function or a sphere of operation.

The Privy Council's test for determining what actions are subject to judicial review is similar to the 'public effect' test which has been developed in recent United Kingdom cases such as *R. v. Panel On Takeovers and Mergers,* ex parte *Datafin Plc'*.[13] As the Privy Council stated in *Mercury Energy*:

> Judicial review involves interference by a court with a decision made by a person or body empowered by Parliament or governing law to reach that decision in the public interest.[14]

This definition of judicial review brings the statutory test for action subject to judicial review under the JAA closer to the test for common law judicial review. Common law judicial review continues to apply to the exercise of public duties which do not derive from, or under, any Act, or under the constitution or other instrument of incorporation, rules or bylaws of any body corporate conferring the rights or powers detailed in the definition of 'statutory power' under s.3 of the JAA. The key is a sufficient public law element if the extraordinary remedies provided in Part VII of the Act (except for the remedy of injunction) are to be activated.

The result is a broadening of the scope of decisions capable of being subjected to judicial review under s.4 of the JAA. This reading appears consistent with the reform agenda of Lord Woolf, one of the members of the Privy Council sitting in this case. In 'Judicial Review: A Possible Programme for Reform', Lord Woolf stated:

> A body should be subject to judicial review if it exercises authority over another person or body in such a manner as to cause material prejudice to that person or body and if judicial review were available, that person or body could show the decision-maker had acted unlawfully.[15]

Challenges Under S.4 of the SOE Act

The second major difference between the Privy Council's approach to SOEs and the Court of Appeal's approach is the former's willingness to determine whether individual acts of SOEs have complied with the SOE's principal objective of operating as a 'successful business' under s.4(1) of the SOE Act.

In contrast, the Court of Appeal in 'AEPB' found that 'particular acts in the conduct of the business of SOEs cannot be isolated and characterised as the exercise of a statutory power of decision in terms of section 4(1)(c)' since:

> There is nothing in the section to suggest a statutory intention that particular acts or transactions of an SOE may be isolated and subjected to judicial scrutiny. On the contrary in considering whether an SOE is achieving its objective it is necessary to assess its performance overall and over a period of time . . . *Read as a whole section 4(1) contemplates a large picture approach* to the determination of whether the SOE is operating as a successful business. There is nothing to suggest that Parliament ever contemplated that someone affected by a particular act or omission of an SOE, e.g. a charity whose application for a donation was refused or any employee refused permission to attend a work related educational seminar, could claim a duty to it in respect of a *single* transaction. (Emphasis added.)[16]

The Court of Appeal thus concluded that '[s]ection 4(1) of the SOE legislation does not provide an additional public law challenge of particular decisions through the court processes'.[17]

Broadcasting Assets Cases

The Privy Council's willingness to contemplate a challenge of particular decisions for failure to comply with s.4(1) could be particularly potent, in the light of Lord Woolf's observations about the equal importance of the objective of social responsibility with the objective of an SOE being profitable, in the recent Privy Council decision of 'New Zealand Maori Council & Ors v. Attorney-General & Ors'.[18] That case concerned an appeal from the New Zealand Court of Appeal decision that a transfer of broadcasting assets to an SOE, Television New Zealand, would not impair, to a material extent, the Crown's ability to take reasonable action to comply with the principles of the Treaty of Waitangi under s.9 of the SOE Act. The applicants submitted that, as the principal objective of an SOE under s.4 of the SOE Act is to operate as a successful business, that would be inconsistent with the SOE becoming voluntarily involved in a non-commercial activity such as promoting the Maori language on television. However, Lord Woolf took the view that the objective of social responsibility and the objective of an SOE being profitable were to be accorded equal importance. Speaking on behalf of the committee, he stated:

What can amount to operating as a successful business has to be determined in the context of the three requirements set out in paragraphs (a), (b) and (c) of section 4(1). *There is nothing to suggest that those paragraphs are not to be treated as being of the same weight.* The creation of profit is of no greater importance than the other objectives identified in the subsection. The language of (c) makes it clear that, as long as the state enterprise has the necessary financial resource, it is perfectly entitled to be involved in a loss or non-profit making activity.

Therefore, subject to any financial constraints, it would not be inconsistent with section 4 for the state enterprise to encourage the use of the Maori language by broadcasting television programmes in that language. By doing so the state enterprise would be exhibiting 'a sense of social responsibility' and would be 'having regard to the interests of the community'. Section 4 with its reference to 'successful business' reflects the general intent of the Act that the performance of state enterprises should be efficient and business-like. While in the foreseeable future there is little prospect of Maori broadcasts being profitable, there is no reason why they should not be presented in an efficient and in a business-like manner. (Emphasis added.)[19]

This is directly contrary to the finding of Greig J. in *Wellington Regional Council* v. *Post Bank Ltd.* In that case, the judge observed of s.4(1) of the SOE Act that:

It is plain, in my view, that the overriding consideration is commercial . . . It is obvious that the three matters in s4(1) are matters which require balancing. They may be, as it is said, antithetical. *It is not always the case that social responsibility and profitability can always be in harmony, so there is a balance that has to take place.* I attach some importance to the phrase in para (c) that the endeavour to accommodate and encourage the interests of the community is 'when able to do so'. It is not 'as far as it is able to do so' but 'when'. (Emphasis added.)[20]

Lord Woolf's observations also appear contrary to parliamentary intent as reflected in s.7 of the SOE Act. That section provides:

7. *Non-commercial activities* — Where the Crown wishes a State enterprise to provide goods or services to any persons, the Crown and the State enterprise shall enter into an agreement under which the State enterprise will provide the goods or services in return for the payment by the Crown of the whole or part of the price thereof.

It is difficult to predict how successful challenges to SOE decisions for failure to comply with their social responsibility obligations will be. It may well depend on the composition of the New Zealand court. However, the approach of the Privy Council to s.4(1) and the weight Lord Woolf gave to 'social responsibility' under s.4(1)(c) will undoubtedly have relevance to SOEs as well as non-SOE Crown companies created under legislation with similarly worded 'successful business' provisions to s.4(1)(c) of the SOE Act.

Challenges to Crown Health Enterprise Decisions Made Under Judicial Review

An example is Crown Health Enterprise (CHE) decisions under the Health and Disability Services Act 1993 (HDS Act). Decisions concerning the type, quantity, quality and price of health and disability services depend on the terms and conditions of purchase agreements CHEs have entered into with purchasers. CHEs are not specifically empowered to enter into contracts under the HDS Act as the exercise of such powers arises under the Companies Act. However, the Privy Council in *Mercury Energy* broadened the scope of actions subject to judicial review under s.4 of the JAA to those where the statute merely conferred a function or an area of operation as opposed to the specific power. By and pursuant to the HDS Act, CHEs are empowered to operate the business of providing health and disability services and, for that purpose, to enter into contracts with purchasers of such services, such as the Regional Health Authorities (RHAs) and the Public Health Commission (PHC). CHE decisions on the type, quantity, quality and price of health and disability services may thus be capable of being subjected to judicial review.

Lord Woolf's observations about the equal weight to be given to social responsibility under s.4(1)(c) of the SOE Act may also embolden judges to give the requirement to exhibit social responsibility equal weight with CHEs being as successful and efficient as comparable non-Crown-owned businesses under s.11 of the HDS Act. Although s.11(2) lists these factors as equal objectives of CHEs, it also provides that subs.(2) is not to limit subs.(1). Moreover, s.11(1) provides that:

> The principal objective of every Crown enterprise shall be to:
> (a) Provide health services or disability services or both; and
> (b) Assist in meeting the Crown's objectives under section 8 of this Act by providing such services in accordance with its statement of intent and any purchase agreement entered into by it — *while operating as a successful and efficient business.* (Emphasis added.)

It will be difficult, however, for courts to determine whether CHEs have acted consistently with the statutory objectives in s.11. The type, quality, quantity and cost of health and disability services that a CHE provides depend on the purchase agreement which the CHE has entered into with the RHA and/or the PHC. The nature of the purchase agreement is, in turn, affected by the nature of the funding agreement which the RHA or PHC entered into with the Minister of Health. The reasonableness of CHE decisions will need to be assessed in the context of these constraints.

Is Expansive Judicial Review Appropriate?

The approach of the Privy Council in *Mercury Energy* does not refute, but indeed reaffirms, that there are limits to the appropriate scope of judicial review. It is arguable that some recent challenges to the commercial decisions of SOEs have tried to reverse government policies which transfer certain state trading functions into the private sector. Attempts have been made to use judicial review to achieve policy outcomes which this legal tool was never intended to achieve.

Although good arguments can be made for the greater accountability of SOEs and CROCs, the courts are not always the appropriate mechanism to bring this about. There is a very real question whether the courts are better equipped than SOE or CROC boards to assess the reasonableness of commercial decisions. Rather than rushing to the court in the first instance, effort should instead be focused on improving the effectiveness of the non-judicial accountability mechanisms already in place to exact greater accountability from SOEs and CROCs.[21]

One important non-judicial accountability mechanism, scrutiny by parliamentary select committees, could well become more effective once the Mixed Member Proportional Representation system (MMP) of electing MPs is implemented, and there are more MPs to serve on such committees.[22] MMP is also likely to result in a changed balance of power in Parliament so that select committees may not always be chaired by government members or comprised of a government majority, and MPs may feel freer to act on their independent opinion as opposed to following the party line.[23] The Standing Orders Select Committee is currently reviewing the rules of the House of Representatives to determine, *inter alia*, whether changes need to be made to accommodate the new electoral system.

Changing Government Policy

At the most general level, legislation is an implementation of policy. Those who object to a certain government policy should seek to change it, and the law which implements it, instead of using inappropriate judicial review challenges as a backdoor method of reversing it.

Rather than advising clients to take a judicial review challenge to the courts, lawyers should help their clients to put together a case to key ministers and public servants as to why policies should be changed, and then offer advice as to how that policy can best be implemented. It is arguable that MMP will increase the opportunity to change policies such as those concerning corporatization and privatization, since it will open up the constitutional system to greater contestability of policy advice. Certainly, one potential scenario in the future is that a coalition government under MMP may be more likely to give greater weight to social responsibility, as opposed to profitability, for CROCs and SOEs in response to the trend of public demand for greater accountability from public and private institutions.

If courts are to have a role in determining whether SOEs and CROCs are acting consistently with their statutory objectives in making commercial decisions, Parliament needs to state more clearly the exact relationship between profitability and social responsibility. What *is* the balance? What weight is to be given to profitability as opposed to social responsibility? The courts should not be left to determine the legal validity of controversial SOE and CROC decisions which private individuals think are contrary to social responsibility. Rather, policy-makers need to think through the relevant issues, make the decisions, and be prepared to answer for the decisions they have made in Parliament and to the electorate.

There is, however, a legitimate role for courts to play, even if it is not in determining, via judicial review, the validity of SOE and CROC commercial decisions. The courts should ensure that Parliament, having delegated trading functions to SOEs and CROCs, leaves these bodies to perform their functions without political interference. Thus, under section 7 of the SOE Act, for example, ministers wishing an SOE to provide goods or services to any persons must enter into an agreement with the SOE and pay for such services. Furthermore, under section 25 of the HDS Act, the Minister of Health can give an RHA or the PHC a direction only if it is by written notice published in the *Gazette* after consultation with the RHA or PHC. Such a direction is likely, in turn, to affect the purchase agreements the RHA or PHC enters into with providers of health and disability services such as CHEs.[24]

Notes

1   See A. R. Galbraith, 'Deregulation, Privatisation and Corporatisation of Crown Activity: How Will the Law Respond?', New Zealand Law Conference, Wellington, March 2–5, 1993, p.226; R. E. Harrison, 'Deregulation, Privatisation and Corporatisation of Crown Activity: How will the Law Respond?' New Zealand Law Conference, Wellington, March 2–5, 1993, p.102; M. Taggart, 'Corporatisation, Privatisation and Public Law', *Public Law Review* 2 (1991), p.77; M. Taggart, 'Recent Developments in Administrative Law', *Legal Update Series*, University of Auckland, May 1994, p.1.

2   See Sir Patrick Neill, 'A Reply to Professor Sir William Wade's "New Horizons in Administrative Law" ', in 9th Commonwealth Conference Papers (Commonwealth Law Conference, Auckland, 1990), p.443.

3   These include the Official Information Act, the Ombudsman Act and the scrutiny of parliamentary select committees.

4   See, for example, *Clutha Leathers Ltd (in rec) v. Telecom Corporation of New Zealand Ltd* (1988–89) 4 *New Zealand Company Law Cases*, 64,249; and *New Zealand Optical (in rec) v. Telecom Corporation of New Zealand Ltd* (1990) 5 *New Zealand Company Law Cases*, 66,457.

5   [1994] 1 *New Zealand Law Reports*, p.55.

6   [1994] 2 *New Zealand Law Reports*, p.385ff.

7   *Ibid.*, p.388.

8   *Ibid.*, p.391.

9   *Ibid.*

10 *Ibid.*, p.390.

11 [1984] 1 *New Zealand Law Reports*, p.699ff.

12 *Ibid.*, p.707.

13 [1987] *Queen's Bench*, p.815.

14 [1994] 2 *New Zealand Law Reports*, p.388.

15 [1992] *Public Law*, p.220, p.235.

16 [1994] 1 *New Zealand Law Reports*, p.558–59.

17 *Ibid.*, p.591.

18 [1994] 2 *Weekly Law Reports*, p.254 ('Broadcasting Assets').

19 *Ibid.*, pp.261–62.

20 Unreported, High Court, Wellington Registry, CP 720/87, December 22, 1987, pp.14–15.

21 See further, M. Chen, 'Judicial Review at the Crossroads', *Victoria University of Wellington Law Review* 24 (1994), p.51.

22 The number of MPs will be increased from 99 to 120 under MMP.

23 See M. Chen, 'Remedying New Zealand's Constitution in Crisis: Is MMP Part of the Answer?', *New Zealand Law Journal* (1993). p.22; M. Chen, 'The Introduction of Mixed Member Proportional Representation in New Zealand — Implications for Lawyers', *Public Law Review* (1994), p.104; Phil Goff, 'Select Committees: a new player in negotiating policy outcomes or an old role revisited?', AIC conference on 'Strategic Policy', Wellington, September 22–23, 1994.

24 At the time of writing, the Minister of Health had just announced that the PHC would be disbanded.

CHAPTER SIX

Interpreting Contemporary Contractualism

ANNA YEATMAN

Introduction

Over the last twenty or so years the Anglophone liberal democracies have witnessed the revival of contractualist doctrines of governance. Interpreted narrowly, contractualist doctrines are those which locate the legitimacy of social obligation in the legally sanctioned and freely undertaken contractual choice of individuals. Interpreted more broadly, in a way which suggests the ethos of contractualism, contractualist doctrines are those which require social obligation to be mediated by some form of individualized consent. This means that social processes, outcomes and relationships have to be made accountable to individualized enquiry and judgement. Such accountability may or may not lead to individualized assent or dissent. Writ large, as in the social contract, or writ small, as in individual contracts, contractualism appears to have a peculiar salience in the governance of self-regulated social life.

However, just exactly what this all means is currently highly debatable. I will argue shortly that it is the broad meaning or ethos of contractualism which is at issue: most instances of contemporary contractualism have no legal standing and, it turns out, the legal doctrine of contractualism itself depends on this ethos.

What might one point to as evidence of this so-called 'new contractualism'? A mix of examples indicates readily the different kinds of contractualism in view.

First, there is the increasingly influential idea that services should be designed around the needs of individuals, not the other way around.

This was a principle adopted for the Australian Home and Community Care programme in 1989, it is a core principle of the British Citizens' Charter, and it influenced the 1994 Australian white paper on the needs of the long-term unemployed in its insistence that labour-market assistance should be tailored to the needs of the individual job-seeker. Why or how is this idea contractualist? Contractualism is indicated in the requirement for the individual user of a service both to choose what they require of that service, and to make that choice explicit in such a way that it can be determined whether or not the service has responded effectively to it.

Second, there is currently a plethora of contractualist instruments of public management. These include performance agreements between ministers and chief executives of public agencies, performance appraisals as negotiated between the appraiser and the appraised, competitive tendering for publicly funded services, and the contracting-out of publicly funded services to external suppliers. Some of these contracts have legal standing, others do not. What they share is a contractualist language making explicit the reciprocal expectations between the parties concerned. Such explicitness is reached through a mixed process of contract and negotiation, often of course in the context of established policies, guidelines or procedures. By situating these policies, guidelines and procedures in relation to a dialogical explicitness about tasks and processes, they themselves become subject to the principle of rational accountability. Explicitness and the kind of information-sharing it presupposes fuel consent. Thus contractualist explicitness and consent are linked principles. This does not mean that the consent is unconstrained, or that there are not different kinds of inequality in the relationship between the negotiating parties.

Third, there are a number of relatively new statutes which work in terms of the norm of a self-regulated relationship. In this connection we can mention the New Zealand 1991 Employment Contracts Act, where the employment contract by statute is radically individualized in two senses: first, each party, employer or employee, can choose to negotiate on their own behalf or to be represented 'by another person, group, or organization'; and second, each has freedom to negotiate whether the contract is an individual or collective employment contract.[1] This is not to argue that the 1991 Act is itself fully adequate to contractualist values — it is not, as I shall show below — but to suggest that it is symptomatic of the new contractualism, as is also the Australian government's dilution of a centralized wage-fixing system in favour of enterprise bargaining.

Whatever else may be said about these developments, one thing is clear: as much as they legitimize self-regulated modes of employment, in the same measure they contribute to the delegitimizing of established paternalistic legal and policy discourses of worker protection. The delegitimizing of paternalistic principles of protection in the employment arena needs to be seen in the context of other important statutory developments, such as equal employment opportunity, anti-discrimination and equal pay legislation. The directional force of such measures is to constitute the parties to employment relations as equal persons in terms of their contractual capacities, rights and obligations. Contractual equality of this kind is an equal entitlement to individualized personhood. It requires the disestablishment of all state legislation and policy which 'protected' certain categories of person precisely because they were assumed to be incapable of protecting themselves from harm. Thus, for equal pay for women workers to be possible, protective legislation limiting the hours women could work had to be abolished.

Entitlement to status as an individual has been extended to those belonging to social categories that were in some or all ways excluded from the older discourses of contractualism. This extension has not occurred without the mobilization of social movements which have both protested against these exclusions, and unambiguously rejected the paternalistic principle of some speaking on behalf of others. In this way the so-called 'new social movements' — feminism, the gay and lesbian movements, the various anti-racist, multicultural and indigenous people's movements — have all contributed to the resurgence of contractualist principles.

In what follows, first, I want to say a little more about this broader ethos of the new contractualism, then to show how it operates in current theoretical discourses of contractualism, and finally to address the critiques of the new contractualism. In conclusion, I will suggest that whatever else we do we cannot help taking the new contractualism seriously, and, paradoxically enough, one line of critique may lie in working to make the new contractualism more adequately contractual.

The Ethos of the New Contractualism

Nineteenth-century utilitarianism crystallized what we might call the classical doctrine of contract — certainly as understood in law.[2] 'Contract' refers to a legally enforceable exchange of promises. It is binding because the parties to it intended to be bound; 'it is their will or intention which creates the liability'.[3] The contractual obligation resides in honouring the promises once made. The emphasis in this doctrine of contractualism is on the nature of the obligation that flows from freely given choice. By the same token, if it turns out that the choice was not freely given, the courts may determine that the contract was not a fair or proper one.

Given contemporary democratic expectations, a contractualist emphasis on a legally consequentialist choice must inevitably lead into questions about the conditions under which a freely chosen obligation can be assumed to be given. If contract law is necessarily and inevitably oriented to the issue of whether or not choice has been freely exercised, then we are likely to see a range of developments in law which specify the conditions under which such choice may be assumed to be exercised. These can include what P. S. Atiyah problematically regards as paternalistic protection 'for those who make rash and ill-considered promises', as in the provision of cooling-off periods and the like.[4] Such conditions may come increasingly to include the requirement that, for example, banks explain the fine contractual print of different mortgage interest-rate options, and plastic surgeons the risks of silicon enlargement of bodily parts, to their respective consumers.

The legal emphasis on a freely assumed or voluntary undertaking makes it appear that the origins of this relationship reside in choice. This may be an appropriate way of looking at a whole range of contractualist relationships, where the issue of entering the relationship in the first place is, or should be, a matter of choice. As we know, this is not true of many relationships: the chief executive of a government agency cannot choose whether or not to contract with his or her minister; the student taking a university topic cannot choose whether or not to be assessed; the person who lacks an independent income and who is ineligible for public income support cannot choose whether or not to be employed; the person who is medically advised to remove some skin cancers normally does not choose whether or not to have surgery. In all these cases it is a question not so much of choice as of whether the person concerned is effectively and appropriately participating in these relationships.

This is still in many, if not most, contexts a radical demand. Too few doctors involve their clients in an informed relationship to medically oriented decision-making, far too few employers work with their employees in an explicitly negotiated co-producing relationship, and far too few academics engage students in the formation and negotiation of an assessment contract. At the same time, the direction of legislative and normative change appears to be clear: the expectation is that parties to a negotiated, contractualist type of relationship be adequately informed about the nature of this relationship, and that there be ways of making each accountable to the other. A good statutory example of this expectation is the New Zealand Official Information Act 1982 which states as its purposes in section 4:

(a) To increase progressively the availability of official information to the people of New Zealand in order —
   (i) to enable their more effective participation in the making of laws and policies; and
   (ii) to promote the accountability of Ministers of the Crown and officials, and thereby to enhance respect for the law and to promote the good government of New Zealand:
(b) To provide for proper access by each person to official information in relation to that person:
(c) To protect official information to the extent consistent with the public interest and the preservation of personal privacy.

At this point, it is useful to distinguish the principles of consent and choice. In many instances, even if a relationship is entered into by choice, once entered into it is not choice but consent that becomes the operative contractualist principle. Consent can be argued to be operating when the parties to a relationship are adequately informed about their relationship, and their respective entitlements within it, and they have the right to negotiate the substance, process and direction of this relationship. This right of negotiation involves the right to discussion, debate and contestation in respect of the relationship. Negotiation entails the additional principles of explicitness and accountability. A relationship can be adequately negotiated only if the parties concerned make explicit what they see as issues to be addressed, issues in relation to which they have distinct and separable, i.e. individualized, interests. Explicitness will often demand that one party become accountable to the other — and possibly to third parties — for their actions.

Informed consent, negotiation by mutual adjustment[5] and accountability, then, are the central components of this looser, non-legal ethos of contractualism. In some cases, as we have seen, a statutory entitlement will underpin a right to information, and there will often be a legal contractual aspect to such relationships. In general, however, the ethos of contractualism works off a shared set of commitments to self-regulated relationships which do not have legal standing.

Theoretical Discourses of the New Contractualism

The new contractualism is evident in a number of theoretical discourses which model institutional design and governance. These are the discourses of public choice, rational choice, agency theory and the new institutional economics.

Most of their critics have wrongly assumed that these discourses are essentially economistic in character. However, they represent a wider intellectual movement in contemporary political and social science, where the nineteenth-century utilitarian calculus of individualized rational action has been turned into a sophisticated instrument of institutional design in all contexts, not just economic ones. If there is a master discourse among these, it is rational choice.

Rational choice is far more sophisticated than most of its critics appreciate. It works in terms of a calculus of self-regulated, rational adaptation of individuals to a highly complex set of circumstances, including the complexities that attend extensive and intensive inter-dependencies between actors. Jon Elster's portrayal of rational action is helpful in understanding what is involved here:

> An action, to be rational, must be the final result of three optimal decisions. First, it must be the best means of realizing a person's desire, given his [*sic*] beliefs. Next, these beliefs must themselves be optimal, given the evidence available to him. Finally, the person must collect an optimal amount of evidence — neither too much nor too little. That amount depends both on his desires — on the importance he attaches to the decision — and on his beliefs about the costs and benefits of gathering more information.[6]

It should be emphasized that this conception of rational action does not preclude using the categories of culture, discourse, ideology or psycho-analysis to explain how the individual forms and ranks his or her desires. This is not at issue. What is at issue is the rational choice theorist's normative insistence on the individualized nature of desire. This does not in itself make such desire self- as distinct from other-regarding;

individualized desire can be oriented in terms of all types and modes of social relationship, including those which we term 'ego-centric'.

The unit of desire is an individual actor not a collectivity.[7] Or, rather, desire functions to individualize an actor. On this approach, institutional design should enable actors rationally to pursue their individualized desires in ways which make informed acknowledgement of the terms of their co-existence with other desiring individuals. These individualized actors can be either empirical individuals or corporate actors such as firms. Agency theory and the new institutional economics can be seen as theorizing rational choice on behalf of such corporate actors in budgetary and/or economic contexts.

Rational choice espouses a methodological individualism which is expressed in the proposition that 'there do not exist collective desires or collective beliefs'.[8] It is arguable what this means. Taken literally, it is both empirically and normatively false. It neither explains how there are shared or intersubjectively maintained democratic values which enable such a theoretical orientation as that of rational choice, nor how these values provide a normative framework for individualized or self-regulated social relations. Yet, if this proposition means the idea that, in modern society, collective desires and beliefs exist only as they are mediated through individualized choice, consent, judgement and commitment, then this methodological individualism commands some purchase. It is, however, a purchase limited to modern democratic contexts, and, this being the case, there is a circular relationship between the methodological premise and the types of explanation for which it is offered as a ground.[9]

The current theoretical discourses of the new contractualism can be criticized from two different directions. They can be criticized for what, by the terms of their construction, they cannot accommodate: we can call these external criticisms. Or they can be criticized for what their assumptions could accommodate if they were transformed by internal criticism. Let us take the latter first.

Internal Critiques of Theoretical Contractualist Discourse

This is a large topic, and it will be enough to suggest the nature of the work required to be done here. It is fair to say that both the theoretical expositors of the new contractualism and their external critics tend to take for granted the very category that should be problematized: namely, individualized agency. I have suggested above that rational choice requires desire to operate in such a way that it individualizes the actor — that is, it turns this actor, non-corporate or corporate, into an intentional unit of action, whose agency in relation to other such units is assumed to be bounded and, in this sense, is independent. This is a self who understands selfhood as his or her separability from other selves in such a way that he or she can be treated and treat himself or herself as a distinct locus of judgement, volition and decision-making. This self's oppositional other is a tribal or patrimonial self: namely, one whose selfhood is organically derived from the identity of some kind of communal self.[10]

Because confusion is so rife in this area, it is important to emphasize that the individualized self exists only in terms of its relationship to other selves. Individualization, in other words, is a type of social relationship. Thus, it is not the case that the tribal or patrimonial self is a self in relationship, where the individualized self is a self not in relationship. Rather, we have two different kinds of self in relationship. Tribal selves, for example, are communalized selves, while modern contractualist selves are individualized selves.

Liberals and their socialist critics, historically, have made just this mistake: namely, to assume the individualized self is an individual outside social relationships. For Marxists and socialists, this meant that an emphasis on the social nature of selfhood led to the assertion of collective identities which subsumed individuals at the expense of individualized social relationships. Either way, the individual has been left as a natural category.

Until we have an adequate theoretical account of how individualized social relationships work, and what makes them possible, we will not be able to check the individualistic and asocial excesses of liberal contractualist approaches. We need to ask questions like these: How is the individualized capacity to choose developed? What does it mean to choose? Is choice necessarily an individualized capacity? What is the relationship of choice to informed consent and the intersubjective properties of dialogue, negotiation and contestation? How does choice work in relation to accountability, and what is accountability in the context of individualized social relationships? How are the capacities to do all these things developed, and what kinds of knowledge and skill are required for these capacities to operate?

External Critiques of Contractualist Discourse

The external critiques tend to reject the assumptions of contractualism. They can therefore be seen as critiques of theoretical and practical contractualist discourse. These critiques generally conflate contractualism with its liberal, not to say libertarian, versions. To this degree they over-look their indebtedness for the very terms of their critique to contrac-tualism understood in its broader sense — that is, as referring to the ethos of self-regulated social relationships. At the same time, to a degree, it is reasonable for these critiques to mistake their object since the tendency to reduce contractualism to its liberal versions is widespread.

The first critique rejects contractualism as a libertarian or free-market doctrine of 'economic rationalism', where the value of equality is subordinated to the right of survival of the contractually fittest. That there is a vulgar libertarian version of contemporary contractualism which deserves such critique in the name of equality cannot be doubted. The social welfare policies of the Reagan, Thatcher and Bolger governments, in part at least, appear to have been designed according to a libertarian–contractualist doctrine of the survival of the fittest, accompanied by a non-egalitarian defence of employer prerogative within the employment contractual relationship. It is this which explains the section in the New Zealand Employment Contracts Act which makes the rest of that Act incoherent by contemporary contractualist standards: namely, section 57, which states that alleged 'harsh and oppressive' employment contracts can be determined by the Employment Court 'only on the application of a party to the contract and not of its own motion', nor it would seem of any third party. The section concludes with an extraordinarily arbitrary assertion of the non-contractualist and patrimonial principle of employer prerogative: 'Except as provided in this section, the Court shall have no jurisdiction to set aside or modify, or grant relief in respect of, any employment contract under the law relating to unfair or unconscionable bargains'.

Abandonment of the value of equality, however, is a minority position which cannot command legitimacy under contemporary conditions of liberal democracy. Contemporary contractualism can be made to serve, not to undermine, the value of equality. Consider, for example, the principle of designing services around the needs of individuals, rather than the other way around. Thus, the dismissal of contemporary contractualism as an inegalitarian, economically rationalist ethic is inadequate to the terms of the current debate.

The second critique is a feminist one. Liberal contractualism assumes that individuals are always already 'individuals', i.e. independent people who possess a mature, autonomous capacity for rational choice. As classical liberalism and utilitarianism argue, this rules out of the contractualist picture all those whose contractual capacity is neither sufficiently developed nor sufficiently autonomous. This obviously excludes children, and traditionally it has also excluded those whose cognitive or mental capacity is held to be so impaired or immature as to prevent them from making autonomous judgements of their own interest.

The feminist theorists who talk in terms of a combined ethic of care and empowerment appear to address and correct these exclusions. Theorists such as Virginia Held or Carol Gilligan counterpose to contractualist assumptions of an independent, even autarchic, individuality an individuality that is relational. They use the mothering relationship as their ethical model, a relationship which is socially and morally adequate only if the mother is oriented to the well-being and development of her child as a particular other. Virginia Held counterposes contractualism and maternal morality in this way:

> Morality, for mothering persons, must guide us in our relations with actual, particular children, enabling them to develop their own lives and commitments. For mothering persons, morality can never seem adequate if it offers no more than ideal rules for hypothetical situations: morality must connect with the actual context of real, particular others in need. At the same time, morality, for mothering persons, cannot possibly be a mere bargain between rational contractors. That morality in this context could not be based on self-interest or mutual lack of interest is obvious; that a contractual escape is unavailable or inappropriate is clear enough.[11]

Held's argument that mothering involves an ethic which cannot be accounted for by liberal contractualism is correct as far as it goes.[12] By emphasizing the inability of the child to contract in or out of this relationship, and the correlative inability of the ethical mother to contract in or out of allowing this child to be dependent on her, Held is effectively restating the classical liberal exclusion of children from contract. However, by her insistence on the effects of this exclusion for the adequacy of political and ethical theory, this is more than just its restatement.

Yet Held is involved in a difficulty which reflects her inability to develop an internal critique of contractualism. Let her speak, for the moment:

> The relation between mothering person and child is not voluntary and therefore not contractual. The ties that bind mothering person and child are affectional and solicitous on the one hand, and emotional and dependent on the other. The degree to which bearing and caring for children has been voluntary for most mothers throughout most of history has been extremely limited . . . The relation should be voluntary for the mothering person, but it cannot possibly be so for the young child, and it can only become, gradually, slightly more voluntary.

> If we begin with the picture of rational contractor entering into agreements with others, the natural condition is seen as one of individuality and privacy, and the problem is the building of society and government. From the point of view of the relation between the mothering person and child, the problem is the reverse. The starting condition is an enveloping tie, and the problem is individuating oneself. The task is to carve out a gradually increasing measure of privacy in ways appropriate to a constantly shifting interdependency. For the child the problem is to become gradually more independent. For the mothering person, the problem is to free oneself from an all-consuming involvement. For both, the progression is from society to greater individuality rather than from self-sufficient individuality to contractual ties.[13]

'The starting condition is an enveloping tie, and the problem is individuating oneself.' By this statement, Held turns the process of parenting into one of nurturing the progressive empowerment of individualized agency. Thus, mothering as care–cum–empowerment is a derived rather than an independent or complementary ethic in respect of contractualism taken in its broader sense. This is precisely why modern liberal–republican discourse distilled the idea of 'republican motherhood',[14] and why, generally, liberalism has left mothering as a relatively unspecified, privatized relationship.

To argue that the individual qua unit of individualized action requires, in Talcott Parsons' famous formulation, 'to be made not born'[15] only goes so far in challenging liberal contractualism. Liberal contractualism is oriented to the fully formed contractual capacities of the individualized actor, not to how they were acquired. To show this to be a serious theoretical and practical problem requires something different from what Held is up to. She concedes the territory of the fully formed contractual individual — even though she does not approve of its individualistic ethic — and thereby seems to suggest that liberalism is adequate to its own turf at least. Logically, this forces those who have less than fully adequate contractual capacity to become residual categories.

Held could do something different. This would be to intervene on liberalism's own ground, to show that its contractualist understanding is less than adequately contractualist. Held concedes that empirical mothering persons are not all that she — and we — would have them be: 'the relation may in a degenerate form be one of domination and submission'.[16] At this point she needs to enquire into the grounds of her standard of adequacy for the mothering relationship. If they are the nurturance of an empowered, individualized agentic capacity in the one who has been child to this relationship, then she is using contractualist standards for the ethic of this relationship. This is a modern ethic for the parent–child relationship which social contract theorists like Locke and Rousseau had already conceived. Held does not enquire into how a mothering person contributes to, even constitutes, the individualized capacity of a newly emergent actor. This enquiry can proceed only as it is informed by enquiry into what it would mean simultaneously to deform this emergent individualized capacity by tying it to the needs of the mothering person's personality — that is, tying it to ongoing symbiosis. In this, Held, like the liberal contractualists she criticizes, tends to take individualized agentic capacity for granted.

In this connection, incidentally, Talcott Parsons' insistence that the second and contractually oriented parent (the father) must intervene in the maternal symbiosis, and draw the young child away from this locus of identity towards an individualized one, does not explain how individualized agentic capacity is possible. All it explains is a specific gender formation of contractualist identity, where individualization is mistakenly identified with a masculinist insistence on an autarchic model of independence in relation to others.[17]

This brings us to the third external critique of contractualism, that offered by the neo-Foucaultian theorists of governmentality. Contract for these theorists is a technology of what they term neo-liberal government. The virtue of this perspective is that it understands the relational character of individualized or, as it would say, autonomized action.[18] Thus, marketization, privatization, devolution and contractualization are all technologies of government which fit the modern regime of regulation, where government works by means of the self-regulating capacities of citizens as these are informed by the normalizing effects of professional expertise, among other things.

The critical value of this perspective is its ability to see through the rhetorical fictions of liberalism, to show how it legitimizes a particular regulative regime even when it is talking the language of de-regulation. It can do this precisely because of its interest in the discursive practices by which individualized units of contractual capacity are formed. However, this interest turns out to be more formal than substantive in character.

Because this perspective is oriented to the sociological project of inverting liberalism's assumptions — to the proposition that the individual's capacity for autonomous action is socially determined — it does not enquire into the substance of what it means to be an individualized unit of agency. It does not provide a criterion whereby we can discriminate between different kinds of individualizing governmental practices. Or, if it can in principle do this, it cannot provide a criterion for discriminating when individualizing governmental practices are adopted on behalf of non-contractualist principles, and thus suborned by principles contrary to them. I have in mind such cases as when a doctor or social worker uses contractualist protocols, but makes them over to paternalistic or maternalistic principles of speaking on behalf of another in the determination of their needs and interests. To be able to recognise when this is occurring requires a substantive criterion of individualizing governmental practice which, in turn, cannot evade normatively oriented analysis.

Conclusion

I have argued that the new contractualism is a broader ethos of self-regulated social relationships than is adequately captured in liberal contractualist discourse. This ethos informs the terms of oppositional critique and contestation of contemporary social movements in the liberal democracies. It is not clear, however, whether these traditions of critique, or the more established left traditions of critique of liberal contractualism, understand this, or whether contemporary contractualism has broken out of its traditional liberal frameworks.

Instead of anti-contractualist discourse of the kinds represented by the external critiques I have identified, we would be better off asking questions which critically accept the pervasiveness of the contemporary ethos of contractualism, and of our difficulty in escaping it. Such questions would be: How should we understand this contractualism? What are its many and different permutations? Can an orientation to a democratically oriented, individualized agency escape contractualist norms and assumptions? In what ways do contractualist protocols both reproduce and contest inequalities of power? What are the limits of contemporary contractualism, and how might we test them?

These are questions of considerable practical significance. For example, feminists currently have to decide their position on the extension of enterprise bargaining, and its implications for women workers, especially those in low-paid and often casualized jobs. Generally, in Australia at least, the feminist response has been the nostalgic gesture of holding onto a centralized wage-fixing system. This is a nostalgic gesture because, empirically, it is to lock the stable door after the horse has bolted and, normatively, it means holding onto a patrimonial–paternalistic principle of wage fixing. It is not clear whether this is in the interests of women regarded as individualized agents. And, if we do not want to regard women as individualized agents, where does this leave them?

At the same time, we can grant the premise that, in enterprise bargaining, most women workers are poorly positioned to be effective contractual agents. There is an alternative response to this difficulty, and that is to argue that the new contractualism should be more adequately contractual: specifically, that women's (as all individuals') entitlement as effective contractual agents in enterprise bargaining be statutorily recognized, the presumption of employer prerogative in the employment relationship be statutorily disestablished, and that employment contractual capacities of both employees and employers be socially developed and resourced.

I have suggested here also that our theoretical understanding of individualized or self-regulatory social relationships is not all that developed, because of our tendency to naturalize the freely contracting individual which liberalism celebrates. Where sociology intervenes to insist on the social determination of individualized capacity, we have a good start on a more serious theoretical enquiry into the nature and conditions of individualized agency. However, this is the case only if we take this individualized agency seriously — that is, not cancel it because it is both socially determined and a particular type of social relationship.

Notes

1 The relevant sections of the 1991 Employment Contracts Act are 5, 9, 10 and 18.

2 See P. S. Atiyah, *Essays on Contract* (Oxford, Clarendon Press, 1986), especially chapters 2 and 6.

3 *Ibid.*, p.12.

4 *Ibid.*, p.128. Atiyah's conception of cooling-off periods and the like in terms of the discourse of 'consumer protection' fits the general view of these things. However, we might question the use of the metaphor 'protection' to refer to instances of regulation which have as their purpose the extension or resourcing of people's capacities for self-regulation. If this question makes sense, then it is not paternalism we have in view but the use of the state's power of legitimate domination for democratic purposes.

5 See G. Majone, 'Professionalism and Mutual Adjustment', in F. X. Kaufmann (ed.), *The Public Sector: Challenge for Coordination and Learning* (Berlin, De Gruyter, 1991), pp.451–69.

6 From Jon Elster, *Nuts and Bolts for the Social Sciences* (Cambridge, Cambridge University Press, 1989), p.30.

7 This is not the case with tribal identities, as Perrett remarks in the traditional Maori case. See Roy Perrett, 'Individualism, Justice and the Maori View of the Self', in G. Oddie and R. Perrett (eds), *Justice, Ethics and New Zealand Society* (Auckland, Oxford University Press, 1992), pp.27–41.

8 Jon Elster, 'Introduction' to Jon Elster (ed.), *Rational Choice* (Oxford, Blackwell, 1986), p.3.

9 As Roy Perrett argues, the purchase of methodological individualism cannot extend to tribal societies such as traditional Maori society: see Perrett, 'Individualism, Justice and the Maori View of the Self'.

10 Roy Perrett's characterization (p.29) of the non-individualistic nature of the traditional Maori view of the self is a useful counterpoint here: 'A person's identity is determined predominantly by his or her inherited status and relationship to the larger social group, membership of which is genealogically determined. This is carried to the point where what Pakeha would think of as an individual is identified with the kinship group — hence the use in Maori of the personal pronoun *I (au)* to refer to either the individual or the tribe. A chief, for example, will often speak of his tribe as himself . . . The kinship *I* reaches both backwards and forwards in time. A chief narrating a piece of tribal history relating events before his own birth will nevertheless speak in the first person of the *I* that underwent them, i.e. the kinship *I* which absorbs the individual *I* . . . Kairangatira, when alone and surrounded by enemies about to slay him, is reported to have said: "You will kill me, my tribe will kill you and the country will be *mine*." Here the *mine* implies his identity with the tribe in the future which follows his own death.'

11 Virginia Held, *Feminist Morality: Transforming Culture, Society and Politics* (Chicago

and London, University of Chicago Press, 1993), p.211.

12 Held deliberately uses the phrase 'mothering person' not to suggest that men cannot mother, but to emphasize (a) that this is not a biological but a social relation in which men can participate, and (b) that our conceptions of what it is to nurture children are not free from our preconceptions that this is women's business. See Held, *Feminist Morality*, pp.197–98, p.200.

13 *Ibid.*, p.204 and p.208 for these respective passages, emphasis in the original.

14 See Joan Landes, *Women and the Public Sphere in the Age of the French Revolution* (Ithaca, Cornell University Press, 1988).

15 'It is because the *human* personality is not "born" but must be "made" through the socialization process that in the first instance families are necessary.' Talcott Parsons, 'The American Family: Its Relations to Personality and the Social Structure', in T. Parsons and R. F. Bales, *Family, Socialization and Interaction Process* (New York, Free Press, 1955), p.16.

16 Held, *Feminist Morality*, p.209.

17 Parsons' analysis is of course indebted to that of Freud, but, more generally, it recapitulates the schema to be found in all classical sociological theory where, in order to be individualized, the child has to be wrested out of an originary community of identity with the mother and inducted into contractualist, civil society. Compare Tönnies's *Gemeinschaft and Gesellschaft*. Parsons' analyis is to be found in chapters 1 and 2 of Parsons and Bales. It is restated by this time through the lens of feminist critique by Nancy Chodorow in *The Reproduction of Mothering* (Berkeley, University of California Press, 1978); there Chodorow shows that Parsons' assumptions about individualization apply only to boys, and that they presuppose a gender division of labour as a given. This is further support for my general point here that individualized agency tends to be more naturalized than it is problematized. It is problematized on this account only insofar as it is assumed that boy children require to be wrested out of their originary symbiotic identity shared with the mother, an identity which it is further presupposed she has a vested interest in maintaining.

18 See Nikolas Rose and Peter Miller, 'Political Power Beyond the State: Problematics of Government', *British Journal of Sociology* 43: 2 (1992), p.199.

CHAPTER SEVEN

Who Signs the Contract?
Applying Agency Theory to Politicians

GLYN DAVIS AND MARGARET GARDNER[1]

The contract state appears imminent. Agency theory, stressing the advantage of legally binding performance agreements over more traditional bureaucratic structures, sweeps all before it. New Zealand demonstrates the power of the agency model, the way a single, simple idea can be applied across the range of state activity, from the delivery of the largest services, such as defence and health, to the precise details of individual relationships between ministers and chief executives.

Yet amid the cascading stream of contracts from Parliament down to the most humble public servant and private contractor, one group has conspicuously escaped being caught in the flow. While politicians sign contracts with agencies and agents, parliamentarians are not held to account as the logic of the contract model requires. Yet why should those imposing the contract state be immune from its rigours?

This question of consistency evoked controversy in Australia in the early 1990s, when the parliamentary opposition announced its intention to follow New Zealand and replace traditional arbitral systems with individual contracts between the buyers and sellers of labour, allowing no role for third parties. The proposal was clearly based on the principal–agent model, yet it was never explained how politicians would avoid the charge of proposing policy which applied to everyone but themselves. This chapter explores that dilemma of applying agency theory to members of Parliament. Though the example is drawn from Australia, the argument might work in any parliamentary system — just as the weaknesses of the agency model become evident wherever it is applied to employment relations.

A Contract Model of Employment

In 1992, John Howard, the Shadow Minister for Industrial Relations, offered the electorate a radical reshaping of Australia's employment relations. The Liberal/National Coalition policy document *Jobsback!* argued for an end to compulsory arbitration. It would be replaced by enterprise bargaining, in which employers and employees negotiate directly, recording their agreement in an employment contract. Industrial relations would become the province of contracts and the 'ordinary courts', with little further role for trade unions acting as representatives of groups of employees. Despite a subsequent poll loss, *Jobsback!* remains Coalition policy.

The Liberal proposal is clear about its underpinning: employment is a contract arrangement between consenting parties reached in private. Soon after the policy release, the following exchange occurred:[2]

> Journalist: How will you set pay rates for politicians, and avoid the accusation that it's one rule for everyone else and a different one for you?
>
> John Howard: I would love to find a device whereby you could negotiate with representatives of the electorate. The problem is we're the representatives of the electorate and if we are seen to be negotiating with ourselves, everybody says that that's a fix. Um, I think probably relating salaries to movements in community levels, which is in a sense what we have now, is about the best you're going to get.
>
> Journalist: Isn't that comparative wage justice which you are ruling out for other people?
>
> John Howard: No, I don't think so. We're in an unusual position, because we are the governors as well as the supplicants, if I can put it that way. I state the principle. I am perfectly happy to have our pay governed by the policy that I am proposing for the Australian population. And if someone can divine an effective workable way of doing that, I will grab it with both hands.

John Howard has a reputation for honesty, and in this exchange with the journalists of *Meet the Press* he frankly confronted the difficulties of applying his policy proposals universally. At issue is the logic which underpins the Coalition's industrial relations policy. For, if the policy cannot embrace those who propose it, why should the electorate accept the deal on offer? As the reporters imply, there is a moral responsibility on politicians to demonstrate by example rather than exhortation their commitment to major policy changes.

In *Jobsback!*, released on October 20, 1992, Howard proposed the most radical reshaping of Australian employment relations since the prime ministership of Stanley Bruce. *Jobsback!* offered 34 pages of argument and prescription based on direct negotiations between an employer and employee 'without the mandatory intervention of trade unions, employer organisations or industrial tribunals'.[3] Howard preferred contractual relationships to the traditional award system. These relationships would be subject only to minimum conditions, including a minimum hourly rate of pay, to provide 'effective safeguards against exploitation by any unscrupulous employers'.[4]

The effect of these changes, according to the Coalition, would be high productivity and high wages, with workplace reform enhancing 'personal freedom and flexibility'.[5] *Jobsback!* derived its direction and coherence from applying the principal–agent model to industrial relations. The principal–agent theory seeks to take into account the conflicting interests of two players in a negotiation, and then to specify pay-offs for each in a contract.[6] Each player is assumed to pursue their self-interest, with exchanges governed by competition between those interests. Because both sides can state their expectations precisely, and make these binding, maximum return to each is ensured if a contract is reached. The principal, the employer, can hire agents on terms appropriate to the enterprise. The market, in principle, clears at a freely determined price of labour, rather than following the dictates of a centralized arbitration body.

For this logic to prevail, the Coalition must ensure that employment becomes a private, contractual arrangement between two parties, rather than a regulated exchange by representative organizations with state instrumentality as the final arbiter. To this end, *Jobsback!* proposed a significant winding-back of arbitral institutions. The scope of industrial awards, reached through the Australian Industrial Relations Commission (AIRC), was to be 'sharply' reduced.[7] The AIRC would assess the economic impact of its remaining functions according to objectives set by government. There would be no further national wage cases, and the power to award strike pay would be removed. Consistent with an emphasis on individual contracts, authority over individual matters should be dealt with by courts rather than specialised industrial relations jurisdictions.

Jobsback! was explicit about which parties have a legitimate interest in employment contracts. The policy required that 'workplace agreements can be concluded only between individual employers and one, some or all of their employees. Unions or employer organisations — or any other agent of the signatories — cannot be parties to a workplace agreement.'[8] In particular, *Jobsback!* was concerned that unions should no longer be effective players in setting employment conditions. The range of proposed restrictions, or removal of legislative supports for unions and employer associations, included an end to compulsory membership, abolition of monopoly representation rights, discarding minimum union size restrictions, strengthening sections 45D and E of the Trade Practices Act to provide companies with 'protection against the predatory conduct of certain trade unions',[9] ministerial deregulation of unions following AIRC investigations, sequestering of union funds to ensure payment of fines, and a five-year bar on office holders of deregistered unions. These were to be separate from the fines to be levied against unions which break 'the rule of law'.

Cumulatively, these proposals were designed to remove appeal to the state, through arbitral commissions, and to take trade unions and employer associations out of the employment relationship. This would become the preserve of individual principals and their prospective individual agents, as Australia followed the New Zealand precedent of individual employment contracts.

Howard's policy acknowledged that some employers and their employees might jointly elect to remain within the arbitration system, though little incentive was provided for employers to do so. Parties who stayed in the system would be encouraged to restructure their current award as an enterprise bargain, and the policy assumed that employment relations would eventually be conducted exclusively within the Coalition's framework. The document was presented as tending to the universal, rather than as specific to particular industries, workplaces or categories of employer. Certainly the restrictions on the AIRC, and the threat to use commonwealth constitutional powers if state governments did not pass complementary legislation, suggest an expectation that the new framework would be comprehensive. In *Jobsback!* the Coalition signalled a belief that contractual arrangements between principals and agents would be the dominant model for Australian industrial relations. It must be of concern, therefore, if this model could not potentially accommodate some employment situations.

To succeed, principal–agent relations require clear identification of the employer and employee, definition of the tasks which are the basis of the contract, and agreement on indicators to use when monitoring performance and, on expiry, renegotiating the contract. As John Howard acknowledged on *Meet the Press*, politicians appear to fail those tests. In Howard's assessment, the distinction between principal and agent is blurred. Politicians both work to a salary and define that income. If asked to sign a contract they would be 'negotiating with themselves'. Similarly, one might argue that the tasks involved are not well defined. Further, few performance indicators exist for members of Parliament. There are, of course, proxy measures such as local reputation, but in a party-dominated parliamentary system elected representatives largely stand or fall with the fortunes of their party.

Clearly, for a policy based on individual contracts rather than collective performance, current employment arrangements for members of Parliament are unsatisfactory. It does not help the Coalition's cause if one group of workers, our elected representatives, escape the requirement for direct negotiation with their principals which will be expected of others. The problem is politically embarrassing, since it may imply different standards within the community. More significantly, the omission may indicate a gap in principal–agent theory, since it suggests that at least one group — and therefore perhaps others — cannot be encompassed within the model.

If this gap is to be plugged, the Coalition must define the enterprise of being a member of Parliament, and the principal who is qualified to sign a contract. The issue is not just of philosophical interest. The Kennett Government in Victoria made the question of politicians' salaries one of immediate political salience. Some of Premier Kennett's first actions were of immediate benefit to parliamentarians. These included a substantial wage increase in some Coalition MP salaries, introduced in the Parliamentary Salaries and Superannuation Bill 1992. Media comment focused on the apparent incongruity of Industrial Relations Minister Phil Gude being awarded an annual $8,900 increase in the same week as Parliament was asked to abolish the 17.5 per cent holiday loading and weekend penalty rates for Victorian workers under state awards. Minister Gude defended his windfall as part of a new 'career structure for MPs' but, recognising the political damage, quickly announced he would not accept the salary increase. Premier Kennett conceded it had been 'wrong' to push the pay rises through Parliament, and the issue appeared over.[10]

Yet the real question is not the merit of particular wage settlements, but acceptable process. By repudiating the rises, Kennett only deferred the problem. For Victoria was just the first Australian jurisdiction to face this particular conundrum: how, in an age of principal–agent contracts, should the salary of MPs be set? If parliamentarians 'negotiate with themselves', the public may be less than impressed. Yet other mechanisms, such as an independent tribunal, offend against the principal–agent model by allowing a third party to intervene, at the cost of flexibility and the loss of real market rates. Any federal Coalition ministry now faces the same dilemma of how to increase the salaries of its own members without apparently violating the rules imposed on the rest of the community. Finding a way to extend thorough-going enterprise bargaining to members of Parliament is likely to remain a difficult political issue until policy and practice can be brought into harmony.

Current Wage-Fixing Arrangements for Parliamentarians

Along with New Zealand, Australia was among the first democracies to insist on payment of parliamentarians; sections 48 and 66 of the Australian Constitution provide an explicit authority for salaries and allowances to MPs and ministers.[11] The issue, thereafter, has been how such remuneration should be determined.

At first the process was relatively *ad hoc*. Parliament would simply pass legislation setting salaries and allowances, often following agitation from government MPs. From 1952 such legislation usually followed the report of an independent committee of inquiry. Only in 1971 did such an inquiry propose a three-person tribunal to recommend future allowances for parliamentarians. The inquiry report noted the importance of getting such salaries right:

> That the Parliamentary salary should not be so low as to constitute an entry barrier to gifted and highly-qualified people is beyond argument. The salary level at which this barrier may be created for an increasing number of well-educated and experienced persons in the professions and in technological and business pursuits is a matter of judgement. We deem it of special importance that the Parliament attract as Members sufficient numbers of able persons to ensure in the ministries of the future the breadth of expertise and experience required to meet the demands of government.[12]

Here the inquiry panel advanced a familiar argument about members' salaries: while an unregulated market might leave parliamentary salaries low, there is a public interest in paying MPs sufficiently to ensure a reasonable cross-section of talent and qualifications. The panel suggested an independent tribunal as an appropriate mechanism to address this collective action problem, by creating an independent umpire who could take politicians' pay outside the gift of parliamentarians. MPs could be suitably compensated without the accusation of looking after themselves.

The Remuneration Tribunal began operations in December 1973, making annual determinations for members of Parliament, judges and public office holders. The tribunal established a basic parliamentary allowance for MPs, with a detailed schedule of loadings for chairing a parliamentary committee, being opposition whip in the Senate, or occupying posts such as Speaker, minister or prime minister. The tribunal also determined all other allowances for parliamentarians, including money for travel, vehicles and electorate expenses. The formula varied depending on the size of electorate, nights spent in Canberra while Parliament was sitting, travel as a committee member, and so on. Generally governments accepted the recommendations, though on several occasions Cabinet, for reasons of public presentation, resolved to reduce entitlements proposed by the tribunal.

In practice, the tribunal followed the procedures of other specialized arbitral bodies, hearing cases and setting uniform salaries for MPs, with loadings for additional duties. The tribunal mechanism appeared to reduce, though it did not eliminate, criticism of politicians' pay increases. Indeed, in 1990 John Howard complained to Parliament that MP salaries 'lag significantly behind what on any objective analysis would be remuneration that the officers in question are entitled to receive'. The problem, Howard seemed to suggest, is that even with an independent tribunal parliamentarians still shy from the publicity which accompanies a pay rise. 'The measure of self-imposed salary restraint by members of the Parliament', Howard noted, 'at the behest of governments of both political persuasions, has been very considerable and has been greater than that exercised by other sections of the community.'[13]

This pattern of tribunal deliberations and Cabinet nervousness continued until the High Court of Australia unexpectedly ruled that the government did not have power to supplement a determination of the tribunal by providing a postal entitlement to MPs. With that decision, the High Court threw into doubt the validity of payments not explicitly authorized by an Act of Parliament. Accordingly, the government felt compelled to legislate for new remuneration arrangements. Henceforth the income for all parliamentarians would be determined by the Remuneration and Allowances Act 1990. Instead of separately determining an MP's income, the 1990 Act directly ties the annual base salary of a federal member of Parliament to the maximum annual salary of a band 1 senior executive service officer in the Australian public service.[14] The Act then specifies the loadings payable for higher office, along with electoral allowances. Other expenses, such as travel, photocopying and postage, are covered by the complementary Parliamentary Entitlements Act 1990.

The patterns for state Parliaments vary slightly, but most jurisdictions simply link local salaries to those paid in Canberra. In New South Wales, for example, the Parliamentary Remuneration Act 1989 defines the basic salary of an MP as $500 per annum less than that of a federal member, with loadings for higher office expressed as a percentage of the basic salary. Similar arrangements have prevailed in Queensland, under the Parliamentary Members Salary Act 1988, and in Victoria, until the Kennett Government, under the Parliamentary Salaries and Remuneration Act 1968. In South Australia the Parliamentary Remuneration Act 1990 establishes the basic salary as $1000 less than that awarded to a federal member. Only in Western Australia is pay still in the hands of an independent Salaries and Allowances Tribunal, while in Tasmania the wonderfully titled Parliamentary Salaries and Allowances (Doubts Removal and Amendments) Act 1988 ties the salary of an MP to that of a state employee working under the Clerical Employees Award who was earning $40,102 per annum on April 1, 1988.

New South Wales, Queensland and Victoria all adopted their current arrangements while the federal Remuneration Tribunal still operated. These jurisdictions, along with South Australia, avoid stating any contestable principle for determining wage rates by relying on the commonwealth; a rise in federal MPs' salaries automatically triggers an increase at state level. While this is a convenient mechanism for local politicians to avoid the opprobrium of voting themselves more pay, it does not resolve the central issue of how federal MPs' rates should be set. Linking salaries to the public service does not overcome the blurring of principal and agent. On the contrary, it provides MPs in Canberra and Hobart with a direct incentive to increase the remuneration of a particular rank of public servants — for, in negotiating with their employees, parliamentarians effectively are negotiating with themselves.

Hence current practice, at both federal and state levels, provides no mechanism consistent with the objectives of *Jobsback!*, or the values of the agency model. Parliamentary salaries everywhere are set either by proxy, through public service relativities, or by the surviving remuneration tribunal in Western Australia. There are no direct negotiations between a principal and the parliamentarian as agent. Further, there is no flexibility in the current system. All MPs are paid the same basic salary, with higher office bringing returns only on a fixed scale for position, with no weighting for performance. Such arrangements exhibit no capacity for individual bargaining, and no opportunity to test prevailing market rates. Finally, there is no binding contract — an MP can resign at any time, without penalty for failing to see through the parliamentary term.[15] If *Jobsback!* is to apply to this important area of endeavour, a new system of employment relations for MPs is required.

Who Do Parliamentarians Work For?

A viable principal–agent relationship must begin with clarity about who precisely is the employer — which organization, group or individual has the right, even duty, to sign a contract with a parliamentarian? For MPs there is a surprising number of candidates: the institution of Parliament, a political party represented, or the electorate. If the right to hire and fire is taken as defining for an employer, then Parliament itself is quickly ruled out as the principal. Rather, Parliament is a workplace, an industrial site with office space and a set of rules for agents chosen elsewhere. Deciding between parties and the electorate, however, is not so easily resolved. Here ancient, conflicting views about the nature of representative government come into play. The role of an MP — and, by implication, the identification of the employer — has always been a contested issue in Australian politics, a matter of fundamental division between the Australian Labor Party (ALP) and the Liberal/National Party (LNCP) Coalition, not to mention any independent members of Parliament.

Debate has turned on the 'Labor pledge'. Though organized political parties were beginning to emerge in the colonial parliaments of the later nineteenth century, coalitions still tended to be fluid and issue-based; if pressed, most MPs might have professed to hold a broadly consistent ideological position, but to follow their consciences on any particular vote. When Labor MPs first entered the NSW Legislative Assembly in 1891 and found themselves holding the balance of power, they immediately realized that success in achieving the objectives of a minority party depended on discipline and solidarity. If Labor MPs hung together they could make or break majorities in the Assembly. To this end, these Labor parliamentarians signed the first 'pledge' guaranteeing to vote 'as a majority of the party may agree'.[16] In effect, the Labor MPs fashioned themselves as delegates of a political party, rather than as individual representatives of various electorates. The pledge ensured solidarity; voting against the party meant expulsion, and so a loss of official Labor endorsement.

Leslie Finn Crisp identifies two sources for the party pledge: the tactical necessities of the early parliamentary years, and the influence of trade unions in emphasizing solidarity once a decision had been democratically reached.[17] For non-Labor politicians, however, the pledge was a challenge to the very sovereignty of Parliament. As Joseph Cook, briefly an NSW Labor MP but subsequently a Liberal Prime Minister, argued, 'the pledge destroys the representative character of a Member and abrogates the electoral privileges of a constituency'.[18] The charge that Labor parliamentarians were not their own masters but simply agents of a shadowy external organization would be levelled at the ALP through most of this century, culminating in Menzies' clever 'faceless men' campaign of 1963, which invited the Australian electorate to pass judgement on a party which would not allow its parliamentary leaders to participate in internal party debates. Only with the Whitlam-led reforms to the party's governance structure in the late 1960s did the balance of influence shift toward Labor's elected representatives. Yet, while the accusations of external control have diminished, the pledge remains, along with the threat of expulsion for those Labor MPs who do not see the party, and its parliamentary caucus, as their principal.

Non-Labor MPs point to a different, older tradition. They emphasize two aspects of their job: one the responsibility to represent their electorate, but the other duty to their conscience. If these interests clash, conscience is to prevail. Typically, this philosophy is attributed to the English parliamentarian Edmund Burke, who declared that a member of Parliament owed the electors 'his [*sic*] unbiased opinion, his mature judgement, his enlightened conscience' but not the slavish following of their wishes.[19] This independence eventually proved too much for the electors of Bristol,

who threw Burke out of Parliament after just six years, but he returned
as a representative of a rotten borough to serve in total nearly three
decades in the House of Commons. Burke's ideas on representation
remain a significant influence on conservative thought, along with his
scepticism about precipitate change in civic institutions.[20] Burke suggests
a complex relationship between the elected and the electorate: MPs
must strive to advance the values they espoused at the polls, regardless
of the fickle views of voters. Thus the electorate is clearly the principal,
but it selects an agent who cannot be expected meekly to take instruc-
tion.[21] The contract made on polling day must override other, later
considerations.

Echoes of this commitment to electorate and conscience are still heard
on the non-Labor side of politics. In his maiden speech to the House
of Representatives on September 26, 1974, for example, John Howard paid
the obligatory homage to the people who put him into Parliament:

> I want to record, very simply, a sense of honour and privilege at being elected
> to represent the people of Bennelong. I do not profess for a moment that I
> now know all the problems of the electorate of Bennelong. I can only promise
> that in the time ahead I will do my very best to represent those people and
> to look after and cater for their needs.[22]

Though speaking at a time of great political tension, Howard then
characteristically demonstrated his conscience by supporting a number
of initiatives contained in a recent Labor Government budget, including
a new $10 a week handicapped child's allowance. Such concessions were
firmly nestled within an overall condemnation of Treasurer Crean's
handiwork, and an eloquent affirmation of loyalty to the Liberal Party
of Australia.

Other Liberals were less expansive about their conscience and their
role. While Liberal Party founder Sir Robert Menzies devoted his maiden
speech in the Commonwealth Parliament to the potential link between
unemployment and industrial relations,[23] on other occasions he stressed
the different understanding of a parliamentarian's role held by the non-
Labor parties. His speeches to the October 1944 Canberra meeting which
created the Liberal Party balanced the need for an effective national party
organization with the importance of the Liberals not becoming the
captive of any external group. Indeed, Graeme Starr argues that this
difference in belief about representation is linked fundamentally to the

origins of the various Australian political parties.[24] While Labor and the Country Party represented incursions into Parliament by organized interests, 'the Liberal Party was conceived as a parliamentary group in need of organizational support, rather than as an extra-parliamentary body seeking legislative representation'. In his admiration for the technical efficiency of the ALP, but his distaste for the cage of the pledge, Menzies might have been paraphrasing Burke, who advocated the party system on the principle that 'when bad men combine, the good must associate'.[25]

The non-Labor tradition thus identifies the electorate as the employer, with the parliamentarian obliged to serve its interests whenever these do not clash with his or her conscience. As Christopher Publick and Robert Southey see Liberal Party philosophy, it supports 'a party system in which the maximum freedom of individual expression, conscience and action is encouraged. This means a rejection of iron laws of party discipline in favour of responsible individual initiative.'[26] Should conflict arise, the Liberal MP votes according to principle, then submits to the discipline of the polls — even if, as in Burke's case, this independence proves more than the electorate will abide.

This consensus among Coalition MPs about the identity of their employers is central to the successful implementation of a principal–agent model. If the ALP had proposed the policy, there would be an important question about whether it is the electorate or the party itself which should meet the expense of maintaining MPs. The Coalition, however, operates within a tradition of more direct accountability links between a parliamentarian and voters. This heritage proves unexpectedly useful in reshaping employment relations since, at least for those on the Coalition side, it settles any ambiguity about the nature of the enterprise and so who can sign the contract. It now remains only to identify a mechanism by which MPs as agents can meaningfully negotiate contracts with their electorates as principals, and so honour the logic of *Jobsback!*

A Contract for Parliamentarians

Within days of the *Jobsback!* announcement, correspondents to major newspapers were expressing concern about consistency. As Henry Haszler from Eltham in Victoria told the *Australian Financial Review* on October 29, 1992:

I agree we need a more flexible labour market, so I do support the general thrust of the policies announced by Mr Howard. But to convince me I would like Mr Howard, and Mr Kennett, to tell me what system they propose for setting their own salaries . . . Who will act as the 'employer' in their case . . . will there be different rates of pay for individual backbenchers . . . what criteria will apply in setting salaries of individual MPs . . . will MPs be sackable at short notice on the same basis as other people? If, in the end, MP's salaries and perks continue to be set by some tribunal or arbitrator, why is that not also good enough for the rest of us?

Other correspondents suggested answers to these challenges. L. G. Norman of Naremburn in New South Wales told the *Sydney Morning Herald* on November 10, 1992 that a committee of electors should negotiate an individual contract with any successful electoral candidate. This would almost certainly lead to differential rates for MPs doing the same job — 'unfair, perhaps, but such are the joys of the marketplace', noted Norman. The proposal included productivity bonuses for intelligent contributions to public policy debates, and penalties for early resignation. In the same edition of the *Sydney Morning Herald* G. J. R. Seeger of Port Macquarie, New South Wales also urged that parliamentarians be required to negotiate with their constituents, and should be answerable for honouring their election promises. 'Politicians', suggested Seeger, should not 'be exempt from their own radical legislation'.

These are promising starts, since each proposal seeks to fulfil the conditions of the principal–agent model: an individual employment contract with specified expectations, a performance monitoring system, and sanctions for failing to meet the terms reached in negotiation. More problematic is how the electorate should express its will as the principal. A representative committee of voters does not resolve that difficulty, since a committee in turn could not be certain of expressing the majority view and would, in any case, constitute a third party negotiating on behalf of the parties to an agreement. What is needed is a procedure which offers the electorate clear options so that, in selecting a candidate, the voters are also nominating the terms of a binding contract. While several such arrangements are feasible, we suggest that the following rules could satisfy the requirements of *Jobsback!* with minimum additional cost or regulation.

The key is the Commonwealth Electoral Act 1918 and its many successors, which already include disclosure requirements for candidates, albeit only in terms of name, address, party affiliation, solvency and so forth. The legislation could be extended so that candidates present the full terms of the contract they offer the electorate. This would include the real costs of electing that person (salary, entitlements, electorate office expenses) plus the additional increments they would expect if elected to a party leadership or ministry position. Would-be MPs could pitch their bid to the capacity of the particular electorate to pay, so that Australia's distribution of incomes would be broadly reflected inside Parliament.

Further, candidates could be required to list the services they would offer the electorate if selected. These must be services directly in the candidate's control, and paid from the total cost package put before the electorate. Items might include electorate office locations, opening hours, turn-around on electoral enquiries, guaranteed annual attendance at community organization meetings, and so on. Excluded would be benefits beyond the direct gift (and budget) of an individual MP, such as a new school or hospital for the electorate.

The objective of these minimum contract terms, which should be required by electoral legislation, is to quantify the costs and returns to the principal if they select a particular candidate. If they wish, candidates could go beyond these minima, and commit themselves to any level of detail on services or substantial policy. They could, for example, pledge themselves to the ALP platform as interpreted by caucus, or promise to follow only their conscience. One stricture only would apply: in principal–agent relationships, contracts specify property rights and are enforceable in the courts. The more detailed the commitment to provide particular services to the electorate, or to take specific policy positions, the more scope for successful legal challenge if contract provisions remain unfulfilled.

The Electoral Act, as amended, could also include penalties should an MP break his or her contract by not seeing out its term, which would be coeval with the term of Parliament. Mitigating circumstances might include death, grave illness or criminal conviction. Otherwise an appropriate sanction would be the cost of conducting a by-election to replace the errant parliamentarian.[27]

Information is the key to a mutually beneficial contract, and so the offers of candidates would be collated and distributed to electors before polling day, just as the cases for and against a referendum proposal are circulated at present. Indeed, it may even be possible to print the total cost of the contract on offer against each name on the ballot paper, just as party affiliations appear at present for federal elections, so that voters can be reminded of the 'bottom line' as they make their choice.

Performance information on an MP would be provided by rival candidates, just as American aspirants for higher office devote much of their campaign to exploring each other's record, so no additional public expense need be incurred in monitoring contract compliance. Of course, as elsewhere in *Jobsback!*, any part of the principal — that is, any voter — would be entitled to seek damages through the courts for a breach of contract.

Overall, then, this proposal should satisfy John Howard's wish to apply his industrial relations model to parliamentarians. Because each candidate would negotiate an individual contract with the electorate, there would be flexibility, with differential salaries reflecting market estimations of value. Contracts would regulate the employment relationship, obviating the need for an external tribunal or for politicians to 'negotiate with themselves'. The principals, on the other hand, would get only those services they wished to pay for. Administratively, this would require little more than a minor modification to the tax system, so that electors who hired a relatively cheap MP would receive an appropriate tax rebate. A similar state-wide rebate, or charge, could accommodate the character of Senate representation. As agents of their electorate, politicians need no longer worry about applying one standard to the community and another to themselves.

Those committed to older systems of employment regulation may object on various grounds. They could note the relative complexity of procedures required to achieve a meaningful contract. They might dislike the notion of differential pay for people performing the same tasks. They may be concerned about the expense of using the courts to enforce contract conditions. And they may, above all, worry that a public auction for parliamentary seats, subject only to a minimum hourly rate, will drive the price down until, as the 1971 inquiry noted, politics ceases to attract 'the breadth of expertise and experience required to meet the demands of government'. Such are the consequences of policy consistency.

Conclusions

There is, in my opinion, no perfect system for adjusting members of Parliament's salaries and remunerations. I have a view that it is something of an impossible dream to imagine that we can ever take politics out of parliamentarians' pay rises no matter what system we adopt, no matter what time of the year or political cycle it is and no matter who happens to be in power.[28]

In so saying, John Howard points to a fundamental problem for politicians. Theirs is an unpopular profession, whose salaries are always resented. If allowed simply to float to a market-set level, parliamentary incomes (along with those of other unpopular public officials such as judges, bailiffs and commissioners of taxation) may become very low indeed. The traditional response has been to use non-market mechanisms for setting such salaries, as insurance that a suitable range of talent will entertain politics as a career and so that poorly paid politicians are not tempted into corrupt practices.

Christopher Hood examines the rewards which attract politicians to public office. Using the 'economics of politics' approach which is associated with rational choice theory, and which underpins the principal–agent model, an observer might expect rent-seeking behaviour from politicians — that is, parliamentarians who are 'opportunistic, calculating and self regarding' and use office to maximize their own income, unless constrained by institutional arrangements.[29] However, Hood finds little support in the data for this proposition. Relative to managerial and professional salaries, the income of MPs has declined over the last two decades in both Australia and the United Kingdom. This may reflect the transaction costs for politicians of pursuing their own wage rises. It may also be that politicians structure their returns for maximum tax benefit, or make the job less stressful through increased research and support staff, rather than face controversy over personal income. But it may also be that the essential rewards of political life are non-economic, relating instead to power, influence and a sense of contribution. Such motives are not easily modelled — and may not be well served by subjecting parliamentary salaries to a market mechanism in the interests of policy consistency.

Indeed, questions can be asked about the appropriateness of the principal–agent model as a guide to much in economic and social life. Certainly, understanding interactions between people as a series of contracts is a neat analytical device. As Terry Moe observes:

> . . . the whole of politics can be seen as a chain of principal–agent relation-
> ships, from citizen to politician to bureaucratic superior to bureaucratic

subordinate and on down the hierarchy of government to the lowest-level bureaucrats who actually deliver services directly to clients. Aside from the ultimate principal and the ultimate agent, each agent in the hierarchy serves a dual role in which he [sic] serves as both principal and as agent.[30]

Given that all players end up as both principals and agents, the question must be whether this abstraction of political life is of much help in framing employment policy. The principal–agent model was developed to deal with a quite specific problem, that of companies which separate ownership and management. When owners no longer direct operations, but rely instead on a professional hierarchy, they may worry that company executives are pursuing their own interests rather than those of the firm. In fact, much vital information about performance is held by the managers, who can conceal their own benefit from distant owners. A contract is one way of reducing that risk. By specifying expected performance in exchange for rewards, the principal can seek to reduce opportunistic behaviour by agents. Because a contract is enforceable in law, it ties managers to an agreement about their actions and so, it is hoped, maximizes returns for both parties.

Beginning from this narrow base, the principal–agent model has been applied ever more widely, whenever principals need to induce an agent to perform some function. First in New Zealand, and now in Australia, this theory has been imported into industrial relations. Replacing an older model, in which employment was both an economic and social exchange, justifying the participation of a range of interested parties, principal–agent-based policies seek to confine employment negotiations to just two actors: an employer and their agent. The theory is not applied in its pure form, since *Jobsback!* allows for a minimum wage and some mandatory health and safety standards, but in essence the policy seeks to redefine what notion of the public interest is to be served by employment relations.

The consequences of excluding non-economic considerations from the employment contract become clear in the case of MPs. By forcing parliamentarians to negotiate with the electorate, we establish an unfair relationship. All the advantages reside with the principal. We control the price, provided one or more candidates will come forward. Voters are under no obligation to reward sustained hard work or achievement, or to recognize past service. We can use the force of the state to penalize our agent if they break any condition of the contract. This is not a bargain between equal partners. A principal–agent relationship requires the relatively powerless to negotiate with the strong. It does so without the benefits of collective bargaining, since numerous provisions in *Jobsback!* unapologetically diminish the influence of collective organizations and remove the legitimacy of tactics such as strikes and pickets. Our would-be MPs would have to stand alone, each individually negotiating with an impersonal principal concerned only to maximize its own returns.

When power is asymmetric only one side consistently benefits; when that asymmetry is enforced through the state, using provisions which suppress collective industrial action, that imbalance is rendered permanent. Yet we are likely to attract better candidates, and be better served, by MPs with salaries linked to senior executive service grades, or determined by a remuneration tribunal, than by parliamentarians who must engage in a public auction for their seat at the end of each term. When price is held constant, we can choose between policies. This is an important, non-economic, consideration, since some choices should not be made on price alone. Kenneth Arrow noted the divergence between the predictions of the principal–agent model, and its effects in the real world.[31] He identified as difficulties the complexity of establishing contracts, the vagueness of monitoring and the importance of socially mediated rewards — all of which 'go beyond the usual boundaries of economic analysis'. There are important externalities in the employment relationship which cannot be accommodated within the simple abstraction of the principal–agent model.

Notes

1 An earlier version of this paper was published in *The Economic and Labour Relations Review* 2 (1993), pp. 279–98.

2 John Howard, Shadow Minister for Industrial Relations, interviewed on *Meet the Press*, Network Ten television, November 1, 1992.

3 Liberal/National Party Coalition, *Jobsback! The Federal Coalition's Industrial Relations Policy* (Policy Paper, Canberra, 1992), p.3.

4 *Ibid.*, p.5.

5 *Ibid.*, p.iii.

6 See Jonathan Boston, 'The Theoretical Underpinnings of Public Sector Restructuring in New Zealand', in Jonathan Boston, John Martin, June Pallot and Pat Walsh (eds), *Reshaping the State: New Zealand's Bureaucratic Revolution*

(Auckland, Oxford University Press, 1991), pp.1–26; Oliver Hart, 'An Economist's Perspective on the Theory of the Firm', in Oliver Williamson (ed.), *Organization Theory: From Chester Barnard to the Present and Beyond* (New York, Oxford University Press, 1990), pp.154–71; Charles Perrow, 'Economic Theories of Organization', *Theory and Society* 6 (1986), pp.11–45; John Pratt and Richard Zeckhauser (eds), *Principals and Agents: The Structure of Business* (Cambridge, Mass., Harvard Business School Press, 1985).

7   *Jobsback!*, p.22

8   *Ibid.*, p.10–11.

9   *Ibid.*, p.20. Perrow ('Economic Theories of Organization', p.14) notes that most economic theories of organization, including principal–agent theory, 'almost invariably assume that it is the agent that is opportunistic, even to the point of cheating, rather than the principal'.

10 The controversy is described in 'Coalition Defends MPs' Pay Rises', *The Australian*, October 31, 1992, p.4; 'Pay-Rise Push for Coalition MPs', *The Age*, October 31, 1992, p.3; and 'Premier Admits He Was Wrong on Pay', *The Age*, November 2, 1992, p.1.

11 Alan Browning (ed.), *House of Representatives Practice* 2nd edn (Canberra, Australian Government Publishing Service, 1989), p.182.

12 Quoted in *ibid.*, p.182.

13 John Howard, *Commonwealth Parliamentary Debates, House of Representatives*, May 31, 1990, p.1016. Announcing pay cuts for politicians remains always good politics, as then opposition leader John Hewson acknowledged by foreshadowing cuts to ministerial salaries in his revised *Fightback!* policy, launched on December 18, 1992.

14 This mechanism has now been thrown into chaos by the introduction of performance pay for the senior executive service, and the difficulties of translating this into MPs' salaries.

15 While a specified term is usually part of contracts for service, Richard Epstein notes that in practice many employment contracts are made 'at will' — that is, either side can resign from the employment relationship 'at any time, without having to give any reason for termination, and without being subject to a suit for damages'. See Richard Epstein, 'Agency Costs, Employment Contracts, and Labor Unions', in Pratt and Zeckhauser (eds), *Principals and Agents*, p.135.

16 Leslie Finn Crisp, *Australian National Government* 4th edn (Melbourne, Longman Cheshire 1978); Ross McMullin, *The Light on the Hill: The Australian Labor Party 1891–1991* (Melbourne, Oxford University Press, 1991).

17 Crisp, *Australian National Government*, p.192.

18 Quoted in *ibid.*, p.195.

19 Quoted in George Catlin, *A History of the Political Philosophers* (London, Allen & Unwin, 1950), p.325.

20 See R. A. D. Grant, 'Edmund Burke', in Roger Scruton (ed.), *Conservative Thinkers:*

Essays from the Salisbury Review (London, Claridge Press, 1988), pp.77–92; Crawford Macpherson, *Burke* (Oxford, Oxford University Press, 1980); and Conor Cruise O'Brien, *The Great Melody: A Thematic Biography and Commented Anthology of Edmund Burke* (Chicago, University of Chicago Press, 1992).

21 As Terry Moe has argued, there are problems even in this formulation since politicians, as agents, can set voting rules for the electorate, their principals. See his 'Political Institutions: The Neglected Side of the Story', *Journal of Law, Economics, and Organization* 6 (special issue 1990), p.233.

22 John Howard, *Commonwealth Parliamentary Debates, House of Representatives,* September 26, 1974, p.1911.

23 Robert Menzies, *Commonwealth Parliamentary Debates, House of Representatives,* November 2, 1934, p.164ff.

24 Graeme Starr, 'The Liberal Party of Australia', in G. Starr, K. Richmond and G. Maddox (eds), *Political Parties in Australia* (Melbourne, Heinemann, 1978), pp.11–101.

25 Quoted in Catlin, *A History of Political Philosophers,* p.325.

26 Christopher Publick and Robert Southey, *Liberal Thinking* (Melbourne, Macmillan, 1980).

27 Following Epstein ('Agency Costs'), this should be an optimal feature of the system, since it is not an expectation enforced in many real-world employment contracts — though one may note the earlier Australian tradition of master–servant relationships, in which terms of service were indeed enforced by the courts.

28 John Howard, *Commonwealth Parliamentary Debates, House of Representatives,* May 31, 1990, p.1016.

29 Christopher Hood, 'Looking After Number One? Politicians' Rewards and the Economics of Politics', *Political Studies* 40 (1992), p.209.

30 Quoted in Boston, 'The Theoretical Underpinnings', p.5.

31 Kenneth Arrow, 'The Economics of Agency', in Pratt & Zeckhauser (eds), *Principals and Agents,* pp. 49–50.

CHAPTER EIGHT

Measuring Performance
When There Is No Bottom Line

Donald Kettl

Around the world, measuring government performance is like the weather. Everyone talks about it. Everyone agrees on the need for improvement. But there is no consensus on how to do it. In the US, the storms have been even greater. As with disgruntled travellers everywhere, someone else's weather has always seemed better. American reformers have, in particular, looked longingly at performance management systems installed in New Zealand and Australia. Vice-President Al Gore's 1993 campaign to 'reinvent government' relied heavily on these models in proposing to 'empower' bureaucrats in exchange for holding them accountable through new performance management systems.

The US, especially at the federal level, has lagged substantially behind the rest of the industrialized world in developing performance management systems. One of the reasons is the configuration of political power in America, especially the division of responsibility for administration between constitutionally separate executive and legislative branches. Another reason is the particularly complex administrative environment of the US, in which administrative responsibility is widely shared and accountability is hard to define.

In this chapter, I will describe the American federal government's renewed efforts to develop an effective performance management system, examine the implications of American constitutionalism for the system, and assess the ability of the system to cope with the complexities of the American administrative system.

Timid First Steps

Like most industrialized nations, the US has launched a major campaign to reform the management of its federal government. Although the American federal government has lagged behind the efforts of many other countries, and indeed behind the efforts of many of America's sub-national governments, the Clinton Administration has placed management reform near the centre of its domestic policies. Indeed, Vice-President Gore has taken on the job of co-ordinating the movement, a rare show of high-level political support for a problem so prosaic.

In 1993, Gore led the National Performance Review (NPR), an intense six-month effort to examine how the administration could create a government that 'works better and costs less', as the NPR's report put it.[1] The NPR's recommendations focused on solving four problems: cutting red tape; putting customers first; empowering employees to get results; and cutting back to basics. In just its first year, Gore's campaign produced some remarkable successes, but it also identified important problems, especially in how to link the effort with the nation's broader political environment, which threatened its long-term success.[2]

One of the NPR's recommendations called for an aggressive strategy for forcing federal agencies to develop and use objective measures for defining their goals and assessing their performance. In the midst of the debate over the NPR, in fact, Congress passed the Government Performance and Results Act (GPRA), which committed the federal government to a ten-year programme of applying performance measures to its programmes.

The Endless Campaign for Performance

Proposals for improving performance management in the federal government, and to better link objectives with budgets, have circulated for years. Most have been short-term experiments with clearly political aims. In the mid-1960s, President Lyndon Johnson enthusiastically embraced the Planning–Programming–Budgeting (PPB) System as a way to escape line-item budgeting and begin focusing on broader objectives. President Richard Nixon scrapped PPB and replaced it with Management by Objectives (MBO), which his top advisers saw as a way to focus managers' attention more clearly on broad objectives set by top officials. MBO evaporated with the Nixon presidency, only to be replaced by Zero-Based Budgeting (ZBB) during Jimmy Carter's presidency. Carter believed that ZBB would give his budgeters greater leverage over spending by forcing managers to rethink their priorities each year and to justify spending increases in terms of value added. Ronald Reagan predictably ended ZBB when he assumed the presidency and focused simply on holding the budgetary line.

Throughout this long campaign, elected officials and policy analysts alike were unhappy with the inability to control the budgetary process better or to escape the tyrannical politics of short-term budgeting. They took to heart the enduring lesson of budget reformers, to focus on what government money buys instead of how much is spent, but they had a difficult time devising a system that matched the nation's political realities. Instead, presidents tended to impose, from the top down, sweeping new measures to replace the system of their predecessors and to assert their control over the executive branch. Each system added a different bit to presidential leverage, and some of those bits endured. The Pentagon, for example, continues to budget in the five-year, programme-based terms envisioned by PPB, although for political reasons the department's budgeters have long since abandoned the label. Managers quickly learned, however, that any new system imposed by the White House would soon pass. The cycle of reforms thus developed the seeds of their own destruction, and each new presidential reform only increased the cynicism of the career bureaucracy and members of Congress alike. Yearning for reform, in fact, grew as the barriers to achieving it increased.

Despite such despair, some members of Congress waged a continuing campaign for reform that focused more sharply on improving government performance. Senator William V. Roth (Republican, Delaware), in particular, had campaigned for years on the need to link the outputs of government — the results of public programmes — with its inputs — the budget. Few of his colleagues took him seriously. But in 1993, support for his initiative grew. Several American scholars, notably Harry Hatry, Joseph S. Wholey and Allen Schick, had quietly been collecting information about performance management systems around the world to help hone the concept. The head of the General Accounting Office, Comptroller-General Charles A. Bowsher, strongly endorsed performance measurement as 'an important tool in managing for results'. He told Congress, 'Public officials must be able to better ensure our citizens that the government can effectively account for where their tax dollars go and how they are used. But doing this will require that federal agencies and Congress change the way they do business.'[3]

Senior career officials within the Office of Management and Budget (OMB), meanwhile, began building their own case for reform. Federal managers, they argued in the government's management report for fiscal year 1990, tended to be judged by their conformity with procedures. They had little incentive to worry about results. As the report argued:

> Unless actions are taken soon, there exists a danger that the Government will become more inefficient and programmes less effective. Skilled employees and competent managers will be in great demand nationwide. If the Government does not hire and retain qualified staff over this time, its workforce could drift into mediocrity, with its management burdened and frustrated by layers and layers of controls that attempt to ensure that things are done right.

The solution, the report concluded, required 'disciplined planning, monitoring, and evaluation', built around 'central control and decentralized responsibility'.[4] Meanwhile, Gore's task force on 'reinventing government' developed its own separate case for better performance-monitoring. Its final report echoed the earlier OMB arguments:

> . . . management in government does not judge most programmes by whether they work or not. Instead, government typically measures programme activity — how much it spends on them, or how many people it has assigned to staff them.[5]

The Government Performance and Results Act

The odds had long been against the passage of a government performance act. Members of Congress, in particular, have rarely been excited about 'good government' legislation. But in July 1993, Congress overwhelmingly passed the GPRA. President Clinton eagerly signed it as one of the first fruits of the NPR. Members of Congress embraced the bill in part because of its promise; no one wanted to vote against a bill that promised performance and results. They were also swept up in reform fever. But there was little evidence that they fully understood the ambitious programme on which they had launched the government.

GPRA commits the federal government to a sweeping ten-year reform programme. If results match the promise, Congress's role in policy-making will fundamentally change. Budgeters within the OMB will have to transform the budgetary process. Managers throughout government will have to link clear performance indicators to their work. Hardly anyone disagrees with the Act's goals. Who, after all, could oppose the idea of committing the government to performance and results? But no one really knows how to do it. No one really knows what would happen to government if the Act worked. And no one wants to consider the implications if GPRA fails. GPRA, in short, represents the central problems of applying performance-based approaches to management throughout the government.

GPRA builds on three steps. Each federal agency, by the end of the ten-year phase-in period, will establish five-year strategic plans, performance measures to gauge their success in meeting the plans, and annual reports, based on those performance measures, on how well they have met their performance goals. The process includes:

• a five-year plan that is updated every three years;

• a comprehensive mission statement that links the agency's current operations with its long-term goals;

• an identification of the goals and objectives, along with the resources, systems, and processes required to achieve the goals;

• a description of the most important external factors that could affect the agency's success in achieving the goals;

• annual programme evaluations to help agency officials assess their success, explain why goals might not have been met, and revise the goals if necessary; and

• use of evaluations by OMB and the president to set future budgets and to revise programmes, if necessary.

Although GPRA allows a decade for all agencies to develop the process, most agencies have already launched pilot projects to test the system. Most observers have been surprised by the overwhelming enthusiasm that has greeted the programme to date.

GPRA's planners have focused attention on outcomes (how well a programme meets its mission) over outputs (a measure of the activity in the programme itself). An OMB planning document uses a hypothetical case to illustrate the difference:

One mission of the US Park Service is to meet customer service demands.
Output Measure: In the Northwest, at Silverstone National Park, they recently hired 30 people to clean restrooms twice as often, empty garbage cans daily,

and they also increased the size of the staff at the customer service desks to answer questions from park visitors.

Outcome Measure: Customer satisfaction improved from an 'average' rating to an 'excellent' rating during this period. These ratings were based on customer surveys using a five-point scale.[6]

The illustration makes several important points. The process begins with a mission statement that flows from the agency's legislative mission. It uses output measures, but only as an intermediate step. The outcome measure assesses results in terms of the mission (customer satisfaction) according to a measure (customer satisfaction).

OMB does not expect the transition to performance-based management to come easily. OMB officials, in fact, expect that change will require a long-term process and, in turn, fundamental changes in the culture of government management and the assumption of more responsibility by managers throughout the government. Moreover, OMB officials have repeatedly stressed that agency officials will be the leaders in GPRA. They do not intend this to be a top-down management reform. The Republican victories in the 1994 mid-term congressional elections underlined that point.

The federal government's ragged experience with management and reform, from PPB and MBO through ZBB and Total Quality Management, suggests caution in drawing conclusions too quickly from GPRA. But several things are clearly different this time. First, this is the first of the reforms launched by law instead of executive order or administrative action. GPRA's base in law ensures both congressional and executive branch involvement and makes it harder for its sponsors to retreat. Second, unlike previous reforms which began with an across-the-board effort, GPRA builds slowly from pilot programmes to government-wide implementation. This provides an opportunity for learning along the way. Third, the early evidence suggests that this reform enjoys broader support throughout the bureaucracy than earlier efforts. Finally, GPRA speaks with unusual clarity to problems that citizens want to have solved. It would be hard to find anyone who thinks that government performance is satisfactory, or that linking budgets with results is not a good idea. The 1992 presidential campaign by independent H. Ross Perot underlines that point. The American voters registered strong disapproval for government-as-usual, and expressed strong support for bringing more business-like processes to government.

GPRA thus begins with an unusual level of support. The critical questions are how well the considerable measurement problems are solved and, even more important, how performance management will connect with the process of political communication within American government.

Performance Management in the American Constitutional System

Performance management systems in the US have always struggled with a dilemma: the analysts framing such systems have often been more eager to promote the analytically powerful to the exclusion of the politically useful; the elected officials for whom they performed the analysis have rarely had much taste for the details. The technical side of performance management is daunting.[7] And political communication talents have rarely been the strongest assets of management analysts.

Indeed, the biggest difficulty in American performance management has been that far too often it has been considered simply as a problem of *measurement*. Committing the government to performance-based management, of course, requires that officials throughout government identify and measure results. The more fundamental question, however, is what to do with these measures. In reality, performance management is most fundamentally about *communication*, not measurement. Such communication occurs within a broader political process, in which the players have a wide array of different incentives. Performance management will have meaning only to the degree to which it shapes and improves those incentives. If we think about performance-based management only as a measurement problem — how can we gauge the results that public programmes produce? — we will miss the big questions: How does what we know about results shape how we manage public programmes? How can an audience for such analysis be cultivated? How does the separation of powers, with administrators' responsibility pulled between presidential and legislative influences, affect the discourse? And how does the process of measuring results affect the behaviour of political institutions? Put simply, performance management is about political communication. It has value only to the degree to which it improves that communication.

Political discourse about the results of public programmes occurs on four different levels: within the agency (where the vehicle is the strategic planning process envisioned by GPRA), between the president and the agency (where the vehicle is the budgetary process), within OMB (where the vehicle is the linkage between management and budget), and between the executive branch and Congress (where the vehicle is the connection between the oversight and legislative processes).

An understanding of performance management as political discourse, moreover, underlines the self-evident fact that communication is two-way. Performance measurement as traditionally practised, however, tends to look on the process as more mechanical and one-way: managers measure what they do, and then pass the information along to their overseers. For the process to work well, the participants have to understand the stakes and the incentives of those on the other side and supply information that will be heard. That, in turn, requires considerable sophistication about the nature of the political relationships. An analysis of these relationships identifies several significant problems that performance-based management must solve if it is to be successful.

Communication within Agencies

The rhetoric of strategic planning presumes a relatively straightforward process: managers read the legislation affecting their agencies and set priorities among the goals they are charged with pursuing. The process, of course, involves far more than strategic choice. It requires building consensus within the agency over goals, communicating decisions to managers throughout the agency, backing the choice with budgetary decisions, and overseeing results. Strategic planning therefore imposes huge burdens on executive leadership. And, since it demands such different behaviour from what characterizes most bureaucratic activity, it also requires, as OMB argues, fundamental culture change within the agencies.

The communication process, moreover, requires avoiding three traps. First, it is tempting for managers to retreat into existing planning processes instead of taking the big and innovative steps that GPRA requires. The government, after all, has been experimenting with planning for decades. PPB in the 1960s, for example, required managers to write and follow five-year plans. Many managers know the lore of PPB, know how to satisfy sweeping demands by using standard procedures to create paper trails, and how to wait out big reforms until they wither and blow away. The ten-year trial of GPRA makes it less likely that performance-based budgeting will simply go away. Managed reflexively, according to existing processes, however, it will be unlikely to produce real results. GPRA requires managers, for the first time, to link planning with results, and then to use the results to alter the plans. This imposes new demands on managers at all levels of government.

Second, it is tempting for managers to plan for what can most easily be measured. In the lore of performance-based management, this is known as the 'looking for the keys under the lamp-post' reflex. If I drop my keys on the pavement at night, it is easiest to look for them under the lamp-post because the light is better, even if that is not where I dropped them. What is most easily measured is not always what is most important to measure. Tackling the considerable measurement problems is part of this issue. Dealing with the natural bureaucratic reflex of seeking to measure what is easiest to measure is just as fundamental.

Third, it is tempting for managers to plan for the results they can most easily control. That is only natural if managers are going to be held accountable for their performance. Complex service delivery patterns, however, characterize the federal government. Apart from running the federal prisons, the air traffic control system and social security, there is little that the federal government itself does directly. Most of what the federal government does is done in close partnership with state and local governments and with contractors in the private and non-profit sectors. From building highways to fighting crime, the inter-organizational networks on which the outcomes of public programmes rest often present staggering complexity.

That creates two big problems for performance-based management. On the one hand, it is hard to hold federal managers responsible for results they cannot directly control and, at best, can only indirectly influence. The management of Medicare, for example, depends on the skills of the private contractors who handle the paperwork. Job training programmes depend on how well local governments and non-profit organizations run the programmes. On the other hand, if performance-based management is to have any meaning, it must include a mechanism to assign to managers responsibility for results, and determine ways of measuring their contribution to outcomes. The problem is hard enough when a manager is directly responsible for results. It is far harder, both technically and politically, within the federal government because of the tools on which it relies. Solving these problems requires redefining the culture of federal managers.

Communication between the President and the Agencies

GPRA presumes that the president and OMB will want to review the performance-based information that GPRA produced. It is an old joke about PPB, however, that the only ones helped by the flood of paper it produced were those who manufactured filing cabinets. Presidents and their staffs have huge demands on their time. Moreover, presidents and their staffs tend to concentrate far more on framing than managing policy. When the electorate and the news media look to the White House, they focus more on presidential pronouncements than on the bureaucracy's results. The image of the president as chief executive, furthermore, is founded far more in fiction than in fact. The president is not a corporate executive; executive-branch officials often spend far more time dealing with members of Congress than with the White House.

To be sure, OMB argues that GPRA will be driven by federal executives from the bottom up. The problem is that incentives need to flow from the top down to induce executives to tackle the considerable political, managerial and technical problems that GPRA creates. For over a generation, management has been an issue of only fleeting importance for presidents. There are other ways of creating top-down incentives for performance-based budgeting, notably through the budgetary process. But most performance-based systems presume, in both rhetoric and reality, a heavy reliance on top managers. Such presumptions are often ill-founded.

Even worse, there are often powerful temptations for top managers to use or distort performance measures as political cover. 'Give me something I can run with' is a frequent cry. The risk is that the president and his staff will demonstrate little care about performance management except when they have an immediate political need. Then the temptation will be to distort the long-term focus of the process to short-term political demands. Skilled managers will be able to reconcile political realities with the management process, the short term with the long term. But it will require considerable skill to make the leap. Otherwise, performance-based management could founder: because elected officials do not find it politically useful and do not support the managers who are conducting it; and because managers, without top-level support, find it easy to go through the motions until it is abandoned. Unless performance-based management finds a way to negotiate through these difficult tensions — to develop a language that has meaning for both sets of actors — it is easy to predict that it will go the way of PPB, MBO and ZBB.

Communication between Management and Budget

One solution is for OMB to integrate closely the management and budget functions. The annual budgetary process is the club that every manager recognizes. Linking performance management with budgeting puts muscle into management. Within OMB, however, the problem has always been that management has been the weak sibling to budgeting. The management branch has gradually withered, while deficit politics has strengthened the leverage of the budget branch.

In March 1994, OMB director Leon Panetta and deputy director Alice Rivlin launched a major initiative to attack this problem. Their reform, 'OMB 2000', is designed to combine the budget and management branches into new resource-management units. They plan to conduct annual management reviews of each agency and programme to complement the traditional budget reviews, and to combine the results in OMB's recommendations for future spending.[8]

If the culture change within the agencies is the most important micro-level step in performance-based management, OMB 2000 is the most important macro-level step. It is the biggest change in OMB since it was created during the Nixon Administration; it promises to be the most significant step in top-level management of the federal government since the Hoover commissions. OMB 2000, however, imposes major burdens on OMB's leadership and staff. It requires nothing less than the redefinition of the role of the budget examiner, who has always been the building block of OMB's power. The reform puts the examiners on the front lines and asks them simultaneously to assess the long-term management issues along with the short-term budget implications, to gauge how well an agency hits the strict targets of legislative budget ceilings while worrying about the overall performance of its programmes.

One risk is that short-term budget pressures will drive out examination of long-term results. Another risk lies in training: can OMB find, recruit and promote individuals with the huge range of skills that the new job will demand? The problems are solvable, but doing so will require clear leadership and sustained commitment from top OMB officials. It will require them to redefine the role of the budget examiner, to send clear signals about what that role will be, to provide training to allow examiners to understand their role, and to reinforce that training with incentives to make clear how the role ought to be played. Most of all, it requires integrating management with budget decisions.

The job is daunting. OMB 2000 is a necessary (but, as we shall see, not in itself a sufficient) condition for making performance-based management work in the federal government. To make it work requires nothing less than a redefinition of OMB's role and of the jobs its employees perform.

Communication with Congress

The most fundamental issue of performance-based management is how managers communicate with Congress. Control over the bureaucracy and its programmes has always been a tug of war between the Congress and the presidency. From congressional dominance throughout much of the first century of the US, the president has gradually but increasingly asserted his dominance in the second century.[9] GPRA is, potentially, a powerful instrument for accelerating presidential dominance. It creates a new language of performance, links it with the president's budget, and provides strong sanctions through the budgetary process against managers who do not behave as the president and his senior staff desire.

What role does Congress play? Within GPRA, the executive branch dominates the process and Congress barely plays a role except as recipient of the information. It is inconceivable, however, that agency managers would dare chart a strategic plan on their own. They are charged, after all, with executing the law as passed by Congress. The choice of objectives is defined in law and therefore is not theirs to make. Nor, for that matter, do they have broad options about priorities. Strategic planning assumes that managers will choose to make some objectives more important than others. Congress, however, sets many priorities, some conflicting; all, in the minds of members of Congress, are equally important. Therefore, for government managers to set priorities is to risk offending a member of Congress whose treasured programme is not selected as a top priority.

Skilled managers will solve the problem by making implicit bargains with members of Congress and their staffs. Managers, for example, could negotiate quietly with key oversight committees over which programmes to set as top priorities. That would forestall later attack from Capitol Hill and ensure that the managers would not be undercut as they seek to define a five-year plan. GPRA could therefore produce an unintended irony. The agreements that department heads reach with the president over priorities could reflect congressional more than the president's priorities. The final priorities could be the result of quiet behind-the-scenes agreements between managers and key members of Congress rather than between managers and the president. The process could also transform congressional oversight from after-the-fact hearings to before-the-fact negotiations.

The irony is that, while the process of GPRA enhances the potential for executive control, the incentives it creates could actually increase legislative influence over executive-branch operations. That influence could be more subtle than in the past, and occur more in advance of agency operations than after the fact through oversight hearings. The nature of the incentives and the form of the communication could easily shape the process and the flow of power.

This, of course, depends on whether the language of GPRA will translate well between federal agencies and the Congress. Congress has no obligation to pay any attention whatsoever to the process that it has mandated federal managers to begin. Indeed, there is substantial evidence that, beyond a handful of key congressional staff members who helped draft the legislation, virtually no members of Congress have any idea of what they have created.[10] Congress tends to think in bite-size terms: projects, especially as they benefit their constituencies, rather than long-term programmes; and short-term effects, especially those that will be felt before the next election (members of the House must stand for re-election every two years), rather than long-term effects. The biggest risk to GPRA and its ambitious effort to transform federal management is that Congress itself will have little interest in it, provide little support for it, and therefore encourage this reform to evaporate away like its predecessors.

But the question is open. On its answer will ultimately depend the success of performance-based management in the federal government. The president might be 'chief executive', but Congress often has far greater influence on executive action. OMB is an important counterweight, but how it exerts its influence will depend heavily on the results of GPRA.

Through the Administrative Lens, Darkly

The entire performance management system in the US builds on a relatively straightforward assumption: that managers' responsibility can be delineated, that the results of their decisions can be measured, that inputs can be linked with outcomes, and that they can therefore be held accountable for their behaviour. And, on the face of it, who could disagree with this formulation? The reverse of any of these propositions appears absurd. Indeed, the fundamental appeal of performance management is the apparently unarguable power of its logic.

The problem is that this logic does not match the administrative structure of American, and especially federal, government. The federal government spends less than 14 per cent of its budget on programmes it manages itself, and half of this goes to operate and maintain the armed forces.[11] Most federal money goes to transfer payments to individuals, grants and contracts. Most federal employees work to write the rules, supervise the contracts, and process the paper to get the money out the door. Federal housing programmes work through grant programmes to local governments. Federal human service programmes operate through grants to state governments; the states combine federal money with their own and typically make grants to local governments and negotiate contracts with non-profit organizations. Federal regulatory programmes, from new labels detailing the nutritional value of food to the quality of air and water, depend on compliance by private manufacturers. The trend, moreover, is likely to continue. As Congress debates a fundamental reform of the American health system, the only predictable result is that the administrative process it produces will be mixed.[12]

The American administrative system, especially the federal administrative system, depends on complex interconnections among the federal government, state and local governments, private contractors and non-profit partners. Other nations have, under the banner of privatization, spun off public enterprises into the private sector. In the US, successive reforms — even those advanced as privatization — have increasingly tied the public, private and non-profit sectors together. Most federal employees are intermediaries in a system where their role is to facilitate the work of others. Relatively few federal employees directly control the outcomes of the programmes they manage. The federal government, in the meantime, has committed itself to measuring performance when, in fact, there is no bottom line or clear lines of responsibility.

Holding managers accountable for programmes they do not control is a difficult venture. Measuring their marginal contribution to success or failure in programme implementation is a daunting challenge that managers of GPRA have only dimly begun to explore. The logic of performance management is well known. The system's administrative complexities are recognized, at least by insiders. The problem is that the ambitious GPRA system does not recognize the inescapable challenge that lies just under the surface. This does not mean that GPRA is doomed. In fact, working through the large challenges of assessing individual performance within an environment of shared responsibility offers great potential for better understanding these inter-organizational networks and for managing them more effectively. But it does mean that the interconnections of the American administrative system further complicate the problem of measuring results, assessing responsibility and making GPRA work.

Conclusion

GPRA — indeed, performance-based management in the federal government — sits squarely between complex cross-cutting pressures. To make it work requires linking the levels of communication, sending the right signals to reinforce the basic message, building the capacity to do the job, and speaking a language that is useful and can be readily interpreted by those who hear it.

The measurement problems are themselves daunting. Indeed, as this chapter suggests, there are hidden measurement problems for which reformers have not yet developed good answers. Managers must determine ways of assigning responsibility for results in the many programmes where responsibility is shared. Moreover, they must develop mechanisms for linking programmes and results with authorizations and appropriations. Building the technical capacity to tackle these problems is a prerequisite to real reform.

More fundamentally, however, performance-based management must be understood as a problem of political communication. To focus narrowly on the measurement problems, interesting and difficult though they are, misses the far more important political issues. To be effective, performance-based management requires managers to think about their jobs in new ways. This bottom-up process requires reinforcement from the top, especially from OMB, which in turn requires OMB to succeed in reinventing itself. It requires a sophistication in understanding that the performance management process might sometimes be undercut in the rough-and-tumble of the political process. It requires developing new linkages with the legislative process, on both law-making and oversight. It ultimately depends on devising a way to connect the performance of complex administrative structures with the administrators who run them.

Although performance management advocates usually view the problem as a technical one — how can we devise the best indicators — the process is fundamentally a political one. The special features of the American political system make that process especially difficult. There is nothing that can truly be described as a 'government' programme. The constitutional system of separated executive and legislative powers produces compromises that blur the definition of goals. Likewise, tensions between Congress and the president over the conduct of bureaucrats, whose actions in the end truly define 'policy', often further blur the definition of policy goals.

All political systems have a difficult time digesting the technical information that performance management produces. In the US, however, the multiple channels of political influence — the plethora of interest groups, the many points of access into the system, and the hyper-sensitivity of the political process to micro-level concerns — can sometimes drown out discussion of performance or results. The American system seems peculiarly designed to frustrate the steps that true performance management requires.

This is not a brief against performance management. But it is a caution against focusing too narrowly on the measurement issues, against over-promising its potential or ignoring the political audience for the results. Indeed, the strongest potential for performance management is in informing, and even perhaps shaping, the broader political debate that shapes American public policy.

In sum, performance-based management is one part measurement. It is one part political savvy. It is one part administrative sophistication. And, most of all, it is one part communication, with the communication process driven by a clear understanding of the needs and incentives of the listener. Performance-based management has the potential for dramatically improving the results of public programmes. If it succeeds, it will also, just as dramatically, transform the behaviour and processes of the most important political institutions in American politics. On one level, therefore, performance-based management is a way of thinking about how to improve what government *does*. On another level, it is a way of thinking about what government *is*. Given the keen interest of elected officials and the electorate in improving government performance, few questions in the governance of the US today are more important.

Notes

1   Al Gore, *From Red Tape to Results: Creating a Government that Works Better and Costs Less* (Washington, Government Printing Office, 1993), p.76.
2   See Donald F. Kettl, *Reinventing Government? Appraising the National Performance Review*, CPM Report 94–2 (Washington, Brookings Institution, 1994).
3   Statement of Charles A. Bowsher, *Performance Measurement: An Important Tool in Managing for Results*, GAO/T-GGD–92–35 (May 5, 1992).
4   US Office of Management and Budget, *Budget of the United States Government: Management for Fiscal Year 1990* (Washington, Government Printing Office, 1989), pp.2–28 to 2–31.
5   Gore, *From Red Tape to Results*, p.72.
6   Office of Executive and Management Policy, US Office of Personnel Management, 'Government Performance and Results Act of 1993: Briefing Package' (photocopied, August 16, 1993).
7   One useful review is James E. Swiss, *Public Management Systems: Monitoring and Managing Government Performance* (Englewood Cliffs, NJ, Prentice–Hall, 1991).
8   'Making OMB More Effective in Serving the Presidency', OMB Office Memorandum 94–16 (March 1, 1994).
9   Francis E. Rourke, 'Whose Bureaucracy Is This, Anyway? Congress, the President and Public Administration', *PS: Political Science and Politics* 26 (1993), pp.687–92.
10 Interview with the author.
11 See Donald F. Kettl, *Government by Proxy: (Mis?)Managing Federal Programs* (Washington, Congressional Quarterly Press, 1988); and Frederick C. Mosher, 'The Changing Responsibilities and Tactics of the Federal Government', *Public Administration Review* 40 (1980), p.542.
12 See John J. Dilulio Jr, Donald F. Kettl and Richard P. Nathan, *Making Health Reform Work: Implementation, Management and Federalism*, CPM Report 94–1 (Washington, Brookings Institution, 1994).

CHAPTER NINE

Rationality, Efficiency and the Market

T. M. WILKINSON

In economic markets, people buy and sell goods and services at various prices. Not everything can be bought or sold and sometimes transactions can take place only if they follow certain rules. For example, the government does not allow a market in human kidneys, and it permits buildings to be constructed only if they satisfy certain health and safety regulations. The government is not alone in determining the extent of the market, but it is a major influence. How that influence should be exercised is controversial.

In New Zealand in the last few years, the tendency of government has been to extend the market. The deregulation of broadcasting, for instance, has allowed some groups of people to set up TV and radio stations and sell advertising to other groups of people. There are many who would like to see the market extended still further. Roger Douglas, for example, favours giving people the option of forgoing health and superannuation payments above a certain level of insurance, the power to purchase education for their children from schools that compete with one another, and the greater use of private firms in the provision of many of the services that the state currently provides.[1] There are some who would go even further than Douglas, preferring that people not be forced to contribute anything to their old age or their health needs, being instead left with the freedom to spend their money as they wish. It is important to see that the issue here is not whether the state should *redistribute* money. The issue is how far people should be able to use their money to buy things and how far others should be able to sell them things. One could favour an equal distribution of wealth and yet reject any interference with what people should be allowed to buy or sell. The question here is how far the market should be allowed to extend.

One common argument for extending the market appeals to efficiency. Resources are scarce, and how they are distributed makes a difference to how well off people are. Behind the efficiency defence of the market is the claim that markets provide the best way of allocating those scarce resources so that people are as well off as they possibly can be. This defence supposes both that efficiency is a good thing and that markets are efficient. Here is a simple (and simplistic) version of the efficiency defence.

People perform lots of different actions in a market — buying things for consumption, selling things for profit, investing, and so forth. These actions are tied to the efficiency defence of the market by supposing that, when people perform these actions, they do so for good reasons. The basic idea is that, when people buy and sell things, they know what they are doing. In each given transaction, the parties are acting for good reasons. In some way, they must be better off after the transaction, otherwise they would not have agreed to it. A market is made up of many such transactions between many different people, and so the result of these should be that many people are better off than they were before. If we stop people making these transactions then they will be worse off than they need be. If we care about how well off people are, we should leave them to buy and sell what they want. So we ought not to interfere with market transactions by regulating, requiring or prohibiting economic actions.

The basic idea is highly appealing, but plenty needs to be said about the assumptions it depends on. A major result of welfare economics is to show that, in certain ideal conditions, market outcomes will be efficient. The ideal conditions are those that obtain under perfect competition, such as the absence of externalities, free entry and exit into the market, perfect information and, crucially for this chapter, the condition that economic actors are rational. The demonstration that markets in these conditions will be efficient is often cited in defence of actually existing markets. Clearly, if actual markets were efficient, that would be an important reason to have them. Do we have that reason? In actual markets, many of the conditions for a perfectly competitive market are conspicuously absent. The existence of externalities and the resulting public goods problems are perhaps the most frequent objections to the efficiency defence of the market.

The assumption of rationality, though a less common target for criticism, is controversial. Its role is to link what people do in the market with the satisfaction of their preferences. There are two extreme views about the rationality assumption. One holds that people in markets always act for good reasons, or at least we ought to assume they do. The other holds that people do not act for good reasons at all; rather, whether producers or consumers, they act on a misperception of their true interests because, for example, they are the victims of false consciousness. My aim here is to defend a position somewhere in between these two extremes.

This chapter explores the rationality assumption and its role in the defence of the market. It begins with a more detailed description of the relationship between the economists' conception of rationality and their version of efficiency. Next, it explores some of the implications of their conception of rationality before noting its inadequacies. The conclusion here is that there are more ways of being irrational than the economists' conception allows, and so economic actions have to satisfy further conditions before one can appeal to an efficiency defence of the market. But, although there are more stringent conditions for rational action than economic orthodoxy holds, it does not follow that people do not satisfy them. It will often be hard to tell, however, whether they do. This leads into one response to irrationality, common to economists and many others, which claims that we ought not to attribute irrationality to people and so we ought not to interfere with market transactions. To do so would be unacceptably paternalistic. The chapter examines this view, and the support offered for it by the well-known view that people are the best judges of their own interests. It concludes that, while the 'best judge' view has considerable force, there are some types of decision to which it often does not apply and there may be some reason to reject the extension of markets to include them. The final conclusion is somewhat equivocal: that the bulk of market transactions are probably rational and so the efficiency defence applies to them, but that we should be much less sure of certain types of transaction, where there may be reason to interfere with the market.

Rationality and Efficiency in Economic Theory

There were many unexplained terms in the simple defence of market transactions as a means of satisfying efficiently people's rational interests. This section gives the more specific interpretation in economic orthodoxy of terms like 'acting for good reasons', 'rational interests' and 'efficiency'. It first considers the requirements in economic theory that actions must satisfy to count as rational, and discusses some of the implications of those requirements. It then considers the relationship of rational actions to efficiency.

In the economists' treatment of economic action, an action is rational if it displays the right link between a rational preference ordering and behaviour. In outline, someone's action counts as rational if it is the result of their doing what they most prefer. This sounds like a pretty easy condition to satisfy, and it often is. Let us break down that simple description of rational behaviour. First, in economic theory, there are certain axioms that preferences have to satisfy for an agent to count as rational. Second, once the preferences have satisfied those axioms, actions have to follow preferences, in that they have to be actions to achieve the most preferred options.

There are two major conditions that preferences have to satisfy to form an ordering. First, all states of affairs are assumed to be comparable by agents. Someone must be able to rank all states of affairs by preferring some to others or being indifferent between them. This is sometimes known as the *completeness* axiom. Second, preferences must be in a transitive ordering. An ordering is transitive if, when someone prefers A to B and B to C, they prefer A to C. This is sometimes known as the *transitivity* axiom.[2] There are other axioms which deal with rational choices under risk and uncertainty, but here I shall discuss only choices under certainty.

The completeness and transitivity axioms give a specification of people's rational interests. People have an interest in getting what they most prefer. These interests are then connected to action by a further axiom, which is that agents choose the highest-ranked options available to them. It does not immediately follow that, because an agent prefers A to B, they will choose A, even if it is in the feasible set.[3] Maybe they suffer from weakness of the will and act against their considered preferences. This further axiom is important because it shows that there is more to rationality than merely having a rational preference ordering. After all, it is economic *action* (which implies behaviour) that comes within the scope of the efficiency defence of the market. How people act on the assessment of their interests is independently important. This point recurs in the discussion of the 'best judge' principle.

I shall now say a little more about the status of these axioms. The completeness axiom is philosophically controversial, since some claim that not all bundles are comparable because some are incommensurable. Joseph Raz, for example, claims that one often cannot compare the value of different careers for deep reasons to do with the nature of value.[4] In any case, it is not especially plausible to suppose that it is a rational requirement that individuals can compare every bundle. The axiom is often assumed for reasons of convenience and not because it is thought to be a failure of rationality if it is violated.[5] The completeness axiom will be mentioned no further here. By contrast, some economists do claim that having transitive preferences is a requirement of rationality, and the claim has a certain plausibility.[6] I shall here accept that transitivity of preference is a necessary condition of rationality.

Economists generally claim more than that their axioms are necessary conditions for rational action — they also claim that they are sufficient. This is a remarkably weak conception of rationality. It puts the content of preferences almost entirely beyond rational scrutiny.[7] There are two important effects of this, one desirable, the other perhaps less so.

First, it follows from the refusal to scrutinize the content of preferences that selfishness is not rationally required. If you prefer giving all your money to charity to retaining it, the state of affairs where all your money is given to charity is preferable from your point of view or, in other words, better satisfies your preferences. According to the economists' conception, you ought to try to satisfy your preferences, which in this case requires giving the money away. Clearly, then, whether satisfying preferences will result in selfishness depends not on the injunction to satisfy preferences as such but on the content of the preferences. As we have seen, there is nothing irrational about altruistic or otherwise selfless preferences.

This point should remove some misguided objections to what economists say. It is true that many economists have endorsed Francis Edgeworth's view that 'the first principle of Economics is that every agent is actuated only by self-interest'.[8] But the assumption of self-interest is just that — an assumption. It does not follow from the economists' principles of rationality and is usually adopted for convenience. Even then, the assumption that, for instance, households aim to maximize their utility or that firms aim to maximize their profits does not entail selfishness. Consider that Oxfam may try to maximize its trading profits in order to do the most good for the needy.

A refusal to scrutinize the content of preferences entails that there is nothing irrational about altruistic preferences. It also entails that there is nothing irrational about a preference for a state of affairs in which one drills through one's foot over a state in which one does not. The second effect of the refusal to scrutinize is that apparently crazy preferences are not irrational. Whether or not this is a sensible thing to say,[9] we should attach less weight to the satisfaction of crazy preferences, even if they are embedded in a transitive preference ordering.

It is implied by the economists' conception of rationality that one can rationally fail to promote one's self-interest, as when, for instance, one has certain altruistic or crazy preferences. Rationality — on the economists' view — means satisfying preferences but these need not be self-interested. This implication is not necessarily to be regretted, and I do not think that the divergence of preference and self-interest offers a decisive objection to the economists' conception. It is not, I think, a requirement of rationality that one aims only at one's self-interest. I shall here assume, because there is not space to argue for it, that what counts in assessing actions is the way in which they satisfy rational interests (not necessarily *self*-interest). What I shall presently show, though, is that the view of economic orthodoxy is not good enough for carrying out that assessment.

So far, I have discussed the economists' specification for rational action. We have yet to see their specification for efficiency. Let us suppose that consumers do have a transitive preference ordering and do what they most prefer. Economists make a connection between rational choice, markets and efficiency. Markets are characterized by voluntary choice and some initial set of property holdings. Individuals can trade these holdings for other things that they prefer. In any given trade, both parties ought to gain. They each prefer what the other is offering (otherwise they would not agree to trade) and as a result of the trade each is in a more preferred situation. Each has what they prefer relative to what they had before. According to economists, this is a gain in efficiency.

That there is a gain in efficiency follows from their account of what efficiency is. The most widely used standard is Pareto-optimality. In its preference-based form, it states:

> A state of affairs is Pareto-optimal when there is no feasible alternative which someone prefers and no one disprefers.[10] A state of affairs is Pareto-inferior when there is a feasible alternative state of affairs which at least one person prefers and which no one disprefers. A state of affairs is Pareto-superior to another state when at least one person prefers it and no one disprefers it.

The central claim of welfare economics is that ideal market transactions made by rational consumers will tend towards a Pareto-optimal equilibrium.[11] If two people each prefer what the other has to what they have, and if they can trade, know the other exists and so on, then they would trade. A Pareto-inferior state would have been transformed into a Pareto-optimal one.

Why should we care about Pareto-optimality? If we accept the economists' specification for rational interests in terms of preference, then Pareto-optimality has a certain intuitive appeal. A Pareto-optimal state will be one in which no one can do better to satisfy their interests without someone else doing worse. Furthermore, to the extent that Pareto-optimality has force for us, it will lead us to favour improvements where some people do better to satisfy their interests while others do no worse. How could one resist such improvements? There is no doubt that Pareto-optimality, understood in terms of the satisfaction of rational interests, is not sufficient for the moral acceptability of a distribution, but, in some form or other, it has a good claim to be necessary.[12] My argument here will not be with Pareto-optimality as an ideal of efficiency. Instead, I shall criticize the economists' account of what it is for people to act rationally by arguing that actions must satisfy further conditions before they can be said to be rational. Later, I ask whether a 'best judge' view offers a good reason for thinking that people do satisfy these conditions.

Irrationality

This section discusses the ways in which people's actions can fail to satisfy their rational interests. It first deals with actions which are irrational because they violate the economists' axioms, and then shows why satisfying these axioms is not sufficient to make an action count as rational. These axioms do not cover the possibility that the belief and desire components of preferences can be defective in various ways, and I shall claim that people's rational interests are not solely specified by transitive preference-orderings.

On the orthodox view, there are two main ways in which someone's action could fail to satisfy their rational interests. First, preferences may not be ordered transitively. Second, people may not do what they most prefer. One explanation for the second failure could be a failing of rationality such as weakness of the will, where someone prefers one thing over another yet picks the less preferred thing. Well-known examples of this include smoking cigarettes despite preferring, all things considered, not to. Another explanation could be making a mistake about which options are available. For instance, one could prefer beer to lemonade but choose lemonade because of a false belief that beer is not available.

However, there are other ways in which actions could satisfy economists' axioms and yet fail to advance someone's rational interests. First, preferences might be mistaken. (Mistakes in the belief component of preferences are distinct from mistakes in beliefs about which options are available.) Preferences incorporate belief, and beliefs can be false. Second, beliefs, even if true, can be acquired by irrational processes, such as wishful thinking, which are not caught by the unduly narrow economic conception of rationality. Third, the desire component of preferences may not satisfy certain conditions on their origin which they need to if they are to be rational.

First, I discuss mistakes. Suppose a person prefers an operation to taking a pill because they believe that this is the best way to cure them of some disease. Let us suppose that, contrary to their belief, the pill is in fact the best way. If we were running a private hospital and made more money out of operations than pills, we would gain if they chose an operation. We could come to an agreement with this person. We would perform the operation, they would pay us and we would both have what we prefer. In fact, we would have traded up to a Pareto-optimum. If we refused to give the person the operation and offered only the pill, they would be in a situation they preferred less. Since we could offer them the operation, which they and we prefer, there is a feasible Pareto-superior alternative to their getting the pill. But it is not true that the person's interests are better satisfied by getting the operation than the pill. Hence there is a divergence between their interests and their preferences.

This important point marks a difference between preference satisfaction and desire satisfaction views of interests, two views which are often run together. A desire satisfaction view says that interests consist in the satisfaction of basic desires — desires underived from other desires. On some views of basic desires, these cannot be mistaken. Non-cognitivists, for example, regard basic desires as neither true nor false — they are not capable of bearing truth values. This means that the idea of a mistaken basic desire does not make sense. Consider the ludicrousness of criticizing someone for liking strawberry ice-cream. However, some desires can be mistaken in the sense that they are based on false beliefs; non-cognitivism does not apply to them. Typically, they will be desires derived from other desires. Derivative desires take this sort of form: 'I want to be well at least cost. I believe that having an operation is the best way to become well. So I want an operation.' The 'I want an operation' is a derivative desire, and it is mistaken because it is based on a mistaken belief. But the desire to be well, if that is not derived from another desire, does not bear truth value, according to non-cognitivism.

A desire satisfaction view of interests will claim that interests are advanced by the satisfaction of basic, underived desires. The satisfaction of derived desires will advance interests only to the extent that they serve the basic desires. A preference satisfaction view, by contrast, holds that a person's interests are advanced when they get the state of affairs they prefer. This is equivalent to saying that their interests are advanced when their derivative desires are satisfied. Preferences, like derivative desires, incorporate belief.

Non-cognitivism about basic desires is often thought to support the refusal of economists to make critical scrutiny of preference. But that refusal is not so supported, because preferences and basic desires are not equivalent. As we have seen, non-cognitivists believe that basic desires cannot be mistaken. This view is controversial but has some plausibility. However, non-cognitivists certainly accept the uncontroversial view that beliefs can be mistaken. Since preferences can incorporate beliefs, preferences can be mistaken. What sort of beliefs are there in preferences? One can have beliefs about the best way of satisfying desires, and also beliefs that one has desires or, in the case of other-regarding preferences, beliefs that others have desires.

Beliefs can be mistaken without being irrational. So to say that a person has mistaken preferences is not to claim that they are irrational. Nevertheless, if someone has mistaken preferences, we obviously have reason to doubt whether their actions are satisfying their rational interests. Even if markets tend towards Pareto-optimality, where no one can get what they prefer without someone else getting what they disprefer, Pareto-optimality is less of a defence of a state of affairs if the preference satisfaction is the satisfaction of mistaken preferences.

It is also true that beliefs can be irrational without being mistaken, although if they are irrational they are more likely to be wrong. A view which takes the rationality of preferences for granted fails to take account of the non-controversially irrational ways in which beliefs can be formed. That is why it is false to claim that irrationality of preference is only having an intransitive preference ordering. One could have a transitive preference ordering, yet it could be irrational because the preferences are based on false beliefs.

What sorts of irrationality of belief are there? The common distinction here is between cold and hot irrationality of belief. Cold irrationality consists in having certain biases, such as ignoring prior probability distributions or falling victim to the gambler's fallacy in making probability judgements.[13] Hot irrationality consists in motivated mistakes, such as wishful thinking and cognitive dissonance and probably false consciousness.[14]

So far, I have concentrated on mistakes and irrationality in the belief component of a preference ordering, and this has amounted to saying that our interests are not always advanced by the satisfaction of derivative desires. It is much more controversial to claim that people's basic desires can suffer the same faults as derivative desires. Yet economists are often criticised for ignoring the origin of people's desires and, to the extent that they do this because they think that desires are beyond rational scrutiny, they are probably making a mistake. One need not believe that consumer desires are the result of corporate brainwashing to accept that the origin of desires makes a difference to their rationality. If people want things because they have been brainwashed, or because they have given up desires which they can see no prospect of satisfying, or because of peer pressure only, then we should be sceptical about their rational interests being given by the content of these desires. It is quite hard to formulate the conditions of origin that someone's desires would have to meet for their satisfaction to count as advancing the person's rational interests. Perhaps the desires have to be formulated in circumstances of autonomy.[15] But, whatever the right conditions are, there is no doubt that there have to be some, and the origin of preferences cannot be merely ignored as irrelevant to their rationality.

Interpreting Behaviour

How far the points about mistaken and irrational preferences undermine a Pareto-optimality defence of markets depends in part on how irrational or mistaken people actually are. The mere fact that there is more to making preferences respectable than economic orthodoxy holds does not imply that preferences are not in fact respectable. Saying, for example, that the economists' conception of rationality ignores the possibility of wishful thinking does not entail that people actually do think wishfully. How widespread are mistakes and irrationality? The answer to this question requires empirical evidence beyond the scope of this chapter. However, it is worth reporting that there is a considerable barrier to gathering evidence, and that barrier is that virtually any action or set of actions can be interpreted as rational.

As an example, consider the effects of advertising. These effects are commonly cited by Marxists as a cause of irrational action.[16] They cause people, it is claimed, to act against their own best interests. But how can we tell whether this is true? We might try to compare consumer behaviour before and after an advertising campaign to see how it has changed. But some changes in response to advertising are clearly not irrational. Perhaps the advertising told me about something which I had not known existed and which serves my ends better. It is not irrational of me to consume this new thing.[17] So we cannot tell merely from a change in behaviour whether or not someone is acting irrationally. It depends on the person's wider interests and their beliefs about how best to serve those interests, including whether those beliefs have been formed in the right way.

The general point is that any set of actions is capable of being interpreted as rational. Sometimes, however, the most plausible interpretation of odd actions will be that they are irrational. One example is Tibor Scitovsky's interpretation of data on time-saving and the purchase of DIY goods as evidence of irrationality.[18] There is an inconsistency of behaviour here that could be explained by positing bizarre, but not irrational, preferences by consumers. But it is more plausible, Scitovsky claims, to interpret their behaviour as irrational. Furthermore, there is some evidence from psychological experiments that subjects are persistently prone to errors in probability judgement, for example.[19] Again, the behaviour displayed in these experiments is open to being interpreted as rational, but only at the price of implausible and gratuitous assumptions about preferences.

The 'Best Judge' View

The problem of interpretation is that any action or set of actions which plausibly fails to serve rational interests can also be interpreted as the contrary. But why should we interpret actions as rational?[20] Perhaps we ought to regard actions as rational and correct because we have no business judging others' actions. This answer is given by those who endorse a principle of consumer sovereignty, and they often support it with a claim that people are the best judges of their own interests.

The 'best judge' view is most commonly associated with John Stuart Mill, who used it both to reject paternalism and to support consumer sovereignty.[21] There are several different versions of the 'best judge' view, more than one of which may have been held by Mill himself.[22] I shall take the view to be a claim that people are the best judges of their own interests. The implication is that paternalism, understood as forcing someone to do something for their own good, will frequently backfire. What individuals are forced to do will often not be good for them; indeed, it will often be harmful. Individuals are more likely to be right about their own interests than anyone else, including the state.

The application of the 'best judge' view to the market is simple. People should be left free to engage in market transactions, assuming that only the interests of the parties concerned are affected. Even if what some people do in the market looks, to us, odd or bad for them, we should not stop them on those grounds. Prohibiting or restricting voluntary market transactions on the ground that they harm one or more of the parties directly concerned is paternalistic and wrong. The connection between the 'best judge' view and the rationality defence of the market seems to be this: we should assume that people's preferences are correct and that they know what will best satisfy them. The reference to 'correct preferences' loses its oddness when we recall that preferences incorporate belief as well as desire. To say that a preference ordering is correct is to say that it is suitably transitive, its belief components are neither irrationally formed nor false, and its desire component is not tainted in origin. So, even if people's behaviour looks irrational, we must assume that it is not. Because they are the best judges of their interests, we are more likely to be wrong than right in attributing irrationality to them.

The Limits of the 'Best Judge' View

The 'best judge' view is not the only reason why we should avoid paternalism — some others are given later — nor is it the only defence that can be offered for free market transactions. But it is one of the best known and most commonly cited. The doctrine that people know better than the government how to spend their own money is familiar in party politics as well as in the academy. Roger Douglas, for instance, argues for the application of competition in health, education, housing, retirement and so forth by claiming that markets 'leave individual consumers free to buy the service that *best suits them and their needs*'.[23] Phrases like this appear only as an occasional rhetorical flourish in Douglas's book, but I think their significance goes far beyond that in popular defences of the market. That Douglas makes so little of the doctrine that people are the best judges of their own interests may just show how much that doctrine is taken for granted.

How plausible is such a doctrine? Clearly, the 'best judge' view has some initial plausibility. How could the government tell what is better for me than I can? Not even my parents can do that.

There are three points to note at the outset. First, the doctrine is usually applied only to adults who are not insane. Second, the 'best judge' view is not an 'infallible judge' view. The view does not claim that people can never be wrong about their interests and what will best satisfy them. It does not even claim that people are likely to be right. All it claims is that they are more likely to be right than anyone else. Third, and most important, the 'best judge' view makes claims only about people's judgements of their interests. It does not make claims that people will act on those interests, and so it does not preclude, for instance, weakness of the will.

There are at least two reasons for endorsing the 'best judge' view. First, I clearly have some kind of privileged access to my own basic desires. I am *much* more likely to know what I want than anyone else is.[24] Second, I am more likely to take an interest in the satisfaction of my basic desires, and hence more likely to have invested the necessary effort in finding out how to do this. Thus my derivative desires are more likely to be the right response to my basic desires than anyone else's. Both of these points, if correct, still establish only that people are more likely to be right about their interests and what will satisfy them than anyone else, and not that they are likely to be right, full stop. But I think that they render the latter conclusion plausible.

However, there is no need to take people's preferences as a whole and ask whether they are the best judges of what their preferences are. We can be more discriminating than that. Instead, we can classify people's preferences into various categories and ask of each of those whether people are the best judges. There are three categories in which we might doubt the application of the 'best judge' view: altruistic interests, long-term interests, and interests arising from complexity. I shall consider each in turn.

Earlier, we saw that preferences can be altruistic or self-interested. Market transactions can be carried out with the intention of satisfying either or both of these sorts of preferences. But, as Mill pointed out last century, there is no reason to think that the truth of a 'best judge' view with respect to self-interested preferences also holds for altruistic ones.[25] Altruistic preferences are preferences for the well-being of others: one wants others to do well. But one can clearly make mistakes about what will benefit others — as the 'best judge' view itself implies. The mistakes can be of two sorts, corresponding to the two sorts of beliefs in a preference ordering. One can have mistaken beliefs about the content of the basic desires of others ('you were wrong in giving her that present — really she hates furry dice in cars') and one can have mistaken beliefs about the best way of satisfying others' desires. There is no good general reason to think that one's altruistic preferences are especially likely to be right. One lacks the privileged access into the basic desires of others that one has into one's own basic desires, and one generally lacks self-interested incentives to find out how best to satisfy the desires of others. So the view that one knows one's own interests best does not support the view that one's altruistic preferences are more likely to be right than anyone else's. It is perhaps for this reason that economists often recommend that altruistic acts take the form of giving money as opposed to in-kind goods.[26] Because people know their own interests best, if we are trying to help them we should give them the greatest leeway to do this, and that is what money provides, at least relative to giving food stamps or rent rebates.

It may also be worth mentioning here that the 'best judge' view does not support a system of education vouchers, where parents are left free to decide which schools to send their children to. A defence superficially similar to the 'best judge' view is sometimes given — that parents know best what is in their children's interests. But that, of course, is not a claim about the judgement of one's own interests; rather, it is a claim that some people (parents) know what is in the interests of others (their children). Whether or not that claim is true, it will not be supported by the 'best judge' view, although some of the arguments for that view, with appropriate modification, may offer support for the 'parents know best' claim.

Returning to judgements of self-interest, we might be sceptical about people's judgements of their long-term self-interest. It is a nice question whether the problem here is people's having faulty basic desires or inadequate judgements of how to satisfy them. Whichever is the case, people may cause all sorts of trouble for themselves by making transactions which dramatically affect their later lives. Spending all one's money in youth, marrying too quickly, signing harmful long-term contracts can all be against one's long-term self-interest. I think we are often sceptical about the 'best judge' view when applied to cases of this sort where the bad effects come some time later than the initial action. Mill's explanation for our scepticism is that people are often not judging on the basis of experience. For this reason, we should be reluctant to allow people to bind themselves to long-term irreversible contracts.

We might add to Mill's explanation that some people, at least, are irrational with respect to time. That is, they discount the future at an excessive rate, not justified by the risks of mortality.[27] Here the problem is that people will not save enough or take out enough insurance. One way in which many countries avoid these risks is by having a welfare state, financed by coercive taxation. Apart from any redistributive effects, which are beyond the scope of this paper, such a system might be defended as a form of compulsory insurance. Of course, compulsory insurance is a breach of market principles and the doctrine of consumer sovereignty, which prescribes that people are to be left with their money to spend as they wish. But here we might wish to curtail the operation of that principle, given that people are more prone to make mistakes about time-related matters than others.

The third area in which we might wish to restrict consumer sovereignty concerns complexity. The 'best judge' view may give little reason to attach weight to people's self-interested preferences when those preferences are based on matters of which they have little comprehension. There is nothing more paradigmatically in a person's self-interest than their health, but it is uncontroversially true that others — typically doctors — often know more about how to advance people's health than do the people whose health it is. Often, our own self-interested preferences are not as reliable a guide to our self-interest as someone else's because we lack some kind of specialized knowledge.[28] In these cases, the 'best judge' view is not plausible.

Here, however, we should recall the earlier distinction between judgements of basic interests and judgements of derivative interests. Lack of specialized knowledge constitutes a problem for a claim that people are the best judges of their derivative interests, but it has much less application to the judgement of basic interests. Consider again the smoking example: it is not necessarily irrational to smoke even knowing the risks. One can rationally judge that the pleasure of smoking outweighs the potential harm. The cases to worry about are those where someone does not know the risks or else cannot stop themselves from smoking even though they would like to. Similar comments apply to saving. It is not necessarily irrational to save nothing for one's old age. One could, for instance, try for a life with the highest peaks possible, which requires throwing all one's resources at it in youth; and that aim can be rational. The 'best judge' view is at its most plausible when it states that people are the best judges of their basic interests. Doctors may know more about my health than I do, but they do not know more about the importance of health in my interests. The obvious problem is trying to work out when some action — like a consumption splurge in youth — is the result of picking the right means to satisfy one's peculiar interests, and when it is the result of irrationality or faulty judgement.

This obvious problem is more than just a difficulty in the classification of action. It affects the justifications for what we ought to do. Suppose we decide that people do not save enough for their old age and so we institute compulsory saving. This is, in one sense, an interference with everyone's freedom, but we are supposing that people either do not judge correctly their interests in saving or else do not act on their judgements. However, there may be some who do rationally think it better for them to have all their money to spend now. Yet, if we institute a compulsory scheme, we shall be forcing them to act against their own correct judgements of where their interests lie. What should we do? (Note that the same problem will almost certainly arise wherever there is compulsion.) On the one hand, some people will be forced to act against their own interests. On the other hand, if we do not apply compulsion, some people, who would very much like compulsion, will act against their own interests because of their irrationality or because they do not know where their true interests lie. In some ways, this is a problem of distributive justice. Any choice will be in some people's interests and against others', and we need a broader theory to tell us what we should do.

Of course, there are grounds other than the 'best judge' view for rejecting interference. One cannot say that paternalism is always legitimate when we are not the best judges, so that, for example, we should be forced to take medical treatment we do not want if it is good for us. Here are two such grounds: that we have an interest in shaping our own lives, and that we need to learn from our mistakes. However, neither of these offers much support for the extension of the market.

The value of shaping our own lives is an important reason for not placing our lives in the hands of even infallible experts. We want to live our own lives rather than have others direct us. The central value here is autonomy, and it has considerable force against some paternalistic attempts which governments have made through the ages. However, I do not think it offers much of a defence of consumer sovereignty, simply because most of the things that we acquire or give up as a result of market transactions are not central to shaping our lives. Whatever the demerits of banning smoking, for example, the right to smoke is not plausibly essential to the autonomy of smokers. People do not make smoking a central part of their lives. Similar remarks hold for the bulk of other market transactions for relatively mundane goods.[29]

Quite apart from an interest in autonomy, we have an interest in being allowed to lead our own lives even if we are making mistakes.

One benefit of making mistakes is that we learn from them, as Bismarck said that fools do. This consideration certainly has some force, but only when we can learn from our mistakes and benefit from this. There are two cases where we cannot. One is when the results of what we do are irreversible; the other is when we have no way of telling that we have made a mistake because, for example, we have no feedback. Those who commit errors of probability judgement, for example, may never learn of this.

Some Implications

The previous section was concerned with whether we have a reason to assume that people are rational and have correct beliefs, even when their behaviour appears irrational or based on false beliefs. One reason offered was derived from the 'best judge' view. There were several areas where it is doubtful whether such a view applies, and we might decide to restrict freedom of market transaction in those areas. By extension, those are the areas too in which we should be most sceptical of the force of the rationality defence of market efficiency.

Undermining the 'best judge' view does not imply the legitimacy of paternalism. It does not even imply that people's preferences in the three categories considered are irrational or incorrect. Rejecting the 'best judge' view simply means that we cannot *assume* that they are. This equivocal conclusion means that the implications are not clear for markets or their alternatives. We can safely conclude that the 'best judge' view offers no support for saying that children should be allowed to choose education (or not) in a market system, or that the insane should be free to decide whether to buy treatment. But the 'best judge' view does not apply to them anyway. More controversial areas, such as pension arrangements and the freedom to opt out of health care, require much more thought. The possibility of mistaken and irrational preferences could undermine a Pareto-optimality defence of markets. Whether it does depends partly on how bad are the effects of mistaken or irrational preferences. Here, I think, little of general application can be said. The effects of satisfying some mistaken or irrational preferences could be disastrous; the effects of satisfying others trivial. In fact, satisfying some irrational preferences could even be beneficial. Of course, we could say more than this in particular cases with more information. However, there is not much of a general nature in the literature on the harms likely to arise from mistaken or irrational preferences.[30] As a conjecture, perhaps there should be some kind of compulsory saving programme for old age and health because of the potentially dire consequences of mistakenly or irrationally not putting enough aside to meet those needs.

Note, however, that I have not queried the applicability of the 'best judge' view to what is perhaps the predominant type of market transaction: those relatively mundane transactions made to satisfy short-term self-interested preferences. Buying one's food, paying for transport, selling one's car — these sorts of transactions are the usual stuff of markets, and here I think that the 'best judge' view does offer a good general reason to regard them as rational and correct. At least, the 'best judge' view implies that people are more likely to be right than others, and that is all the reason we need not to intervene in transactions between willing parties. That reason can be overridden by, for instance, a desire to prevent bad third-party effects, but third-party effects are beside the point of this chapter. In many of the transactions that make up markets, we can offer a partial vindication of their defence by economists. When considering only the effects on the immediate parties to a transaction, and excepting those transactions not covered by altruism, long-term self-interest and complexity, we should assume that people will not make mistakes and we should leave them to bargain as they wish.

Notes

1   Roger Douglas, *Unfinished Business* (Auckland, Random House New Zealand, 1993).
2   D. Laidler, *Introduction to Microeconomics* 2nd edn (Oxford, Philip Allan, 1981), p.12.
3   For this supplementary assumption, see K. Arrow, 'Values and Collective Decision Making', in his *Collected Papers*, Vol. 1, *Social Choice and Justice* (Cambridge, Mass., Belknap Press, 1983), p.61.
4   J. Raz, *The Morality of Freedom* (Oxford, Clarendon Press, 1986), ch. 13.
5   See, for example, R. Luce and H. Raiffa, 'Utility Theory', in P. Moser (ed.), *Rationality in Action* (Cambridge, Cambridge University Press, 1990), p.28.
6   See, for example, J. Broome, 'Should a Rational Agent Maximize Expected Utility?', in K. S. Cook and M. Levi (eds), *The Limits of Rationality* (Chicago, University of Chicago Press, 1990). It is controversial to assume that transitivity

is a necessary condition. Scitovsky, for example, claims that insisting on transitivity ignores perfectly respectable desires for novelty. See Tibor Scitovsky, *Human Desire and Economic Satisfaction* (Brighton, Wheatsheaf, 1986), p.21. I think that Scitovsky is probably unfair to transitivity.

7 'Almost', because even this weak conception implies that some preferences could not be classed as rational if the transitivity axiom is to have any bite. See, for example, Broome, 'Should a Rational Agent Maximize Expected Utility?', pp.138–41; and Susan Hurley, *Natural Reasons* (Oxford, Clarendon Press, 1989), ch. 4, for an argument to this effect. Arrow ('Values and Collective Decision Making', p.63) is one example of the refusal to scrutinize the content of preferences.

8 Quoted in A. Sen, 'Rational Fools', in F. Hahn and M. Hollis (eds), *Philosophy and Economic Theory* (Oxford, Oxford University Press, 1979), p.87.

9 For one crazy/irrational distinction, see Donald Hubin, 'Irrational Desires', *Philosophical Studies* 62 (1991), p.23.

10 Someone disprefers A to B if and only if they prefer B to A.

11 See, for example, Sen's account of the direct and converse theorems in 'The Moral Standing of the Market', *Social Philosophy and Policy* 2 (1985), pp.9–12.

12 See Sen, 'Moral Standing', and also John Rawls, *A Theory of Justice* (Oxford, Oxford University Press, 1972), pp.70–1 and section 12 generally.

13 See, for example, Amos Tversky and Daniel Kahneman, 'Judgement under Uncertainty: Heuristics and Biases', in Moser (ed.), *Rationality in Action*.

14 For the view that effects usually attributed to false consciousness work through belief and not desire, see 'Introduction' in F. Hahn and M. Hollis (eds), *Philosophy and Economic Theory*, pp.8–9.

15 For this suggestion, see Jon Elster, *Solomonic Judgements* (Cambridge, Cambridge University Press, 1989), pp.55–6.

16 For a quite sophisticated version of this view, see G. A. Cohen, *Karl Marx's Theory of History* (Oxford, Clarendon Press, 1978), ch. 11.

17 For more examples like this, and an excellent defence of consumer sovereignty against charges of irrationality, see David Miller, *Market, State and Community* (Oxford, Clarendon Press, 1989), ch. 5.

18 Scitovsky, *Human Desire and Economic Satisfaction*, p.76.

19 See Tversky and Kahneman, 'Judgement under Uncertainty'.

20 One answer is that we have to adopt a principle of charity in the interpretation of people's actions. This has been argued by Donald Davidson in many places. See, for example, his 'Paradoxes of Irrationality' in Moser (ed.), *Rationality in Action*.

21 The arguments in the chapter of the *Principles of Political Economy* (London, Pelican Books, 1970) called 'Of the Grounds and Limits of the Laisser-Faire or Non-Interference Principle', where Mill argues for a version of consumer sovereignty, are frequently the same as those offered in *On Liberty*, where

Mill argues for freedom of action.

22 R. Goodin discusses several interpretations of the 'best judge' view in his article 'Liberalism and the Best-Judge Principle', *Political Studies* 38 (1990), pp.181–95. It is hard to see what some of the interpretations have to do with being a best judge.

23 Douglas, *Unfinished Business*, p.3 (emphasis added).

24 Goodin ('Liberalism and the Best-Judge Principle', p.183) seems to overlook this more plausible (because weaker) version of a privileged access view in his criticism.

25 Mill, *Principles of Political Economy*, p.333.

26 For example, Thomas Schelling, *Choice and Consequence* (Cambridge, Mass., Harvard University Press, 1984), p.25.

27 See also Goodin, 'Liberalism and the Best-Judge Principle', p.189.

28 Sidgwick, writing in the last century, thought that this objection to the 'best judge' view increasingly applied to consumer choices as technological development increased their complexity. He also thought that people would not be sufficiently aware of their need to hire expert advice. See H. Sidgwick, *The Principles of Political Economy* (London, Macmillan, 1887), p.417.

29 I do not want to claim that autonomy requires no freedom to make some choices over trivial options, only that it does not require the freedom to make any trivial choices. For a claim that freedom to make some trivial choices is a requirement of autonomy, see Raz, *The Morality of Freedom*, p. 374.

30 Economists do sometimes predict that, with intransitive preferences, someone can be the victim of a money pump. A person is supposed to pay a dollar to get to B, which they prefer to C, another dollar to go from B to A, and then another dollar to go from A back to C, and so on. If this happened, I suppose it would compromise a defence of the market, but the money pump rests on the rather strong assumption that the victims would not realise that they were being taken for a ride. For an example of the bad effects of intransitive preferences, see the story of Hans Christian Andersen cited in Elster, *Solomonic Judgements*, pp.21–22.

Contributors

Jonathan Boston is Associate Professor of Public Policy at Victoria University of Wellington. In recent years he has undertaken research in several fields including aspects of social policy, higher education policy, public sector reform, and moral theology. His most recent books include *Reshaping the State* (co-editor, Oxford University Press, 1991), *The Decent Society? Essays in Response to National's Economic and Social Policies* (co-editor, Oxford University Press, 1992), and *Voices for Justice* (co-editor, Dunmore Press, 1994).

Mai Chen is a partner in Mai Chen and Geoffrey Palmer, Public Law Specialists. She was previously Senior Lecturer in Law at Victoria University of Wellington. She has written extensively on women's issues and anti-discrimination law, constitutional reform, and judicial review. Recent publications include *Women and Discrimination: New Zealand and the UN Convention* (Victoria University Press, 1990) and *Public Law in New Zealand* (co-editor, Oxford University Press, 1993).

Glyn Davis is Senior Research Fellow with the Centre for Australian Public Sector Management at Griffith University, Brisbane. He has previously held senior administrative and policy positions with the Queensland Government, and is completing a study of co-ordination routines in state executives. He is co-author of *Public Policy in Australia* (Allen & Unwin, 1993) and has co-edited a number of books on public management and public-sector reform.

Margaret Gardner is Professor of Industrial Relations and Pro-Vice-Chancellor (Equity) at Griffith University, Brisbane. She has published extensively on industrial relations. Her recent books include *Employment Relations* (co-author, Macmillan, 1992), and she is currently working on a history of Australian trade unionism.

Robert Gregory is Senior Lecturer in Public Policy and Administration at Victoria University of Wellington. He is particularly interested in the nature of modern bureaucracy and in theoretical approaches to public policy-making and policy analysis. He has conducted comparative attitudinal research into political–executive relations in Australia and

New Zealand, and has published extensively on various aspects of public policy and administration, including *Politics and Broadcasting: Before and Beyond the NZBC* (Dunmore Press, 1985) and *The Official Information Act: A Beginning* (editor, NZIPA, 1984).

Donald Kettl is Professor of Public Affairs and Political Science, La Follette Institute of Public Affairs, University of Wisconsin-Madison, and Visiting Fellow, Brookings Institution, Washington. He has written extensively on aspects of American government and public-sector reform, and is particularly well-known for his work on the contracting-out of publicly funded goods and services. Recent books include *Government by Proxy: (Mis?)Managing Federal Programs* (Congressional Quarterly Press, 1988); *Sharing Power: Public Governance and Private Markets* (Brookings, 1993) and *Improving Government Performance* (co-author, Brookings, 1994).

John Martin is Senior Lecturer in Public Policy at Victoria University of Wellington. A graduate in political science from Victoria, he served in a number of departments in the New Zealand public service between 1953 and 1987. Before leaving the public service he was Deputy Director-General of Health. In recent years he has written extensively on public management issues. His books include *A Profession of Statecraft?* (Victoria University Press, 1988), *Public Service and the Public Servant* (State Services Commission, 1991) and *Reshaping the State* (co-editor, Oxford University Press, 1991).

Michael Trebilcock is Professor of Law, Director of the Law and Economics Programme, and Chairman of the International Business and Law Programme at the University of Toronto. He has written extensively on a wide range of legal issues and has a particular interest in the choice of governing instrument. Among his recent publications are *Trade and Transitions: A Comparative Analysis of Adjustment Policies* (co-author, Routledge, 1990), *Unfinished Business: Reforming Trade Remedy Laws in North America* (co-author, C. D. Howe Institute, 1993) and *The Prospects for Reinventing Government* (C. D. Howe Institute, 1994).

Anna Yeatman is Professor of Sociology at Macquarie University, Sydney. She has written extensively on public management, feminism, political theory, biculturalism and postmodernism. Recent publications include *Bureaucrats, Technocrats, Femocrats: Essays on the Contemporary Australian*

State (Allen & Unwin, 1990), *Feminism and the Politics of Difference* (co-editor, Bridget Williams Books, 1994), *Postmodern Revisionings of the Political* (Routledge, 1994), and *Justice and Identity: Antipodean Practices* (co-editor, Bridget Williams Books, 1995).

Martin Wilkinson is Lecturer in Political Studies at Auckland University. His primary interests lie in the area of political philosophy and, at its boundaries, in moral philosophy, economics and law. He has published in *Utilitas* and *Political Science*.

Index